THE BEST C

THE BLUES CD LISTENER'S GUIDE

by Howard J. Blumenthal

Billboard Books
An imprint of Watson-Guptill Publications/New York

A few hundred men, and some women, created the blues. Some people beat the odds, lived to tell the stories, and maybe even earned some fame or fortune. This book is dedicated to the ones who did not.

Senior Editor: Bob Nirkind
Managing Editor (Logical Extension, Ltd.): Sharon Blumenthal
Design: Howard J. Blumenthal
Jacket Design: Barbour Design

First published in 1998 by Billboard Books, an imprint of Watson-Guptill Publications, a division of BPI Communications, Inc., 1515 Broadway, New York, NY 10036

Library of Congress Cataloging-in-Publication Data

Library of Congress Cataloging-in-Publication Data for this title can be obtained from the Library of Congress.
ISBN 0-8230-7675-X

98-86880
CIP
MN

Manufactured in the United States of America
First printing, 1998

1 2 3 4 5 6 7 8 9 / 06 05 04 03 02 01 00 99 98

The blues is about as old as this century, a uniquely American form born from the misery of working in broiling hot fields, letting off steam at Saturday night dances, and expressing the inevitable sorrows. Most early blues records were made by men who could barely afford their own guitars, but the music stayed alive. There were down periods, like the 1930s and the 1970s, and periods of rediscovery, like the 1950s. In recent years, the blues has become more popular than ever before.

This book provides a road map through the blues. It's organized by artist name, so you'll find it to be a useful companion when shopping for CDs. Every review is followed by a suggestion for further listening, which we call a "LINK." A LINK may be an additional CD by the same artist, a various-artists collection based upon a similar style or cultural characteristic, or simply an album that might be entertaining. And every review was written by me—one person who took the time to listen to a great many CDs, select the best ones by each artist, and explain why each one is a worthy addition to a blues CD collection. These reviews are intended to be a starting place, not the final word.

There are no ratings. Every CD in this book is worth owning. And, with a few noted exceptions, every CD in this book is currently available in the U.S.

I sincerely hope you enjoy reading this book. It was a great pleasure to write it.

Howard J. Blumenthal
October 1998

Listening setup:
Loudspeakers: Thiel 3.6
CD player: Meridian 508.20
Pre-amplifier: Balanced Audio Technology VK-3i
Amplifier: Balanced Audio Technology VK-200
Loudspeaker cables: Cardas Golden Cross
Interconnect cables: Cardas Golden Cross

Acknowledgments

A great many people shared their enthusiasm, opinions, and information with me. My family listened, and learned about the blues; my ten-year-old son now understands the connection between blues and jazz. I'm especially grateful to Kevin Mallon at Claris and to the publicity department at Adobe, and to Ted Swanson, who guided me through the wonders of databases. I'm also thankful to Apple Computer for the invention of the Newton; about 1/3 of this book was written on the road, using that remarkable product's handwriting recognition. Mostly, though, it's about the music. A great many music industry professionals helped to make this project possible.

Above all, I'd like to thank Terri Hinte and the staff at Fantasy Records. With a spectacular jazz catalog and a wonderful selection of blues (Original Blues Classics), they deserve special recognition—and an apology for past mishaps.

And, thank you to:

- Ron Stallworth
- Jonny Meister, WXPN-FM, Philadelphia, PA
- Victor Tabinsky, Record Archive, Rochester, NY
- Jeremy Sarachan, Fantastic Records, Rochester, NY
- Robert Palmer
- Bill Low, AudioQuest
- Jerry Gordon, Evidence Records
- Annie Johnston, Arhoolie
- Chris Wheat, GRP/MCA
- Jennifer Levy, GRP/MCA
- Tom Cording, Legacy
- Jeff Walker, Legacy
- Glenn Dicker (formerly of Rounder)
- Steve Burton, Rounder
- Steve Karas, PolyGram
- Mark Pucci
- Meg MacDonald, Vanguard
- Lellie Capwell, Vanguard
- Marylin Egol, RCA/ BMG
- Doug Engel, Delmark
- Cindy Byram, Shanachie
- Ari Eisinger
- Brenda Dunlap, Smithsonian Institution
- David Bartlett, Tone-Cool
- Marc Lipkin, Alligator
- Mike Stefanik, Collectibles
- Cary Goldberg, JVC XRCD
- Kathy DeJohn, Telarc
- Megan Zinn, Red House
- Emilie Liepa, Red House
- Andy Schwartz, Epic
- A.J. Correale, SONY International
- Jennifer Ballantyne - Chess/MCA
- Sharon Levitan, House of Blues
- Alyson Chadwick, BMG
- Joanne Larson, Wolf
- Yvonne Gomez, RHINO
- Cathy Williams, RHINO
- David Dorn, RHINO
- Barbara Shelley
- Jerry Portnoy
- Jim & Selina O'Neal, Rooster Blues
- Don Kent, Yazoo
- Andrew Galindo
- JoAnne Larson, Wolf Records USA
- *and many more*

Born Lathan John Adams in 1932, New Orleans R&B singer Johnny Adams started out as a gospel singer, working locally with groups like the Soul Revivers. In the late 1950s, Adams changed over to R&B, and his 1959 single "I Won't Cry" for the small New Orleans label Ric was locally popular. In 1962, Adams made it to number 26 on the national R&B charts with "A Losing Battle," written and produced by Dr. John. Adams had a few more minor hits in the late 1960s: "Release Me," "Reconsider Me," and "I Can't Be All Bad." In the 1970s, the small flame of national interest flickered out, but a 1985 contract with Rounder changed his life. Still in his 50s, Adams began a regular routine of touring and recording new albums. His R&B songwriter tribute albums have been very well received. He died in 1998.

I Won't Cry — Rounder 2083

These sides come from 1959–63. They were recorded for a small New Orleans concern called Ric/Ron, and they're full-blooded romantic R&B. The title cut "(Oh Why) I Won't Cry," probably the CD's best tune, is a mid-tempo number recalling the 1950s. It's special for reasons that become even more evident on "Life Is a Struggle"—the man sings with heart. Adams's gospel training serves him well; the emotions are honest and rise well above fairly conventional (albeit well-done) accompaniment. Mac Rebennack produced and wrote "Teach Me to Forget," a fine, classy ballad that enjoys a typically stylish vocal.

LINK➤ *Walter "Wolfman" Washington — Wolf at the Door* **Rounder 2098**

Washington can lay down a soulful ballad as well as any contemporary blues man, but he can just as easily slink into a funky groove with big R&B horns. He started by playing guitar in New Orleans clubs, worked some with Adams, and broke nationally in 1991.

From the Heart — Rounder 2044

From 1984, this is probably Adams's finest work. The versatility and range of his singing is matched by very strong material, notably Doc Pomus's tender "From the Heart" (in which Adams adds impact by holding his notes longer than expected) and Hal Jackson's ripping "I Feel Like Breaking Up Somebody's Home." Alvin "Red" Tyler's tenor sax break on "If I Ever Had a Good Thing" is spine-tingling. The whole band is top-flight: Walter "Wolfman" Washington's electric guitar is particularly satisfying on "Your Love Is So Doggone Good," but once again, it's Adams's voice and Pomus's songwriting that carry the day. Throughout, Adams expertly works the space between "blues" and soul.

LINK➤ *Ivory Joe Hunter — Since I Met You Baby: The Best of Ivory Joe Hunter* **Razor & Tie 2052**

Pianist Hunter was one of the top ballad singers in the 1950s, noted for songs like "I Almost Lost My Mind" and "Since I Met You Baby." He could also aim for the heart of rock 'n' roll and boogie with the best of them. This CD is a good sampler.

Walking on a Tightrope **Rounder 2095**

His second-best album. Ten songs written by R&B wizard Percy Mayfield, all excellent. Duke Robillard and Walter "Wolfman" Washington play guitar. Jon Cleary is an inspired jazz/R&B pianist. Adams's voice is also in exquisite form. Listen to the chilling arrangement on the title song, the way Adams wraps that voice around the lyrics, his sincere storytelling. It all comes together here. Cleary's midnight piano and Adams's silky smooth "Danger Zone" make the perilous world all right on a song Mayfield wrote for Ray Charles. "Lost Mind" is the most famous song here, a great jazz vocal with an airtight jazz band's accompaniment. Nice production, too. From 1989.

LINK➤ *Percy Mayfield — Poet of the Blues* ***Specialty 7001***

A good sampling of Mayfield's work from 1950 until 1954 (a period that yielded a healthy number of hits). It includes "Please Send Me Someone to Love," "Lost Love," and "Strange Things Happening," plus over 20 others.

Sings Doc Pomus: The Real Me **Rounder 2109**

Co-produced with impeccable taste by Scott Billington and Mac (Dr. John) Rebennack, this 1991 CD's got a tasty New Orleans feel. When Adams lets loose on "Still in Love," the CD's second-best ballad, he performs to lush, clever accompaniment. Dr. John's keyboard work is very articulate and ideally suited for Adams's exquisite ballad "There Is Always One More Time." Every word Pomus wrote had dignity, and nobody in the world sings Pomus as well as Johnny Adams. Listen to what happens on the Pomus classic "Blinded by Love" or "The Real Me," arranged so simply so that the unadorned honesty of Pomus and Adams shines through. What a wonderful album!

LINK➤ *Dr. John — Mos' Scocious* ***Rhino 71450***

With a stage presence right out of Mardi Gras and a phenomenal talent for producing, writing, performing, and simply thinking about music, Dr. John's story is a fascinating chunk of New Orleans history. This 2-CD anthology covers over 30 years of music.

One Foot in the Blues **Rounder 2144**

For their eighth album together, producer Scott Billington and singer Adams wanted something new in the mix. They found it in Dr. Lonnie Smith, an expert Hammond B-3 organ player. They also added a little funk to keep the sound fresh and modern. "Won't Pass Me By," which begins the 1996 album, sounds completely modern, but Adams's voice keeps that rock-solid soul in its center. And that burst of organ accentuating Adams's slow vocal groove is stunning. Billington and Adams choose their material carefully; two jazz standards, "Ill Wind" and "Angel Eyes," coexist with Percy Mayfield material. And on "Angel Eyes," Smith's sentimental organ bed is sublime.

LINK➤ *Johnny Adams — Good Morning Heartache* ***Rounder 2125***

Adams's jazz album. Extremely stylish, beautifully sung, but not totally devoid of soul or blues. The track list includes "You Don't Know What Love Is," "Come Rain or Come Shine," and "But Not For Me." The band is not exactly a jazz ensemble, but it does the job with real affection.

Luther Allison's earliest memory of the blues dates back to the 1940s, when he and his father would listen to B.B. King's radio program on WDIV, Memphis. The son of an Arkansas country farmer who moved his large family to Chicago, Allison considered playing Negro League baseball and trained as a shoemaker. While in high school, Allison became interested in blues guitar. As a Chicago teenager, he also sang gospel with the Southern Travelers, but shifted his attention to play with his brothers in several blues bands. Friendships with local blues musicians led to gigs with Muddy Waters, Elmore James, and other legends. Allison started recording in 1969, first for Delmark and then for Motown's Gordy label. He attracted a rock audience by fusing blues with rock. Allison moved to France (near Paris) in 1984. Prior to his death in 1997, he appeared at clubs and festivals in Europe (where he was very popular) and in the U.S.

Serious — Blind Pig 72287

Allison started recording in 1969 for Delmark; he was also the only bluesman to record in the 1970s for Motown's Gordy label. It wasn't until this 1987 album, however, that Allison finally found his audience. His package includes a crackling rock guitar (complete with effects and catchy riffs), a powerful rhythm section, and a soulfully hoarse voice. The combination works best on a rocking tune like "Backtrack" or on a slower, organ-based blues like "Reaching Out." The tasty mixture of stinging guitar and late-night piano brings "Show Me a Reason" to life. Keyboard player Michael Carras, incidentally, is a significant contributor throughout this CD. "Parking Lot" sounds like a Rolling Stones number.

LINK➤ *Mighty Joe Young — Mighty Man* — ***Blind Pig 5040***

A top Chicago blues guitar player circa 1980, Young was sidelined with health problems. He did plenty of fine session work and recorded numerous singles over the years. This 1997 album was a decade in the making. Young's classic Chicago blues are fabulous.

Soul Fixin' Man — Alligator 4820

It's 1994, and Allison's a seasoned performer who structures his lengthy guitar solos for maximum effect. "Bad Love" is a textbook example of electric blues. It's illuminated by a rejected, dejected vocal and the deft power of the Memphis Horns. The entire CD follows the path set by this first cut. "I Want to Know" quickly establishes a guitar and organ groove, and Allison slides in, a soulful vocalist yearning for love. "Soul Fixin' Man" boogies with a faster beat, and "Middle of the Road" takes some chances with a sirenlike guitar and an unusual reggaelike rhythm. Solid 1990s blues.

LINK➤ *Luther Allison — Blue Streak* — ***Alligator 4834***

Allison's 1995 Alligator album is more raucous ("All the King's Horses"), but it's also tight and cleverly arranged ("What Have I Done Wrong?" and "Big City"). On these last two numbers in particular, the power and grace of Allison's guitar evoke dark urban evils.

Allman Brothers Band

One argument strongly states that the Allman Brothers Band was influenced by blues, but was not a blues band by strict definition. Another embraces the band because it grew from blues roots. Either way, brothers Duane (lead guitar) and Gregg Allman (organ, vocals) got things started in Florida with a group called the Allman Joys, in the mid-1960s. They moved to L.A., signed with Liberty Records as Hourglass, and returned to Florida a few years later, where they organized a new band with Dickey Betts (lead guitar), Berry Oakley (bass), Butch Trucks and Jai Johanny Johanson (both drummers). Through the early 1970s, the Allman Brothers Band was one of America's hottest rock bands, but Duane Allman's death from a motorcycle accident in 1971 and Berry Oakley's death the following year sapped some originality. By decade's end, the group was no more; various members have performed together several times since and kept the band alive.

Beginnings **Capricorn 531-259**

The first two Allman Brothers Band albums have traveled through time with their integrity intact. The 1969 debut album, named for the band, begins with blues by way of England: Spencer Davis's "Don't Want You No More." The twin lead guitars of Duane Allman and Dickey Betts provided the heart of this group, best exemplified by the slashing "It's Not My Cross to Bear" and on Muddy Waters's "Trouble No More." *Idlewild South*, a 1970 followup album, contains the group's insignia riff on "Revival," a bit of country-rock on the hit "Midnight Rider," and a large-scale houserocking version of Willie Dixon's "Hoochie Coochie Man." Impressive craftsmanship and integration of Southern bar band rock and Chicago blues.

LINK➤ *The Allman Brothers Band — Dreams* ***Polydor 839-417***

Covered in faux rawhide and containing five hours of music, this 4-CD box contains all of the classic Allman recordings, plus a healthy dose of music made before the band was officially formed. Remastering has greatly improved the sound. Expensive, but worth it.

At Fillmore East **Capricorn 531-260**

One of the all-time great live rock albums, this 1971 classic is filled with the best blues the Allmans ever recorded. Duane Allman's slide guitar sculpts Willie McTell's "Statesboro Blues" with agile, muscular lines; his smart, fancy, and on-target solos never tire the listener. A moody version of T-Bone Walker's "Stormy Monday" follows, but three extended tracks form the album's heart. Willie Cobb's "You Don't Love Me" is beaty and bouncy, with a rippling blues arrangement featuring the guitars and organ; it runs 20 minutes. "In Memory of Elizabeth Reed," at 13 minutes, and "Whipping Post," at 23 minutes, are a bonfire of improvisations, spectacular solos, and superb rock music.

LINK➤ *Duane Allman — Anthology* ***PolyGram 831-444***

This popular 2-CD set presents work not only by the Allman Brothers, but also with other bands. Among the many notable tracks: "Layla" (Derek and the Dominos), "The Weight" (Aretha Franklin)," plus session work with Boz Scaggs, Delaney and Bonnie, Wilson Pickett, and others.

Marcia Ball

Singer-pianist Marcia Ball was born in Orange, TX, in 1949, but spent her childhood in nearby Vinson, LA. Her grandmother and aunt were musicians; they taught her to play piano, a skill enhanced by about ten years of lessons. Besides music, Ball spent her afternoons as a cheerleader. By 1966, she was an English major at Louisiana State University, performing on the side in a sometimes psychedelic blues-rock band called Gum. Ball moved to Austin, TX, and started working with a progressive country-rock band called Freda and the Firedogs (she wore a cowgirl outfit). When the band broke up, she went solo. Rounder signed Ball in the early 1980s; she's been recording for the label for more than a decade. Ball has become a very popular blues performer not only in the Austin area, but throughout the U.S. and Europe.

Hot Tamale Baby — Rounder 3095

Although it lacks some of the songwriting chops that became evident on *Gatorhythms*, Ball's second Rounder album is worth a listen. When she attacks Clifton Chenier's "Hot Tamale Baby," Ball is singing and playing atop a relentless beat. She turns a children's rhyme into a full-blooded Lousiana dance tune of her own on "That's Enough of That Stuff," and manages a quote or two from "Iko Iko" along the way. Ball's leadoff number, "Never Like This Before" is a Memphis R&B tune by Booker T. Jones, Isaac Hayes, and David Porter. It gets the total treatment, complete with piercing horns and backup singers. This is good, but Ball gets much, much better.

LINK➤ *Neville Brothers — Fiyo on the Bayou* — ***A&M 4866***

Local Louisiana influences cooked through a rock 'n' roll sensibility make songs like "Hey Pocky Way," "Brother John/Iko Iko," and "Fire on the Bayou" distinctive and uniquely the province of the Neville Brothers. Arguably their best album, it's from the early 1980s.

Gatorhythms — Rounder 3101

On her third Rounder album, Ball starts out spicy with a hot New Orleans jump number written by Mac (Dr. John) Rebennack. The tune is called "How You Carry On," and it's one of those irresistibly fast numbers with hard-driving horns, an R&B saxophone, and Ball pounding away on her piano while singing her heart out. "La Ti Da" is slower, but the ingredients in its boogie-woogie stew are similar. Ditto for "Mama's Cooking," an original variation on zydeco's upside-down tonality. Ball's probably at her best on the mid-tempo "Mobile," an amalgamation of folk, country, rock, and blues that recalls an Alabama home. Ultimately, all of this comes down to solid songwriting, very good piano playing, and a knack for blues-rock singing developed over decades. Lots of fun! From 1989.

LINK➤ *Irma Thomas — Soul Queen of New Orleans* — ***Razor & Tie 2097***

The Rolling Stones took "Time Is on My Side" from Irma Thomas (their arrangement is very similar). Her other songs are as good: "Cry On" and "Wish Someone Would Care" are among the best of two dozen superb R&B sides. A must-have collection of 1960s singles.

Dreams Come True — Antone's 14

This terrific album was recorded in 1989 by Marcia Ball with Lou Ann Barton and Angela Strehli—two Texas singers who are every bit her equal. An extraordinary band led by Dr. John features star cameos from David "Fathead" Newman and Jimmie Vaughan. With top-notch material, this is fine R&B performed by solo voices and in group harmony. Every song sounds familiar, as if it traveled through time from 1961, but many of the songs are fresh and new. Ball's own "Love, Sweet Love" is a highlight, and so is her title track. Ike Turner's "A Fool in Love" is enthusiastically presented; ditto for his spooky "Idolize You."

LINK➤ *David "Fathead" Newman — House of David* **Rhino/Atlantic 71452**

Top R&B saxophone player gets the 2-CD collection that his career deserves. There's plenty of work with Ray Charles, plus tracks with Dr. John, Aretha Franklin, Hank Crawford, and other jazz compadres. One of the few saxmen who successfully straddle jazz, R&B, and blues.

Blue House — Rounder 3131

A coming-of-age for Ball, who adopted a classier, more mature approach to her work for this 1994 album. She starts out with Muddy Waters's "Red Beans," a touchstone for her past. "The Facts of Life" is more telling; it's a reflective, down-tempo consideration of "the high, low, and in between." Blending her country, blues, and rock background, Ball honky-tonks her way through "Down the Road"; it's one of several songs with unusually tight accompaniment from horns and percussion. In many ways, Ball has become an adult contemporary performer, recalling but not focusing on the blues. "St. Gabriel" and "Why Do I?" are quite effective folk-rock tunes.

LINK➤ *Marcia Ball — Let Me Play with Your Poodle* **Rounder 3151**

From 1997, Ball's best shot at mainstream success. With her blues training, she knows how to deal with the sexual innuendo of the title song, and her vocal treatment of Randy Newman's "Louisiana 1927" is also excellent. Such versatility serves her well. Fine listening, great sound.

Sing It! — Rounder 3719

Another successful trio album; it's performed with formidable R&B queen Irma Thomas and blues-rock singer Tracy Nelson. On "Yield Not to Temptation," Thomas really shows her stuff. It's a gospel song with the album's trio as a small choir. Nelson and Ball harmonize on "Heart to Heart," two old pros eulogizing what's left of a love affair. "In Tears" features Nelson on a folk-rock torch song with ample opportunity to show off a big voice. Ball and Thomas's backup vocals are chilling. There's a taste of zydeco in "Sing It," and lots of appealing attitude on "If I Know You." Smart, sassy, and elegant. From 1997.

LINK➤ *Tracy Nelson — The Best of Tracy Nelson / Mother Earth* **Reprise 46232**

Mostly 1960s material from a big-voiced San Francisco blues singer. The best-known track is probably "Down So Low," but there's also a powerfully emotional version of "Need Your Love So Bad" (which Irma Thomas also sings). In the Here and Now *(Rounder 3123), from 1993, is also excellent.*

Many early blues players had nicknames; some were from youthful incidents or habits, some were coined by other musicians, and some came from odd coincidences. Robert Hicks was working and performing at an Atlanta barbeque joint called Tidwell's when he was discovered by a Columbia Records talent scout. His nickname—Barbecue Bob—stuck. In time, Bob became one of Atlanta's most popular blues singers. He was born in 1902 in Walnut Grove, GA. His older brother, Charlie, taught him to play the guitar; the two began their careers together in nearby Atlanta in the early 1920s. They earned a modest living playing at picnics and parties. Barbecue Bob signed with Columbia Records in the late 1920s; by the early 1930s, he had recorded roughly 70 songs for the label. Sadly, Bob died young in 1931 from pneumonia and tuberculosis. Brother Charlie Hicks died in 1963 after several decades of hard times.

Chocolate to the Bone — Yazoo 2005

Barbecue Bob's style isn't anything fancy. He's a man who plays mostly straightforward accompaniment on a twelve-string guitar and sings in a clear, appealing way. The guitar typically carries the rhythm, and Bob simply sings the melody. As a result, this CD is a perfect introduction to old blues records for the newcomer. Bob is especially effective on "Motherless Chile Blues," which is somewhat more complicated than most of his songs; his voice has a near-crying quality as he argues for a lover to straighten herself out. "Twist Your Stuff" is an enticing dance tune. "Yo Yo Blues" has an entertaining up and down quality.

LINK➤ Various Artists — The Georgia Blues 1927–1933 — Yazoo 1012

About a dozen Georgia bluesmen perform on this CD, including "Charlie Lincoln" (Barbeque Bob's brother, Charlie Hicks), who sings lead on "Doodle Hole Blues." This is also the place to hear other delights, such as the wonderful fiddle in the background of Peg Leg Howell's "Rolling Mill Blues."

Complete Recorded Works, Volumes 1–3 — Document (Arhoolie) 5046, 7, 8

With Arhoolie's distribution, Austria's Document label has found its way into many U.S. record stores. Document's mission is to collect and release complete collections of recordings by old blues stars. Since the recordings come from many sources, the sound quality on each release varies widely. For some collectors, the fact that all of Barbecue Bob's recordings are available is primary, and sound quality is secondary. The first CD in this series covers 1927–28, the second is devoted to 1928–29, and the third features 1929–30, plus several cuts from the Georgia Cotton Pickers. Thoughout, Barbecue Bob's performances are engaging and entertaining. Highlights include Vol. 3's "Darktown Gamblin'."

LINK➤ Buddy Moss — Complete Recorded Works, Vols. 1–3 — Document 5123-5

Buddy Moss was one of Georgia's finest early bluesmen. A partner to Barbecue Bob, Moss later worked with Curley Weaver and Blind Willie McTell. He also learned a good deal from Blind Blake. The first two volumes cover 1933 and 1934; Vol. 3 is from 1935–41.

Fort Worth, TX, native Barton was born in 1954. She moved to Austin in the early 1970s and grew up in that city's blues community. By 1982, Barton was recording for the prestigious Asylum label. Her first album was produced that year by Eagles member Glenn Frey and by top R&B producer Jerry Wexler. Unfortunately, the album failed to catch the attention of blues fans. Barton just kept working in Austin's clubs; she tried again with a 1986 album for the small Spindletop label, and again in 1989 with a star-studded album for Austin's highly regarded Antone's record label. Despite a fine voice, considerable talent, and excellent reviews in national magazines like *Rolling Stone*, Barton has been primarily a Texas entertainer. A combination of contract woes, lack of aggressive national touring, and sheer bad luck are some of the reasons why. Still, her work on record is worthy and should be heard.

Old Enough — Discovery (Sire) 74207

Although the personnel varies from one song to the next, several impressive session players provide very consistent support for this 1989 effort. They include Jimmie Vaughan and Derek O'Brien on guitar, David "Fathead" Newman and Mark Kazanoff on saxophones, and Mel Brown on piano. Once again, Barton gets everything right. "You'll Lose a Good Thing" is one of her best tunes; it's a slow dance highlighted by Newman's saxophone wails and Barton's "loo-oo-oose me" vocal emphasis and vulnerability. She returns to Hank Ballard for the rocking "Sexy Ways" and to boogie for "Mean Mean Man." B.B. King's "I Wonder Why" also gets a sexy treatment. Barton's presentation is superb; this is an album worth hearing.

LINK➤ *Omar & the Howlers—Hard Times in the Land of Plenty* Columbia 40815

Omar Kent Dykes and his crew hail from Austin, TX. Their version of the blues is energized, edgy, and exciting. This is the group's major label effort from 1987. For an even better picture of its best work, seek out I Told You So *(on a small local label: Austin 8401).*

Read My Lips — Discovery (Sire) 74217

Recorded at Alabama's Muscle Shoals studio with top-notch session players, this 1982 album should have been a hit. It's got just the right balance of R&B and rock, in addition to a lead singer whose voice has a fine sensibility that recalls every Texas roadhouse and far too many late rock 'n' rolling nights. Marshall Crenshaw's "Brand New Lover" gets the full-scale Jerry Wexler treatment with unexpected percussion patterns, distinctive intonation on the vocal hook, and backup vocals that precisely underline the central idea. It's textbook perfection. "It's Raining" is the slow song equivalent, with an elegant organ and a melancholy horn presenting an emotional chorus. Nods to the 1950s include "Maybe" and "Finger Poppin' Time."

LINK➤ *Deanna Bogart — The Great Unknown* Shanachie 9011

A great 1998 effort by a rocking blues singer and guitarist (she also plays tenor sax), this is a tight, sharp performance with spice from New Orleans and other influences. "Love Funk" gets the guitar right in the midst of a fresh and frisky arrangement. Solid and fun.

Carey Bell

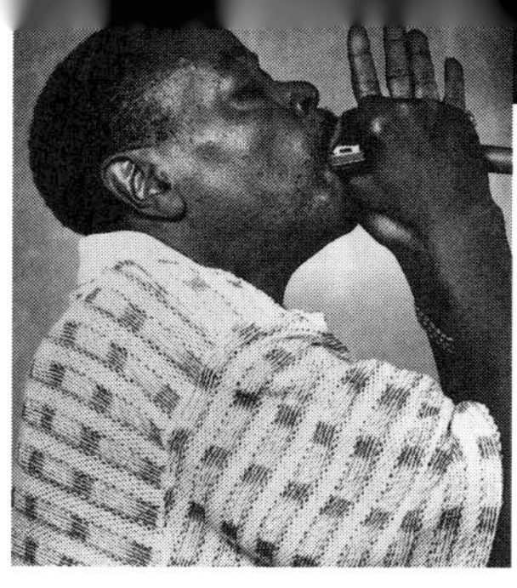

Carey Bell Harrington's hometown is Macon, MS. When he was in his early 20s, his godfather, the pianist Lovie Lee, brought him to Chicago to find work. By that time, it was 1956, and the two had been working together for seven years. Life in Chicago wasn't easy, so Bell taught himself electric bass just to survive; he eventually found work backing up Robert Nighthawk and other local favorites. It wasn't until 1969 that the talented harmonica player was offered a recording contract. Regular road work with Muddy Waters and Willie Dixon followed; back in Chicago, Bell's tireless effort was finally resulting in renown. He appeared on several Alligator anthologies, and in 1990, at age 56, Bell's performance on Alligator's *Harp Attack!* with Junior Wells, James Cotton, and Billy Branch made him a star. Bell continues to record and tour. Carey Bell is the father of Lurrie Bell.

Mellow Down Easy — Blind Pig 74291

Maryland's Tough Luck became Bell's regular band in 1988, and its members are much younger than he is. Bell was 55 years old when he recorded Willie Dixon's "Mellow Down Easy" and the rocking Albert King tune "For the Love of a Woman." Here he is the group's lead vocalist as well as its harpist; he's clear, confident, experienced, wise, leering, or sexual as the lyrics require. The best song on this 1991 album is, inevitably, the one with the most harmonica. That would be "Delta Time," a duet with composer Steve Jacobs offering rhythm harmonica to Bell's lead. "Big Walter Strut" is also one of Bell's better harp numbers.

LINK➤ *Var. Artists — Blues Masters Vol. 4: Harmonica Classics* **Rhino 71124**

An outstanding anthology of blues harp, the tracks here focus on the second half of this century. Artists include Little Walter, Jimmy Reed, Paul Butterfield, Billy Boy Arnold, Charlie Musselwhite, Slim Harpo, and George "Harmonica" Smith. Good liner notes, too.

Deep Down — Alligator 482

Listening to this 1995 album, it's easy to dream about the whole history of the blues. Bell is definitely from the old school: his voice is rough but sincere, aggressive but subdued, and his harmonica is as sharp as a knife. Behind this juke-joint sensibility, however, there's an extremely skilled Chicago band that includes Lucky Peterson on piano, Carl Weathersby on guitar, and Bell's son Lurrie on guitar. When Bell sings "When I Get Drunk," the contrast between the hard-core, no-nonsense instrumentation and his slightly aged, slightly frightened voice is quite affecting. Of course there's nothing like a harmonica master soloing, and Bell doesn't disappoint on "Jawbreaker." In fact, he sounds like a whole horn section.

LINK➤ *Lurrie Bell — Young Man's Blues: Best of JSP Sessions* **JSP 2102**

In the absence of a CD version of 1984's Son of a Gun *(recorded by Bell with his father for Rooster Blues), this CD provides a good look at the younger Bell's talent as a guitar player and vocalist. Try also* 700 Blues *(Delmark 700), released in 1997.*

Jackson, TN, is about 60 miles northeast of Memphis, not too far for Mabel Louise Smith's family to travel so she could compete in an amateur contest at the Memphis Cotton Carnival. Big-voiced at age 8, she won first prize. It wasn't long before Big Maybelle was fronting her church choir—an uninhibited girl praising the Lord with all her might. In 1936, she turned professional; she sang with bandleader Dave Clark and later was an intermission act for a local group called the International Sweethearts of Rhythm. By 1944, Maybelle was singing for big bands in NYC, first for Christine Chatman, then for Tiny Bradshaw. In 1952, she signed as a solo R&B artist with OKeh; she remained with the label for four years. Seriously addicted to drugs, Big Maybelle signed next with Savoy, then with Brunswick. By 1965, her weight problems led to diabetes; she died in 1972 in a diabetic coma.

The Complete OKeh Sessions: 1952–55 — Epic 53417

One of the finest voices in R&B, Big Maybelle brought a combination of Memphis blues, hearty spiritual singing, and a whole lot of soul to her OKeh sides. Her appeal goes well beyond sturdy lungs; her desperation on "Just Want Your Love" is palpable. When Maybelle sings, "One of these days you're gonna wake up and I'll be long gone," it's hard not to believe her. Maybelle swings through the blues on "So Good to My Baby" and disses the singer as if she were a catty, jealous lover on "Gabbin' Blues," a big hit. "My Country Man" and "Way Back Home" were also major R&B hits.

LINK➤ *LaVern Baker — Soul on Fire: The Best of LaVern Baker* **Rhino 82311**

Although oldies radio seems to favor her lighthearted novelty "Tweedlee Dee," Baker is a scorcher for whom 1950s work along the lines of "Jim Dandy" is more typical. On the quiet side, she also makes magic with torch songs like "I Cried a Tear" and the title song.

Blues, Candy & Big Maybelle — Savoy 262

The jazz/pop mood is no surprise here—Savoy was primarily a jazz label, and Big Maybelle's sidemen include Sahib Shihab, Gigi Gryce, Don Abney, and Kenny Burrell. "Candy" is something of a jazz standard; a throwback to the 1940s, the song that became Maybelle's biggest hit. (Considering her drug problems, the lyrics are sadly ironic, too.) Savoy treated Maybelle like a pop singer, a big band songbird gone solo. That's why you'll hear a credible version of "White Christmas" and pop strings behind a torch song, "Until the Real Thing Comes Along." Even the bluesier songs are jazz-blues: "Blues Early, Early" is a midnight jazz tune. Pleasant sound quality.

LINK➤ *Aretha Franklin — The Queen of Soul* ***Rhino/ Atlantic 71063***

Every blues library ought to include at least one Franklin collection. This one's the best. It's a 4-CD box with literate, well-researched liner notes. Songs present a fabulous range of R&B, from "A Natural Woman" and "Chain of Fools" to "Spanish Harlem."

Blake's real name was probably either Arthur Phelps or Arthur Blake. He was born sometime in the 1890s, most likely in Jacksonville, FL, or possibly in the Georgia Sea Islands. By 1926, Blake had been traveling around the South and Midwest for years, performing all sorts of music in theaters and on street corners. That year, he recorded for Paramount in Chicago. His first release, "West Coast Blues," was a hit; over the next six years, Blake recorded about 80 songs for the label. He also performed on a great many Paramount recordings by other artists and was a very popular performer. In 1930 and 1931, Blake traveled with a vaudeville act, then returned to Chicago. Blake's life after 1932 is a mystery; he disappeared and was never heard from again. The consensus among historians is that he died in 1933, either accidentally or at the hands of some rival.

Ragtime Guitar's Foremost Fingerpicker

Yazoo 1068

An engaging musician whose only CD should be in every blues collection, Blind Blake is the quintessential Piedmont blues player. He's bound to raise a smile with the silly double entendre "Diddie Wa Diddie," but the CD gets down to serious work with the glow of four introductory notes on "Police Dog Blues." Those notes return again and again; they are awesome moments in blues history and the punctuation for a sad story of a ne'er-do-well travelin' man. Very quickly, it becomes clear that Blake is an extraordinary guitar player, evident when he performs an instrumental such as on "Blind Arthur's Breakdown" or "Hastings Street" (along with pianist Charlie Spand). Blake talks over a transcendent instrumental bed on "Southern Rag," whose speed, variety, and good-time feeling is among his finest work (and among the best blues guitar on record). The spirit of "Come On Boys, Let's Do That Messin' Around" is generated almost entirely by Blake's guitar. And on "One Time Blues," which seems so calm at the outset, Blake demonstrates double time. It's easy to listen past the scratchy quality that occasionally mars some tracks (Yazoo gathers the best available versions, but some are better than others); at the start of "Skeedle Loo Doo," scratchiness seems a problem, but the music is so compelling that this is soon forgotten. There are 23 tracks in all, on just one CD; nearly every one is worth hearing. Yazoo's liner notes are very complete, but concentrate on guitar technique, with limited attention to music history.

LINK➤ *Blind Blake — Complete Recorded Works, Volumes 1-4*

Document (Arhoolie) 5024-5027

Each of these four CDs is filled with about two dozen songs (a few are alternate takes, but most are originals). As with all Document CDs in this series, the quality varies widely depending upon original source material. Still, Blake is one-of-a-kind and the music is terrific.

Bobby "Blue" Bland

Blues vocalist Bobby Bland came from Rosemark, TN, a small town outside of Memphis. He never learned to play an instrument and became famous solely on the quality of his voice. In 1947, when he was 17, Bland moved to the city and started a gospel singing career. He also performed with the on-again, off-again Beale Streeters, whose members periodically included B.B. King and Junior Parker. Bland served in the Army in the early 1950s, then returned to start recording with Duke, a local label that would be his home for nearly two decades. In the late 1950s, he toured as lead vocalist for Junior Parker's Blue Flames, then worked for most of the 1960s with his own band. Throughout, he recorded a spectacular string of R&B hits and often opened for his friend B.B. King. Duke was sold in 1972, but Bland kept on recording for Malaco and other labels.

I Pity the Fool: The Duke Recordings, Vol. 1 **Duke 10665**

A cautionary note: most of the 44 tracks on this 1952–60 compilation have been slightly overmodulated, perhaps to sound good on AM radio. Bland was in his twenties when these recordings were made, and his maturation over the course of the decade is very appealing. The formula begins to gel on "Wise Man's Blues," with an uncredited organist and vibes player tinkering behind Johnny Board's thick tenor saxophone. The slow, understated groove continues on "You or None," with the sweet innocent voice that sings, "Love is a mystery, but I'll take a chance with you." Bland could also stand out against a rocking blues guitar and powerful R&B horns, his voice forcing the upper ends of its most comfortable register, singing out with tremendous feeling on "I Don't Believe" (which, incidentally, also features a nice solo by Clarence Holloman). These sublime examples of R&B songwriting continue with Johnny Copeland's "I Learned My Lesson," but the showstopper is the "hmm-mm" humming that Bland brilliantly injects into "I Smell Trouble." Nobody puts over a sad song quite the way Bland does; he excels on the slow, lost-boy "Last Night." "Little Blue Boy," is slightly faster and a little more famous. Here, Bland screaches a bit to express emotions in what seems to be a very personal song. The classiest version of Bland's stylish whining finds him growling with annoyance, and yet singing with a satin sheen in his choruses. By 1960, Bland had become a very skillful vocalist, indeed.

LINK➤ *Johnny Ace — Memorial Album* ***MCA 31183***

Pure romance with a gentle tenor voice, sentimental lyrics and arrangements, and honest tenderness. "Pledging My Love" was Ace's best-known song. On occasion, he'll strike out with a jump blues, as on "How Can You Be So Mean?" but most tunes are of the "So Lonely" variety.

Turn on Your Love Light: The Duke Recordings, Vol. 2

Duke 10957

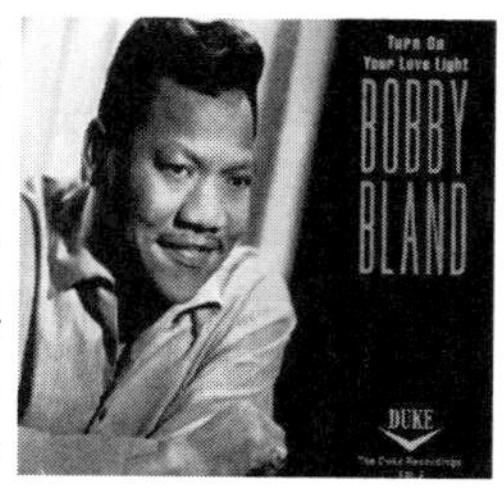

The first volume was little more than a prelude to this 2-CD set. The fidelity is fine, the production is sophisticated and satisfying, the material is chosen with intelligence and taste, and Bland's voice is better than ever. A persuasive version of the old Louis Armstrong favorite "St. James Infirmary" is masterfully executed and just as sad as can be. Bland strikes up a big band feeling on the Earl Hines–Billy Eckstine tune, "Jelly, Jelly, Jelly," which also features some spectacular horn charts. He also does a fine "Blue Moon" and even better versions of Harold Arlen-Johnny Mercer's "Blues In the Night" and Rodgers & Hart's "Blue Moon." The bounce of the horns and the rich grain of Bland's mahogany voice makes "Ain't That Lovin' You" spine-tingling. A gospel rhythm—and a gospel chorus—bring 1962's "Yield Not to Temptation" to the boiling point. The pumped-up horns push Bland higher and higher; this is one of his very best songs. "Turn On Your Love Light," from 1961, includes a taste of the same rhythm and similar horn arrangements, but it's not cooked as a gospel tune. "Share Your Love with Me," from 1963, features strings, the Anita Kerr Singers in the background, and a kitschy romantic vocal from Bland. Slicked-up presentations fill most of CD2 (covering 1963–64); the best is a two-part B.B. King soundalike called "Ain't Doin' Too Bad" and a soulful "Steal Away," with the inevitable lyric, "I've got a right to cry."

LINK➤ *Z.Z. Hill — In Memorium (1935-1984)* **_Malaco 7246_**

A soulful blues singer whose Down Home Blues *album was enormously popular in the 1980s, Hill tended more toward soulful than jazzy blues, but fans of one will no doubt appreciate the other's work. Contains most of Hill's important songs.*

That Did It!: The Duke Recordings, Vol. 3

Duke 11444

It's generally wise to skip past the mid-1960s, when overbearing horns obliterated Bland's honest sentiment on songs like "Angel Girl." Instead, shift to the late 1960s for his handsome, mature vocals on "Lover With a Reputation," "Touch of the Blues," and "Chains of Love." Covering 1965 through 1972, this 2-CD set begins with overblown production, but settles down with time. Wayne Bennett, who appeared on many Bland albums, is a fine accompanist for "Ain't Nobody's Business," which Bland sings wonderfully. There's a good arrangement of "Fever," too, and solid vocal renditions of Charles Brown's "Driftin' Blues" and Hoagy Carmichael's "Georgia on My Mind." Selective listening proves very rewarding.

LINK➤ *Wilson Pickett — A Man and a Half: The Best of Wilson Pickett*

Rhino 70287

Pickett's best is a survey of 1960s soul. Go beyond the songs that crossed over ("In the Midnight Hour," "Mustang Sally") and explore the material that didn't make it on to white radio stations. Some good covers include "Hey Jude."

In the early 1960s, Bob Dylan, John Sebastian, Joan Baez, and Mississippi John Hurt were among many musicians who frequented Alan Block's Greenwich Village sandal shop. Block was a country fiddler whose store was a place where musicians jammed. His wife was a folk singer. Rory Block, who was born in 1949, learned music from her parents and by transcribing old blues records and mimicking what she heard. By 14, she was performing at NYC's Town Hall. At 15, she left home for Berkeley with guitar wizard Stefan Grossman. After a few years of performing, Block found the music business too hard for women; she decided to start a family instead. In 1975, inspired by Carole King's success, Block signed with RCA and later with Chrysalis. Neither experience was a happy one. In 1981, Block settled in at Rounder; there she established herself as a gifted singer-songwriter and an important interpreter of rural blues.

Best Blues & Originals — Rounder 11525

Loving reconsiderations of beautiful songs sung by Tommy Johnson, Robert Johnson, Charlie Patton, Reverend Gary Davis, and Willie Brown fill about a third of this 1987 collection. The others are mostly originals. All come from Block's first four Rounder albums. Her decades of study are evident in wonderfully artistic guitar work evocative of early blues; it's as complex and original as anything these bluesmen performed. Block's singing voice borrows the best from early blues stars and folkies, but she's her own woman, as her eye-opening versions of the traditional "Water Is Wide" and Tommy Johnson's "Travelin' Blues" so artfully demonstrate. With star accompaniment from John Sebastian, Stevie Wonder, David Bromberg, and others.

LINK➤ *Jesse Thomas — Lookin' for That Woman* **—** ***Black Top 1128***

Thomas was born in Louisiana in 1908 and made his way in Dallas alongside Blind Lemon Jefferson. By 1956, he was finished with the L.A. scene and returned to Shreveport. When he started on the festival circuit in the 1980s, Thomas was a revered elder statesman. He's superb.

Gone Woman Blues: The Country Blues Collection — Rounder 11575

Nearly two dozen songs on this 1997 collection are reworked rural blues culled from Block's 1989–95 albums. Celebrating Tommy Johnson, Block opens with his rowdy "Big Road Blues" and punctuates it with Johnson-style falsetto yodels. Next is one of her signature tunes, "Maggie Campbell," plus two more Johnson tunes. There's real depth here, developed by listening and by studies with Skip James, Son House, and others like them. Block imitates and updates Robert Johnson's "Hellhound on My Trail" with two voices—one lead, one chrous—with amazing precision. Her original "Gone Woman Blues" is also excellent. A treasure trove of discoveries, this is an illuminated path through early blues.

LINK➤ *Tommy Johnson — 1928–1929* **—** ***Document 5001***

Johnson was one of the most significant and influential early blues singers, known for songs like "Cool Water Blues" and "Maggie Campbell." "Canned Heat" blues describes the severity of his alcohol addiction (Johnson was known to drink Sterno); somehow, he lived to 1956. Gorgeous blues.

Lonnie Brooks

Although his banjo-playing grandfather taught him to play as a boy, Lee Baker, Jr., didn't take the guitar seriously until age twenty, in 1953. By then, his family had moved from Duboisson, Louisiana to Port Arthur, Texas. He found work with Clifton Chenier, and, by 1957, the musician now known as Guitar Junior was recording his own regional R&B hits like "Family Rules," and "The Crawl." Touring with Sam Cooke in 1959 led to Chicago. To avoid confusion with an established musician, his stage name became Lonnie Brooks. He also swapped his music style from Southern swamp rock to Chicago blues. For the next two decades, Brooks picked up regular gigs, occasionally recorded, and did his best to earn a living. Then, in 1978, his music was included in an Alligator compilation called Living Chicago Blues. This led to an Alligator recording contract, and eventually, awards and critical acclaim.

Roadhouse Blues — **Alligator 4843**

His seventh Alligator album, from1996, finds Brooks in excellent voice and still mired in a mucky Lousiana rhythm, doing his swamp blues thing. The engineering has improved—there's an immediacy here that wasn't present on earlier CDs. Brooks is also sharing lead guitar duties with his talented son, Ronnie Baker Brooks. This is earnest, authentic, refined electric blues, expertly performed. A slight gospel influence by way of Memphis makes "Too Little, Too Late" one of the best tracks. Brooks's guitar still slices through the thick, humid air on "Backbone Man" and "Before You Go," but a more mature approach has replaced sparks with a steady, relaxed flow.

LINK➤ *Clifton Chenier — Louisiana Blues & Zydeco* — ***Arhoolie 329***

When these tracks were recorded in the mid-1960s, Brooks had been gone for several years or more, but Chenier's music hadn't changed much. It's still a blend of Cajun accordion and a shuffling beat, Creole singing, and a good-time approach to musical entertainment.

Bayou Lightning — **Alligator 4714**

With a thick, dark voice and an electric guitar that slices through the swamp-rock arrangements, Brooks's first Alligator album is also his best. The format of "Watchdog" is representative: Brooks sings a verse and a chorus, then solos by sending out shards of energy from his guitar. The image of a bayou storm and the snap of lightning is an apt analogy. The rhythm section overlays some Caribbean tempos and arrangements onto a steady rolling bed. The lowdown "Figure Head" sets up a woman interested only in money; Brooks does a nice job switching tempo and vocal texture to simulate her perspective. "Alimony" also deals with opposite sex issues. From 1979.

LINK➤ *Various Artists — Alley Special* — ***Collectibles 5320***

One reason to buy this CD is to hear Muddy Waters's first commercially released single. Another is to explore some blues history, ranging from Louisana to Detroit with lots of stops along the way. Key artrists include Wright Holmes and Robert "Baby Boy" Warren.

Big Bill Broonzy

William Lee Conway Broonzy was born in the mid-1890s to a family of sharecroppers living in Scott, MS. During his early years, the large family (17 children) moved to Arkansas, where Broonzy was raised. He picked up guitar playing from an uncle, and as a young teen he earned money playing at picnics with his homemade guitar. Broonzy was drafted, served in the army, got married, and worked as a sharecropper. He also played blues, which prompted a move to Chicago in the early 1920s. By the end of that decade, Broonzy was recording for major "race record" labels. He picked up extra cash by working at rent parties and as a maintenance man and janitor. Broonzy worked through the Great Depression, and by the time he sang at the monumental "Spirituals to Swing" Carnegie Hall concerts in 1938 and 1939, he was Chicago's most famous bluesman. After WWII, the electric guitar changed Chicago's blues scene, but the resilient Broonzy transformed himself into a folk-bluesman and worked until 1957. He died of throat cancer in 1958.

Do That Guitar Rag — Yazoo 1035

"Worrying You Off My Mind" has that familiar ring—it's one of those songs that's been reworked time and again. Here, it's a showpiece for Broonzy's full-bodied voice and the nuances of a guitar finding just the right accompanying style. "Mr. Conductor Man" and particularly "C&A Blues" are railroad songs of the highest order. "Leave My Man Alone" is mostly Jane Lucas's song; Broonzy adds guitar and harmony, and Georgia Tom Dorsey (a bluesman who became a gospel singer) plays a bouncy "boom-chang" piano. Lucas and Dorsey also work on the suggestive hokum "Pussy Cat Blues" (with a repeated "meow" sound). Broonzy's guitar work is best on "Big Bill Blues," his recording debut.

LINK➤ *Var. Artists — News & the Blues: Telling It Like It Is* — *Columbia 46217*

Topical blues, covering the W.P.A., pure unadulterated anger ("If I Had My Way, I'd Tear The Building Down," by Blind Willie Johnson), "Unemployment Stomp," "Dope Head Blues," and so on. All classic early blues. Broonzy contributes an army song.

The Young Big Bill Broonzy — Yazoo 1011

The emphasis on this CD is pure country blues and fantastic instrumental work, starting with the first cut, "Long Tall Mama," a pure 12-bar blues. "Stove Pipe Stomp" is a tight instrumental duet featuring Broonzy's sparkling guitar and Steel Smith's six-string banjo. Broonzy's tricky guitar work on "Saturday Night Rub" is supported by flat-picking bassist Frank Braswell. For a textbook example of flat-picked guitar, check out "I Can't Be Satisfied" (also a Braswell duet). Piano-guitar duets are relatively uncommon, but "Good Liquor Gonna Carry Me Down" boogies along comfortably (despite the track's very scratchy sound). "Eagle Ridin' Papa" features both Braswell and Dorsey; it's a bouncy rag with all three men singing.

LINK➤ *Harry Reser — Banjo Crackerjax* **Yazoo 1048**

All-American banjo playing from the 1920s, from the hands of one of the finest banjo players in the history of the instrument. The style is ragtime, by way of string band. Reser worked mainly in NYC; his last job was in the pit orchestra of the Broadway musical, Fiddler on the Roof*.*

Good Time Tonight — Columbia 46219

Most of this work was recorded in 1937–39, and the recordings are somewhat clearer than the Yazoo material. From 1932, there's another version of "Worrying You Off My Mind," and a wonderful slow railroad blues called "Too Too Train Blues." Many of the 1937 songs are performed with Blind John Davis on piano and also with either drums or bass. The suggestive "I Want My Hands on It" begins a sequence of jazz-blues numbers from 1938, the roots of jump blues. There's a jazz horn section (Buster Bennett and others) on "W.P.A. Blues" and "Going Back to Arkansas." On "Too Many Drivers," Broonzy is accompanied by a very soulful clarinet, played by Odell Rand.

LINK➤ *Various Artists — Legends of the Blues, Vol. 1* **Columbia 46215**

Broonzy takes his place among the greatest blues stars in the Columbia, Okeh, and Vocalion catalogs. This extraordinary collection presents superb work from Bessie Smith, Blind Lemon Jefferson, Blind Willie Johnson, Robert Johnson, and more than a dozen more top artists.

Sings Folk Songs — Smithsonian Folkways 40023

What a voice! These are songs from Broonzy's "folk-bluesman" period, and when he tears into "This Train (Is Bound for Glory)," the rafters shake. It's a rich mix of classic Americana, much more folk than blues. Broonzy begins each chorus of "Goin' Down This Road (Feeling Bad)" with a riveting nasal falsetto. The power of "John Henry" is established by Broonzy's guitar, but here his vocal doesn't quite deliver. "Martha" is a country blues with long vocal holds and flashy guitar work. Then there's "Bill Bailey" and "The Glory of Love"—super renditions, but uncomfortable listening because they're so distant from blues. Still, the man had to earn a living. . . .

LINK➤ *Bob Gibson—Joy Joy! The Young & Wonderful Bob Gibson* **Fantasy 9099**

The pure-white side of folk music, a world in which Broonzy had become comfortable. Gibson was a talented songwriter and singer, one who helped built the bridge on which Dylan and others crossed. He's worth hearing, but only if you're a folk music fan.

Charles Brown

Brown's blues are dignified and sophisticated; they're like blues for a late night cocktail lounge. Brown grew up in a middle-class Texas town, took piano lessons, went to college, and taught high school chemistry. He also worked briefly as a chemist in Arkansas; a company transfer led him to the San Francisco area. By 1944, at age 22, music became Brown's life. Now living in Los Angeles, he joined Johnny Moore's Three Blazers. Brown sang and played piano with guitar player Moore and bassist Eddie Williams. The trio started to record, and its "Driftin' Blues" became a huge R&B hit. "Merry Christmas, Baby" followed. Brown formed his own trio in 1949; he was a star for several years prior to the start of rock 'n' roll. Brown kept working, mostly in small clubs and for small labels. In the late 1980s, he was rediscovered and became popular with a new generation.

Driftin' Blues: The Best of Charles Brown — **EMI 97989**

Brown sings two kinds of songs on this album—intimate love songs with his piano and intimate love songs with the quiet accompaniment of a saxophone or guitar. His art matures to perfection on 1953's "Lonesome Feeling" with these instruments taking their disturbing solos behind his unassuming, everyman vocal. "Black Night" follows a similar muse; it reached number one on the R&B charts in 1951, and was one of eleven songs here that made it to the Top Ten. Four late 1940s songs, including the popular "Driftin' Blues," represent Brown's work with Johnny Moore's Three Blazers. "Merry Christmas, Baby," from 1956, never charted, but it's a sweet legacy.

LINK➤ *Charles Brown — All My Life* — ***Bullseye Blues 9501***

Somewhat livelier than Brown's usual stuff, this 1990 album has an R&B feel. While still subdued, it's got a pleasant 1940s-style polish on some cuts. Others feature a gentle funk perpetrated by Dr. John. The two sing together on "A Virus Called the Blues."

Someone to Love — **Bullseye Blues 9514**

Bonnie Raitt's presence on the title song of this 1992 album helped Brown to get airplay on adult rock stations. It's an easy-flowing unaccompanied piano blues (with a movie-style hook). Raitt follows Brown's lead, but adds just a dash of zest with a slightly larger vocal. She gives her heart to the song; the mutual respect is evident as the two trade lines in the final verse. Elvis Costello wrote "I Wonder How She Knows?" which fits smoothly into Brown's style with an especially handsome arrangement. On "Every Little Bit Hurts," Brown delivers his usual lost soul vocal, but this time his singing is echoed and taunted by Raitt's slide guitar. Many more delights are featured.

LINK➤ *Bonnie Raitt — The Bonnie Raitt Collection* — ***Warner Bros. 26242***

Here's a woman long overdue for a boxed set. This 20-track collection presents some of her best-known material from the 1970s and 1980s, including "Finest Lovin' Man," "Sugar Mama," "Angel from Montgomery" (with John Prine), and "True Love Is Hard to Find."

Clarence "Gatemouth" Brown

A versatile performer who often worked jazz, calypso, bluegrass, and Cajun music into an electric blues repertoire, Brown grew up in a musical family. As a teenager, Brown gigged around his Orange, TX, home, then served in the army during WW II. In 1945, at age 21, Brown sat in for T-Bone Walker, who couldn't make his date at Houston's Bronze Peacock. Brown dazzled the crowd and made a management deal with club owner Don Robey. Robey signed Brown to Aladdin Records, but after a few unsuccessful singles Robey formed his own Peacock label; the two worked together there from 1947 until 1960. Then Brown was out on his own, working for smaller labels; for a while he led the band on *The Beat*, a syndicated TV show. Things picked up after several European tours, including one for the U.S. State Department. By the 1980s, Brown was recording for Alligator and then Rounder Records.

The Original Peacock Recordings — Rounder 2039

Most of the dozen songs on this CD were recorded in the first half of the 1950s, before rock 'n' roll, when R&B was the hottest stuff around. It's interesting to contrast Brown's fantastic versatility with the straight-ahead blues of his chief rival, T-Bone Walker. On 1952's "Sad Hour," Brown sings a slow soulful blues in a sincere and sexy style later popularized by Johnny Adams. "Okie Dokie Stomp," from 1954, is an up-tempo instrumental dance number with a very intense electric guitar and rocking horns—very close to rock 'n' roll. Brown's scratchy fiddle leads the stomping "Just Before Dawn," sounding almost avant-garde. Uneven, influential, and worth hearing.

LINK➤ *Guitar Slim — Sufferin' Mind* — ***Specialty 7007***

Famous for the R&B hit "The Things I Used to Do," Guitar Slim's early 1950s sides feature some hotly distorted guitar, empassioned vocals, and R&B horns. "Story of My Life," from 1953, is relentlessly sad, and performed with the over-the-top intensity that makes Guitar Slim so interesting.

Pressure Cooker — Alligator 4745

One time through "She Winked an Eye" should convince even the most skeptical of Brown's extraordinary skills on electric guitar. He clearly belongs on the same plane as the best rockers, and he indulges himself in the improvisational "She Winked Her Eye," with attentive backup from organist Milt Buckner. Ditto for "My Time Is Expensive" with pianist Jay McShann. Brown's vocals are also good, but it's difficult not to focus on that guitar. He even does a credible and remarkably musical job with Louis Jordan's novelty "Ain't Nobody Here But Us Chickens." Fine title cut features Arnett Cobb (tenor sax). Recorded in 1973 for France's Disques Black and Blue.

LINK➤ *Clarence "Gatemouth" Brown — Just Got Lucky* — ***Evidence 26019***

More tracks from those same 1973 sessions include "Caldonia" and "Choo Choo Ch'Boogie," plus some jazzier numbers. The second half comes from 1977 sessions in Nice, France. All tracks feature top-notch jazz sidemen. Very highly recommended.

Alright Again! **Rounder 2028**

A flow of "Frosty" blasts sets the album's pace: here's a tight instrumental with big bursts of brass every few seconds, terrific solos, and Brown jumping in for stunning electric guitar solos. It's the sort of material that goes right to the heart. "Strollin' With Bones" does the same trick again, and with no less effect. "Dollar Got the Blues" is more of an R&B song centered with a very bluesy guitar and vocal, with the horns shaking the house regularly. Some of this, like "Alligator Boogaloo" and "Give Me Time to Explain" feels more like jazz than blues. Brilliant horns, fantastic electric guitar. Energetic recording, too. Great album!

LINK➤ *Various Artists — The Best of Duke-Peacock Blues* ***MCA 10667***

Prior to Motown, Duke-Peacock was the world's largest black-owned record company. It was led by Don Robey, who launched the label with Brown in 1948. Later, the label presented Johnny Ace, Junior Parker, Fenton Robinson, Larry Davis ("Texas Flood"), and Bobby Bland.

Real Life **Rounder 2054**

A 1985 album recorded live in Texas finds Brown and his band in a very coherent groove with some choice material. Brown just keeps driving with that virtuoso electric guitar, one long line with horns that always arrive at the right time and say precisely the right thing; Brown then backs off so the horns can take their solos. Sometimes this is hot blues, and sometimes it's jazz. With Brown, it makes complete sense to find Billy Strayhorn's "Take the A Train" two tracks after a guitar improvisation on the traditional "Frankie and Johnnie." All this is later followed by a boogie-woogie version of W.C. Handy's "St. Louis Blues." Lots of imagination!

LINK➤ *Bill Frisell — Nashville* ***Nonesuch 79145***

Among contemporary guitar players, few cross boundaries—or ignore them—as routinely as Bill Frisell. He zigs from hoedown to country, and country blues, then returns to the rules and structures of jazz. His skills are at the highest possible level.

Standing My Ground **Alligator 4779**

This time it's New Orleans and a distinctly different sound. A tight, distinctive version of "Got My Mojo Working" sets up the album, one of the few Brown didn't write himself. The way Bobby Campo's trumpet slides right in for its "Mojo" solo is outstanding. The rhythm section and Terrance Simien's accordion set a New Orleans mood, and while Brown's clearly a happy visitor and not a native—he does beat it back with a strong guitar solo. Nifty horn arrangements on "Born in Louisiana" are handsome against Brown's bluesy vocal; the horns and singing mix for a while with Brown's fiddle, but all sounds ultimately pale when Brown rocks out on guitar.

LINK➤ *Various Artists — 15 Louisiana Zydeco Classics* ***Arhoolie 105***

The fifth in Arhoolie's formidable (and low-priced) American Masters *series, here's a bluffer's guide to music by Clifton Chenier, C.J. Chenier, and highly regarded locals such as John Delafose and Canray Fontenot. Try also Vol. 3 (Arhoolie 103),* Cajun Classics.

Paul Butterfield grew up in the affluent Hyde Park neighborhood of Chicago and attended the University of Illinois for a while before dropping out to play blues full time. At the university, Butterfield met Nick Gravenites, then Elvin Bishop, who came from Oklahoma with an interest in blues. The three played colleges, sat in at blues clubs, and eventually put together a mixed-race band to play in a white Chicago club. By 1965, fellow student and keyboard player Mark Naftalin and guitar player Mike Bloomfield joined up, and the Paul Butterfield Blues Band recorded its first album. As the 1960s progressed, band members left, and by the end of the decade, the magic had evaporated. Butterfield tried again in the early 1970s with a new band, Better Days. In his later years. Butterfield fought creative frustration and substance abuse. He died of a heart attack in Los Angeles in 1981; he was 44 years old.

The Paul Butterfield Blues Band — Elektra 7294

Proof that white men can play the blues—with the steel, grace, and rhythm of Chicago's best. Butterfield's vocals and harmonica, Mike Bloomfield's lead guitar, and Elvin Bishop's rhythm guitar seek out the heart of darkness—music written by Willie Dixon and Muddy Waters. Remarkably, their own compositions are nearly as durable and offer more space for a very significant contribution to 1960s blues and rock: the extended improvisation. Bloomfield's "Screamin'" totally fits the Chicago blues mold, but it's a step into the future. They do everything well, but "Mystery Train" ("The train I ride is 16 coaches long. . . .") is outstanding. Excellent work from Sam Lay (drummer), Jerome Arnold (bass), and Mark Naftalin (organ).

LINK➤ *Elvin Bishop — Tulsa Shuffle: The Best of Elvin Bishop* — *Epic/Legacy 57630*

To be more accurate, this is Bishop's best from 1969 through 1971, the years that he was associated with the Columbia Records family. Good guitar work on a wide range of material, from Percy Mayfield's "Prisoner of Love" to his own "Hog Bottom."

East/West — Elektra 7315

The ripping combination of guitars and organ creates a sharp, definitive rhythm for "Walkin' Blues," a signature song on this 1966 milestone. Butterfield's updated approach to Chicago blues vocals is extremely effective here—he pays tribute while pushing blues into the future. Ditto for the guitar playing of Mike Bloomfield and Elvin Bishop, who move from urban blues, to 1960s rock, to psychedelic blues on the 13-minute "East West." Nat Adderley's "Work Song" straddles jazz and blues; here again, the band, with extraordinary craftsmanship, redefines contemporary blues. "Two Trains Running" is a more traditional city blues. Aggressive, accessible, and slightly dated, the album retains its status as a rocking blues classic.

LINK➤ *Paul Butterfield — An Anthology: The Elektra Years* — *Elektra 62124*

Long-awaited 2-CD collection of Butterfield's best work (33 songs), notable because it selects the best music from the many later albums (which were spotty); consider this, too, as a possible replacement for the first two albums. Good work from 1968's Pigboy Crabshaw *album, too.*

Leroy Carr & Scrapper Blackwell

Carr and Blackwell were popular for about seven years, but their influence has resonated throughout blues history. Francis Blackwell, who played guitar, was born in South Carolina in 1903. Leroy Carr was born two years later in Nashville, TN. Both men grew up in Indianapolis, IN, and both had colorful adventures before teaming up in 1928 to record for Vocalion. (Blackwell made and sold moonshine; Carr traveled with a circus, bootlegged, and played piano at parties and dances through the South and Midwest.) The pair became a top-rated blues act, but there was trouble ahead. The constant high life led to serious alcohol-related problems for Carr; he died in 1935. Blackwell continued in the business for a few more years, then faded into Indianapolis's labor market until 1959, when he was rediscovered by blues enthusiasts and encouraged to record an album. In 1962, Blackwell was mugged and left to die in an Indianapolis alley; the murderer was never found.

The Virtuoso Guitar of Scapper Blackwell

Yazoo 1019

When Scrapper Blackwell performs "Kokomo Blues," it's easy to understand what the excitement was about. His confidence, polished guitar presentation, and easy vocal style are often copied. Blackwell's delicate guitar accompaniment is both interesting and unusual on "Penal Farm Blues." "Trouble Blues" is elaborate and filigreed. Carr appears only on "Good Woman Blues" and "Barrelhouse Woman No. 2." Their guitar-piano combination on the former is excellent, a perfect balance between the astringent guitar and the flowing piano. Most often here, Blackwell either works alone or with singer Black Bottom McPhail.

LINK➤ *Casey Bill Weldon & Kokomo Arnold—Bottleneck Trendsetters of the 1930s*

Yazoo 1049

A classic R.Crumb cover design introduces two of the 1930s' most popular bottleneck players (each plays seven tracks, but not together). Some of the finest acoustic blues on record.

1929-1935

Best of Blues 10

Considering the historical importance of Leroy Carr and Scrapper Blackwell—and the high quality of their performances—it's surprising to find that their records are largely absent from U.S. catalogs. This collection, from the Best of Blues label (affiliated with Austria's Wolf label), mainly features Carr. His sixteen songs include "Lifeboat Blues," "Gambler's Blues" and some interesting oddities, like "Christmas in Jail—Ain't That a Pain?" The seven Blackwell tracks include "Alley Sally Blues," and "Motherless Boy" blues. The quality of the sound varies widely, but the essence of their spirited presentation comes across without qualification. Keep your eyes open for an out-of-print Yazoo LP entitled *Naptown Blues*.

LINK➤ *Uptown Blues: A Decade of Guitar-Piano Duets* ***Yazoo 1927-1937***

Carr and Blackwell are featured on just one of these 14 tracks, namely 1930's "Papa's on the Housetop." Bo Carter plays with his brother Harry on "When You Left." Roosevelt Sykes is the pianist behind undistinguished guitarist Teddy Darby. A mixed bag.

Armenter Chatmon was born on a Mississippi plantation in 1893. He specialized in songs with sexually explicit or double-entendre lyrics, but such material provides only a limited view of his talents. Carter often performed with his brothers in a family band popular with white audiences; their repertoire included ragtime and dance music as well as blues. (His brother Sam Chatmon, who also played in the band, continued working into the 1960s.) The brothers also performed as the Mississippi Sheiks, with Walter Vinson and another brother, Lonnie Chatmon. Carter was a capable, versatile man who put together his own chauffeuring business, taught himself carpentry, and worked as a farmer. He preferred to play solo acoustic blues, but a sophisticated guitar style did not gain favor with black audiences, and a soloist was not appropriate for the entertainment-minded white audiences. The solution was the recording studio; there, Carter recorded over a hundred sides in the 1930s before interest in his music faded. Bo Carter died in 1964 in Memphis, TN, after several strokes.

Banana in Your Fruit Basket — Yazoo 1064

The blues weren't only about feeling bad. In fact, the very concept of the blues was something concocted by record companies in the 1920s—a small subcategory of folk music performed by Southern "songsters." Many performed songs with suggestive lyrics, but Carter's recordings were among the most popular. Most are obvious and often humorous in their indirectness: "Mashing That Thing" (about masturbation), "Ram Rod Daddy" (oral sex), "Cigarette Blues" ("draw my cigarette until my good ashes come"), "My Pencil Won't Write Any More" ("because the lead's all gone!"). Other songs are more outrageous, like "Banana in My Fruit Basket," and "Pig Meat Is What I Crave." Superb performances, masterful guitar playing.

LINK➤ *Mississippi Sheiks — Stop and Listen* — ***Yazoo 2006***

Walter Vinson, Bo Carter, and Bo's brother Lonnie Chatmon performed under this name on the streets of Jackson, MS (the "Sheiks" name came from a Valentino film). It's fiddle and guitar music, somewhere between string band and blues. Very satisfying.

Twist It Babe: 1931–1940 — Yazoo 1034

While there are more than a few songs with sexual lyrics here ("Baby please let me roll your lemon and squeeze it there all night long"), the music is not as consistently bawdy. Listen closely and examine the work of a very skillful songwriter and performer. "Someday" is a conventional song made special through a highly cultivated falsetto. "Honey" is a superb composition equal to the work of Louis Armstrong, and suitable for an Al Jolson or a young Bing Crosby. "I Get the Blues" is another very "show-biz" blues, intimately performed with a mesmerizing, shimmering style. Start here for some bawdy material and lots of spectacular music-making.

LINK➤ *Mississippi Sheiks — Complete Recorded Works, Vols.1–4* — ***Document 5803-5806***

For collectors. Also seek out the 1979 LP, Sam Chatmon's Advice *(Rounder 2018).*

Cephas & Wiggins

John Cephas, who sings and plays guitar, was born in 1930 in Washington, D.C., and raised in Bowling Green, VA. Phil Wiggins, who sings and plays harmonica, was born in 1954 in Washington, D.C. Cephas grew up singing gospel and learned guitar from listening to blues records. He earned a living mostly by ocean fishing, carpentry, and by singing in professional gospel groups. Wiggins became an accompanist; he worked with local D.C. gospel and slide guitar artist, Flora Molton, and with Mother Scott, an old blues singer. Cephas and Wiggins met at the 1976 Smithsonian Institution Folklife Festival and started playing Piedmont-style blues together. They kept busy in the 1980s on various U.S. State Department tours of Europe and elsewhere, gradually building a reputation at home as well. They're also actors; Wiggins was in John Sayles's *Matewan*, and Cephus was in 1991's Kennedy Center production of *Blind Man Blues*.

Sweet Bitter Blues — Evidence 26050

Of the 17 tracks on this CD, the first 10 probably qualify as a coherent early effort. They were recorded in Virginia in 1983. "Sweet Bitter Blues" is a midtempo acoustic duet with endless space that's filled with Wiggins's inventive improvising. Deep, clear, and just slightly gritty, Cephas's voice is especially well suited to storytelling; he does a terrific job with "St. James Infirmary." The two are also sweet on rags. On "Piedmont Rag," for example, Wiggins's stunningly fast harmonica sounds like a horn. And on the early 1980s live material (from blues festivals in Germany), "Bowling Green Rag" contains the tastiest improvisations. Jimmy Reed's "Running and Hiding" gets the audience cheering.

LINK➤ *Various Artists — Good Time Blues* — ***Columbia/Legacy 46780***

Sub-titled "Harmonicas, Kazoos, Washboards, and Cowbells," this music was made with inexpensive instruments that could be carried to town to town. Several jug bands and string bands, too. It's fun.

Dog Days of August — Flying Fish (Rounder) 70394

On this 1984 CD, the strong suit is storytelling. "Reno Factory" tells the sad tale of losing a love; it is magnificently structured and flawlessly performed. The title song, with its strong lyrics and evocative arrangement, is one of Cephas and Wiggin's best. It's about a "wrong-doing woman," and the heat sizzles from the dirty streets. The two also sketch a vivid illustration of a black folk hero in "John Henry." They look back to Skip James and his high vocal register for "Cherryball" and for the somber, funereal "Hard Time Killing Floor Blues," with choruses sung in unison. Their "I Saw the Light" does Reverend Gary Davis proud. Meticulous craftsmanship meets fine art.

LINK➤ *Guy Davis — Stomp Down the Rider* — ***Red House 80***

He's the son of Ossie Davis and Ruby Dee. He's been involved in theater (notably Mulebone, *a Broadway show scored by Taj Mahal) and sings country blues. Davis knows his influences and plays a mean slide guitar. Try also* Call Down the Thunder *(Red House 89).*

Guitar Man

Flying Fish (Rounder) 70470

"Black Cat on the Line" shows how sophisticated Cephas and Wiggins's urban acoustic blues has become. Wiggins's harmonica provides not only instrumental support, but angry catlike claws in its shape and tone. "Richmond Blues" is a house-party favorite with roots in the 1920s. "Weeping Willow" was inspired by a Blind Boy Fuller tune from 1937. "Police Dog Blues" comes from Blind Blake (he recorded it in 1929). "Corrina" and "Careless Love" are classic old songs, too. These are not museum reproductions, though. Instead, they're living, breathing links in a decades-old chain. And like so many predeccesors, Cephas and Wiggins add virtuoso touches, change lyrics, and make the songs their own. And that's what the blues is all about!

LINK➤ *Harmonica Fats & Bernie Pearl — Blow Fat Daddy, Blow!* *Bee Bump 5*

Two L.A.studio musicians teamed up to explore authentic Southern blues. Pearl picked up blues from other musicians in L.A. This is their third album, reflecting Harvey Blackston's early life on a Lousiana farm. Try also 1991's I Had to Get Nasty *(Bee Bump 2).*

Bluesmen

Chesky 89

The breadth of the Cephas and Wiggins's repertoire and depth of their scholarship is impressive. They are keeping this music alive. That much is clear as the two rip into Big Bill Broonzy's labor protest, "Big Big Boss Man." There's a lot of fine old blues here, from Mance Lipscomb's "Mama Lay It On You" and Willie Dixon's "Little Red Rooster," to Sonny Boy Williamson's "Good Morning, Little School Girl." Once again, the influence of Blind Boy Fuller and Blind Blake guide the way. The ragtime instrumental "Blake's Rag" captures some of Blake's essence. They also remake Guitar Slim's 1954 R&B hit, "The Things I Used to Do." Another highlight is the dance called "Burn Your Bridges." From 1993.

LINK➤ *Corey Harris — Fish Ain't Bitin'* *Alligator 4850*

Performing songs by heroes like Son House, Memphis Minnie, Blind Lemon Jefferson,, the coarse-voiced Harris makes a deep impression with his old-style guitar. Recorded in 1996, this is a remarkable tribute to country blues by a well-educated musical scholar and artist.

Cool Down

Alligator 4838

This 1995 album is a leap forward in the presentation of the duo's original music. "Caroline in the Morning" is a warm and magical sunrise, a loving instrumental definition of the word "home." The title track is a tad preachy; it's a plea to angry, dangerous city gang kids to chill out. "No Ice in My Bourbon," about approaching life head-on, works surprisingly well. New versions of old songs are refined and captivating. Bessie Smith's "Backwater Blues" is stunning partly because the lyrics, heard so clearly here, are so poignant: as a result of five days rain and flooding, "there was a thousand people didn't have no place to go."

LINK➤ *Paul Rishell & Annie Raines — I Want You to Know*

Tone-Cool (Rounder) 1156

Boston-based country blues enthusiast Rishell has recorded several albums (1990's Blues on a Holiday *[Tone-Cool 1144] is also excellent). With harpist Annie Raines, he performs songs by Blind Boy Fuller, Bo Carter, Peg Leg Howell, and others. An original vocal duet, "Got to Fly" is best.*

One of the few rock guitarists with the talent, the versatility, and the inclination to pursue the duality, Clapton was born in 1945 in Ripley, England, about 30 miles from London. Raised by grandparents, he started playing guitar as a young teen; fellow students in art school introduced him to the blues. By spring 1963, he was in a band (the Roosters); that fall, he joined the Yardbirds, an R&B band. He left after the group's first hit to play the blues with John Mayall's Bluesbreakers. Clapton stayed there from 1965 until 1966, when he formed Cream; he then moved on to Blind Faith in 1969. Clapton became one of rock's deities but did not pursue a solo career because he was too shy to sing. With Delaney Bramlett's encouragement, he cut a solo album, then formed his own band, Derek & the Dominoes, in 1970. Drug addiction sidelined his career, but he has worked steadily since his 1973 rehabilitation.

Unplugged — Duck 45024

True to the original conception of MTV's popular concert series, Clapton appears with an acoustic band. From here, it was a short step to country blues, and this 1992 album contains some dazzlers: Robert Johnson's "Walkin' Blues," a cooking rendition of "Alberta" (associated with Leadbelly), and Jimmy Cox's "Nobody Knows You When You're Down and Out" (featuring Chuck Levell's fine piano). There are two hit songs, a slow version of "Layla" and Clapton's very personal blues "Tears in Heaven." The crowd-pleasing "San Francisco Bay Blues" is played partly on kazoo. Muddy Waters's "Rollin' and Tumblin'" closes out a terrific show with just the right tone, and with some of Clapton's best guitar work.

LINK➤ *Yardbirds — Greatest Hits, Vol. 1: 1964–1966* — ***Rhino 75895***

Many of these 18 songs are blues classics like "Smokestack Lightning," "I'm a Man," and "Good Morning, Little School Girl." Originals, like "For Your Love" and "Heart Full of Soul" build on that base. The band that launched Clapton, Beck, and Page.

From the Cradle — Duck 45735

Clapton fans waited for decades to own a complete program of his take on classic Chicago blues. At the heart of this substantial group is Jerry Portnoy (harmonica), Andy Fairweather Low (guitar), Chris Stainton (keyboards), Dave Bronze (bass), and Jim Keltner (drums). Clapton's vocals are gutsy, up to the varied challenges posed by Willie Dixon's "Hoochie Coochie Man" (he's surprisingly steely in the lower registers), Charles Brown's "Driftin'" and Lowell Fulson's "Reconsider Baby." Of course, this is mostly a showcase for Clapton's blues guitar. He rips into every song, particularly Dixon's "Groaning the Blues," Freddy King's "Someday After a While," and Elmore James's "It Hurts Me, Too." Very solid work.

LINK➤ *Eric Clapton — Money and Cigarettes* — ***Warner Bros. 23773***

This bluesiest of Clapton's pop albums was made in 1983 with Ry Cooder, Donald "Duck" Dunn, Albert Lee, and others and begins with a Sleepy John Estes song. The live 1975 E.C. Was Here *(Polydor 531-823) includes long versions of several blues classics as well.*

Crossroads (Box) **Polydor 835261**

Covering five important bands and 15-plus years of solo work, this 4-CD set often blends rock and blues into a hybrid form. Nine Yardbirds tracks launch the story; Billy Boy Arnold's "I Wish You Would" and Jimmy Reed's "Baby What's Wrong?" land somewhere between blues and rockabilly, a style blended with harmonies typical of the British group sound of the early 1960s. Keith Relf is clearly the principal creative force; Clapton's just a talented guitarist. After a few pleasant warm-up tracks with Mayall, three Bluesbreakers songs follow. The degree of added sophistication (and psychedelia) by autumn 1966's "I Feel Free" is stunning; it's one of a dozen Cream songs that reinvent blues instrumentation and blues improvisation. Others in this category include "Spoonful," and "Strange Brew." Decades later, they still stand up to critical listening. Of the three Blind Faith tunes here, Stevie Winwood's "Can't Find My Home" still stands as the group's best. Important transitional work with Delaney and Bonnie is represented only by "Comin' Home." The action briskly moves on to three cuts from Eric Clapton (Polydor 531-819): "Blues Power," "After Midnight," and "Let It Rain"—all hit songs essentially made with Clapton fronting Delaney and Bonnie's band. By now, Clapton's focus is commercial rock, not the unadulterated blues of Cream. Next comes Derek and the Dominoes, which brings a good dose of blues, not only in the choice of songs (Robert Johnson's "Crossroads," the previously unreleased "Mean Old Frisco," and more) but also in the approaches to guitar playing. During the Layla sessions, Clapton and Duane Allman also recorded an unaccompanied duet on "Mean Old World." By 1974, Clapton was solidly out on his own. During this period, he was often guided by the steady producers Tom Dowd ("I Shot the Sheriff") and Glyn Johns ("Lay Down Sally," "Wonderful Tonight," "Promises"). His albums would sometimes feature a classic blues tune as well. *Just One Night*, from 1980, included Otis Rush's "Double Trouble"; it's a bracing breath of very fresh air. The remainder of the 1980s material sampled here is solid commercial rock music with touches of blues. Few boxed sets pack such a good story.

LINK➤ *Cream — Those Were the Days* ***Polydor 539-000***

In 1997, interest in Cream was sated with this comprehensive 4-CD set. The first 2 CDs recap all of the studio work; the rest simulates a live concert. Those with only a passing interest will find 20 of the group's finest songs on The Very Best of Cream CD *(31452-3752).*

Albert Collins

Collins was born in 1932 in Leona, TX, and grew up in nearby Houston. As a teenager, he started playing guitar under the guidance of teacher and cousin Willow Young, which led to gigs with his own band in Houston. By his early 20s, Collins was touring the South accompanying vocalist Piney Brown. Collins replaced Jimi Hendrix in Little Richard's band and before Hendrix's death had planned to play with him on the Band of Gypsies tour. Collins continued to record for small Texas labels and work in clubs. In 1968, he met Canned Heat singer Bob Hite; this encounter led to an Imperial Records contract and Collins's first national exposure. Collins moved to L.A. and toured with rock groups. By the mid-1970s, gigs were harder to find. A 1977 Alligator contract changed everything, and for 20 years, Collins was one of the busiest, most visible blues stars. He died in Las Vegas in 1993.

Collins Mix (The Best of) **Pointblank 39097**

With this sort of collection, it's difficult not to wonder whether the tracks were arranged by some random drawing. Program your CD player to begin with track 7, a ripping instrumental called "Frosty." Recorded in 1962 with B.B. King, it features some chilling solos. A year later, "Don't Lose Your Cool" followed an essentially similar format. It featured tight Memphis horns, a Hammond B3 organ, and the shards of Collins's unusual approach to guitar. Collins's knack for finding a groove serves him well, not only on these early 1960s tracks, but also on the late 1960s Imperial material, and his 1980s work for Alligator. It's all represented here.

LINK➤ *Johnny "Guitar" Watson — Three Hours Past Midnight* ***Flair 91696***

Watson was Collins's rough contemporary, a top-flight innovator on electric guitar. This collection recalls his 1950s work for Flair, but doesn't always sound great. A better choice is Gangster of Love *(Charly [import] 267), which covers the early 1950s and early 1960s.*

The Complete Imperial Recordings **EMI 96740**

This 2-CD set presents 36 tracks that were originally released on three Imperial albums in 1969 and 1970. "Turnin' On" delivers the combination of organ, horns, and guitar that makes Collins so unique: it's something like a jazz jam session, but with rock's energy and blues' expressiveness. His bluesier material is always best; "Got a Good Thing Goin'" is a slow blues accentuated by Collins's guitar and rough vocal with its dramatic sense of sadness. A funky feeling and a harmonica brighten "Lip Service"—one of many songs that deviates from Collins's successful horns-guitar formula. Although it's sometimes repetitive, this is a generally satisfying set.

LINK➤ *John Zorn — Spillane* ***Nonesuch 79172***

One of the great things about Collins was his willingness to try new projects. For example, he appeared with Bruce Willis in a Seagram's commercial. Here, he plays guitar and sings on an avant-garde jazz album from the mid-1980s; the Kronos Quartet also appears on this out-there album.

Ice Pickin' **Alligator 4713**

This is Albert Collins's best album. Released in 1978, it was his first for Alligator. The liner notes are truthful: "a jagged blend of shattering, ringing high notes, icy echo, jarring attack, the blistering power of an arctic storm." The album is engineered so that the guitar pierces through. "Honey, Hush!" is an ideal opener, with ample space for guitar solos. Collins's guitar sings lead; the other instruments, including the horns, hold back. On "Ice Pick," he rocks, but within a very structured, almost manicured setup. The slow, austere blues, "Cold, Cold Feeling," rings true because of the power of Collins's guitar. "Master Charge" is one of the few tunes based mainly on a vocal.

LINK➤ *Jimi Hendrix — Are You Experienced?* **MCA 11602**

Hendrix often claimed Collins as an influence. This was Hendrix's first album (from 1967) that merged influences from British blues and rock innovators into something entirely new. Tunes include "Purple Haze," "Hey Joe," "Wind Cries Mary," "Foxey Lady," other classics.

Showdown! **Alligator 4743**

Albert Collins, Robert Cray, and Johnny Copeland—three top contemporary blues guitarists—share credit on this 1985 Alligator release. The session belongs to Collins and his Icebreakers band; both Cray and Copeland had some history with Collins, so the combination made sense. The material's diversity is very appealing. "Black Cat Bone" is an intense, down-tempo classic from Houston street musician Hop Wilson. Copeland's "Bring Your Fine Self Home" drives a deeply felt harmonica solo from Collins; it feels like a Texas country blues. Cray updates Chicago blues and contributes a lovely vocal on "The Dream." Homage is paid to T-Bone Walker, whose work influenced all three musicians, on "T-Bone Shuffle."

LINK➤ *Albert Collins — Showdown!* **Mobile Fidelity 620**

Is it worth paying twice the price for a gold disc? Listen to Albert Collins's guitar backing Robert Cray's vocal on "The Dream," with the airtight impact of the rhythm section, and you'll sense the enormous improvement offered by Mobile Fidelity's team. The liner notes are easier to read, too.

Frostbite **Alligator 4719**

Starting around 1980 when this album was released, Collins found a formula that worked. Alligator understood how to produce him, and the albums sold. His guitar crackles with a signature snap, and on a tune like "Blue Monday Hangover," the horns are in all the right places, saying all the right things. Years later, listening to Collins is still about those big open numbers, like "I Got a Problem," with the whole band wailing and Collins out in front hanging those stinging icicles. Songs that break through the stereotype are better still; the lounge-style "The Highway Is Like a Woman" is one of this album's best tunes. Extremely skillful music making.

LINK➤ *Doyle Bramhall — Birdnest on the Ground* **Discovery 74201**

Reissue of a 1994 Antone's album, this is the best so far from the Texan guitar player. A mix of originals, a Doc Pomus number, and Johnny Nash's "I Can See Clearly Now" show off Bramhall's dark voice. Bramhall and Jimmy Vaughan are former partners; Smokin' Joe Kubek produced.

The son of a Louisiana sharecropper, Copeland was born in 1937 in Haines, LA. He grew up in Arkansas and Houston, TX. Copeland started his career in Houston, first as a sideman with Joe Hughes and the Dukes of Rhythm, then as leader of his own band. He also boxed as an amateur and picked up his nickname, Clyde. Copeland worked as a regional musician in Texas, Arkansas, and Louisiana for almost two decades before moving to NYC in 1974. Until he could establish a reputation in the city, he worked at a Brew n' Burger restaurant. Eventually gigs in Harlem, Greenwich Village, and in other East Coast cities materialized, and Copeland was working regularly. Rounder released his first major label album in 1981. He worked regularly until the 1980s, when congenital heart problems slowed him down. The NYC blues community helped pay for his care through benefit concerts. Copeland died in 1997.

Texas Twister **Rounder 11504**

This 1986 CD recaps the first four albums Copeland recorded for Rounder (the best records he ever made). From 1977's *Copeland Special* (cassette only, 2025), there's the title cut, with some formidable Texas R&B horn work and a searing solo from saxophonist Arthur Blythe. "It's My Own Tears," a ballad from the same album, is better still: it's a rainy day blues that highlights the emotional range of Copeland's guitar. The most interesting work comes from *Bringing It All Back Home* (cassette only, 2050), recorded in Africa and released in 1986. The jazzy combination of flutes, African percussion, and Copeland's guitar works beautifully; unfortunately, only three tracks are included here. Excellent music making.

LINK➤ *Joe Hughes — If You Want to See These Blues* ***Black Top 1050***

Hughes's big Texas guitar sound and powerful vocals never made him a star, but he has cut several records that will appeal to Johnny Copeland fans. This one was created in 1989. Texas Gunslinger *(Bullseye Blues 9568), from 1996, is also strong and distinctive.*

Shemekia Copeland - Turn The Heat Up **Alligator 4857**

Johnny Copeland's daughter Shemekia got her training as his opening act. She's blessed with a big voice—a confident blues diva's voice—a little Etta James by way of Big Mama Thornton. Recorded in 1998, when she was 19 years old, this was her debut album. Copeland easily keeps pace with the Uptown Horns on the opening "Turn The Heat Up." She belts out her choruses and adds plenty of nuances to make the song her own. She's good on the ballad material, too. "Salt in My Wounds" gets the formula right with a hurt-but-proud woman, sad guitar, and smooth-the-hurt horns. "Married to the Blues" is similar, but it's a better song all around.

LINK➤ *Valerie Wellington — Million Dollar $ecret* ***Rooster Blues 72619***

A spectacular update on the female blues singer, this 1984 album features Wellington's enormous, rapturous voice on a perfect repertoire: Jessie Mae Robinson's "Cold, Cold Feeling," Bessie Smith's "Dirty No-Gooder's Blues," and more. Fabulous sidemen, too.

Cotton first came to prominence as the second of the great harmonica players in Muddy Waters's band (Little Walter had preceded him, although not immediately). As a child in Mississippi, Cotton used to listen to "King Biscuit Time," Sonny Boy Williamson's radio show, on KFFA in Helena, AK. By age 9, in 1944, Cotton was living with Williamson, and the two played and traveled together until 1950. Cotton also worked for Howlin' Wolf; by the early 1950s, he was a highly regarded Memphis blues harmonica player. In 1955, Muddy Waters called, and Cotton moved to Chicago, where he replaced George "Harmonica" Smith in Waters's band. Cotton stayed with Waters until 1966, when he formed his own band and became popular with rock audiences. Cotton has since recorded high-visibility albums for Verve, Alligator, and other labels. He tours constantly, as he has done for decades, and recent problems with his voice have not slowed him down.

Best of the Verve Years — Verve 527-371

Cotton's lively 1967 Verve Forecast debut was co-produced by Chicago blues lovers Mike Bloomfield and Barry Goldberg. "Good Time Charlie" finds Cotton in excellent voice, with a tightly arranged horn section and razor-sharp rhythm. "Turn on Your Lovelight" is a fast, gospel-based shuffle whose choruses build up higher and higher to a frenzied climax. The band is totally on target for Sonny Boy Williamson's "Don't Start Me Talking," which contains one of Cotton's best harmonica solos. There's a great version of Junior Parker's "Feelin' Good" and an even better "Knock on Wood." The second album, 1968's *Pure Cotton*, maintains this very high standard. Among the best blues on record.

LINK➤ *Mike Bloomfield, Al Kooper, Stephen Stills—Super Session* *Sony 64611*

Arguably Bloomfield's best recorded work, this enormously popular 1968 album gives him room to show his stuff. He's magnificent, a brilliant rock-blues musician. But he's only on half the album. The other half features Kooper and guitar player Stephen Stills.

High Compression — Alligator 4737

Half of this 1984 album was recorded by the James Cotton Chicago Blues All-Stars, with Magic Slim on guitar and Pinetop Perkins on piano. There's a wonderful quality about their music. "23 Hours Too Long" provides Cotton with opportunities for long solos and accents, and bandmates add such flavors as special riffs and unexpected rhythm patterns. Cotton's harmonica sounds like a cross between an organ and a saxophone on "High Blues," a pure Chicago blues with amazing special effects. With his regular James Cotton Blues Band, "Superharp" goes for a more modern blues club sound. Cotton's hoarse, gritty vocals make an ideal partner for his street-smart music.

LINK➤ *Various Artists — Chicago/The Blues/Today! Vol. 2* *Vanguard 79217*

Samuel Charters produced this1966 sampler. It includes six tracks by Johnny Young's South Side Blues Band, six more by Johnny Shines', and three by Walter Horton's harmonica band with Charlie Musselwhite. Harmonica player Horton appears on all tracks.

Live at Antone's Nightclub **Antone's 7**

In the late 1980s, Cotton was among Antone's most popular performers; he often traveled to Austin, TX, to play this top blues club. In 1988 he brought along super guitar players Matt "Guitar" Murphy and Luther Tucker, as well as pianist Pinetop Perkins, bassist Calvin Jones, and drummer Willie Smith. Amid sizzling guitars and a no-nonsense rhythm section, Cotton confidently glides to center stage and carries every song with his harp. His control, tone, and musical sense are awe inspiring; "Blow Wind," "Juke," and "Midnight Creeper" are completely dominated by his diminutive organ. His voice is starting to fade, but Cotton's a pro who covers for the inadequacy.

LINK➤ *James Cotton — Mighty Long Time* ***Antone's 15***

Tucker, Murphy, or the Fabulous Thunderbirds's Jimmie Vaughan accompany Cotton on a 1991 outing similar to his work at Antone's. Plenty of energy, perfect balance of guitar and harmonica, and a choice repertoire that includes "Stormy Monday" and "Moanin' at Midnight."

Deep in the Blues **Verve 529-849**

Cotton's voice is so completely blown out that it now possesses the burnished quality of old wood. The engineering is exquisite, and so is the accompaniment: Charlie Haden on bass and Joe Louis Walker on acoustic guitar. Cotton's gleaming harmonica is finally heard properly; on a solo like "Country Boy," it's as if he's sitting on a couch in the same room. The songs were very carefully selected to showcase Cotton's art. "Everybody's Fishin'," "Down at Your Buryin'," and "Dealin' with the Devil" are among many standouts. Walker and Haden also get their unaccompanied solos on "Vineyard Blues" and "Ozark Mountain Railroad," respectively. A work of art from 1995.

LINK➤ *Charlie Haden and Hank Jones — Steal Away* ***Verve 527-249***

A stirring album of spirituals by two top jazz musicians. Mostly Jones's piano carries songs like "It's Me, O Lord (Standing in the Need of Prayer)," but Haden's articulate bass often runs the melody line. This 1994 album is a close kin to Deep in the Blues, *and no less artful.*

Harp Attack! **Alligator 4970**

Four top Chicago harmonica players share credit for this 1990 album: Cotton, Junior Wells, Billy Branch, and Carey Bell. They're accompanied by piano, guitar, bass, and drums. "Down Home Blues," featuring Lucky Peterson on piano, is a rough-hewn rural blues brought up to date with some urban flair. Cotton takes the first vocal and solo, and he's followed by each of the others. Harmonicas take the lead, but they're interwoven with guitar, piano, bass, and drums. "Who" features a harmonica duel between Branch and Cotton. In addition to performing together, each player gets his own featured song. Cotton's 9-minute midnight blues, "Black Night," is quietly effective with a gorgeous harmonica solo.

LINK➤ *Billy Branch — The Blues Keep Following Me Around* ***Verve 527-268***

With guitar player Carl Weathersby, Branch created his long-awaited leap into national renown with this fine 1995 album. The best work here energizes and modernizes older blues material by Willie Dixon and Sonny Boy Williamson; plus, many originals.

Robert Cray is one of a small number of blues performers who saw some local success in the 1970s and helped blues to gain popularity on a national basis in the 1980s. Cray was born in Columbus, GA, in 1953, but his family often relocated because his father was in the military. By 1968, the family had settled in Tacoma, WA. By 1974, Cray and some fellow musicians had a small following. A lucky break led to a taste of the big time: Cray is the bass player in Otis Day and the Knights in the John Belushi film *Animal House*. By 1980 the Robert Cray Band was making records, but it wasn't until 1985's Grammy-winning album *Showdown!* that Cray became nationally known. A Mercury contract followed, along with international touring, respect from fellow guitar players, and shared gigs with Eric Clapton, Buddy Guy, and other legends. Cray is one of the best blues players in today's community.

Bad Influence — Hightone 8001

Cray's roots are worth studying. It's 1983, and his singing is more imitative than original. He hammers his electric guitar long and hard; economy would come later. Some songs, such as "Phone Booth" and "The Grinder," indicate future direction. They update an R&B style that had faded by the mid-1960s, yet Cray's rocking instrumentation makes the style fresh and new. More often, however, he's inventing a new form of contemporary blues that would be endlessly copied. "So Many Women, So Little Time" and "Bad Influence" make use of a smooth voice that goes high for emphasis, marking a contrast with a deep-down rhythm section and a spikey guitar.

LINK➤ *Various Artists — All Night Long They Play The Blues* — *Specialty 7029*

An album of influences, or more officially, a collection of Galaxy Records masters from 1962 until 1971. Much of this blues has an soulful feeling: Little Johnny Taylor's "Part-Time Love," Charles Brown's "I'm Gonna Push On," Philip Walker's "Hey, Hey, Baby's Gone," and more.

False Accusations — Hightone 8005

A model of self-control, Cray's package really comes together for the first time on this 1985 album. His singing voice has never sounded better; "Porch Light" is a mature, soulful vocal that's nicely supported by Cray's extremely tasteful, yet spikey, lead guitar and the soothing effect of Peter Boe's organ. There's a slickness emerging here, too, as on the rueful "She's Gone" and on "Playin' in the Dirt," a song about an illicit love affair. The former is slow, and the latter is sassy. The repeating pattern of Boe's piano, Cray's prickly guitar, and his sad, lost-love vocal on "False Accusations" proves a fitting elegy for a fading relationship. Contemporary blues, done right.

LINK➤ *Paul deLay — Take It From the Turnaround . . .* — *Evidence 26076*

Successfully fighting off drug demons, deLay became one of the most popular blues performers in the Pacific Northwest. This reissue of his 1990 and 1992 albums shows off his emotion-packed vocal prowess and his talent on harmonica. Very satisfying stuff.

Strong Persuader **Mercury 30568**

Cray's commercial breakthrough starts, appropriately, with "Smoking Gun." Producers Bruce Bromberg and Dennis Walker opted for a thicker sound in the mix, with a bottom end that suggests a larger band. Cray's vocals are now fully mature, and his guitar glows red hot. He's beginning to drift from straight blues to rocking blues. "Right Next Door (Because of Me)" is sung from the perspective of the "strong persuader" who seduced his next-door neighbor. Cray's riffs dig deep, but their quantity and placement are spare and intelligent. The Memphis Horns occasionally spice the proceedings, but rarely take center stage. Easy to enjoy.

LINK➤ *Studebaker John — Time Will Tell* ***Blind Pig 5042***

A talented contemporary Chicago guitar player who also plays harmonica, Studebaker John has developed a good following. Other albums worth hearing include Tremoluxe *(Blind Pig 5031) and* Too Touch *(5010). His name comes from the 1963 Studebaker Silver Hawk.*

Some Rainy Morning **Ichiban 526-867**

Cray's 1990 *Midnight Stroll* is credited to the Robert Cray Band Featuring the Memphis Horns (Mercury 846-652). He produced 1993's somewhat pared-down *Shame + a Sin* (518-237) himself, making a transition to this 1995 effort, his most satisfying in several years. The emphasis here is on Cray's guitar, often supported by Jim Pugh's organ, with very effective vocals that add impact to his higher register. Cray wrote most of the songs and gets off to a bluesy start with "Moan," an update of early 1950s R&B songs ("All I do is cry-y-y and moan") with a rock arrangment. "Steppin' Out" also modernizes older blues formulas.

LINK➤ *Dave Hole — Ticket to Chicago* ***Alligator 4847***

No-nonsense, take-no-prisoners attack executed by guitar. Hole's overwrought and the aggression comes out in his music. Nobody combines hard rocking with slide guitar like he does. This dose of pure emotion comes from 1997. Previous albums are generally similar.

Sweet Potato Pie **Mercury 534438**

The horns are back, and the soulful attitude is now expressed with some vocal vibrato. Keyboard player Jim Pugh's "The One in the Middle" is a soulful blues whose meaning is captured in the lyric "Does she ever think of me?" It's a pleasant balance between the Memphis Horns' Wayne Jackson on trumpet and Andrew Love on saxophone, Cray's heartfelt singing, and perfectly timed guitar sparks. They also do a very creditable job with Otis Redding's "Trick or Treat." The best song is the last; "I Can't Quit" is faster and sounds honky-tonky with an impressive solo guitar payoff. Recorded in Memphis in 1997 with reverence for the city's R&B heritage. This CD is among Cray's best.

LINK➤ *Eddie Shaw — In the Land of Crossroads* ***Rooster Blues 2624***

The veteran Chicago saxman performs with his son Eddie "Vaan" Shaw, Jr., on lead guitar. The two of them front a hot band that runs through a dozen songs, all in the Chicago blues mold. Shaw's voice has lots of miles on it; it's subdued but the embers glow with heat.

Debbie Davies

Born in 1952, Davies grew up in the recording studios of Los Angeles where her father worked as a session player (for Frank Sinatra and other top artists) and arranger (for Ray Charles). Davies established herself by playing rock and blues in the San Francisco Bay area; in 1984 she landed a job with Maggie Mayall and the Cadillacs, an all-female R&B band led by John Mayall's wife. Davies gained national acclaim—as well as a valuable education—by traveling with the indefatigable Albert Collins. She became his secret weapon: Colllins loved to surprise fellow musicians and audiences with Davies's slick blues guitar playing. In 1991, she performed in Fingers Taylor and the Ladyfingers Revue, another all-female band. Later that year, Davies started her own band. She signed with Blind Pig in 1993; four years later, she won a W.C. Handy Award. Davies is based in Connecticut.

Picture This — Blind Pig 5004

"Picture This" is a killer song. Davies finds just the right hook and sings it well. Her guitar just bounces from one perfect position to the next. The brass arrangements, so powerfully delivered by the Miami Horns, complement the guitar and voice with precise commercial control. Fortunately, this initital effort is filled with songs almost as good the title tune. "24 Hour Fool" is a grinding "What about me?" song, performed with a cynical attitude and under-the-skin guitar. Albert Collins lends a hand on "I Wonder Why?" a spikey guitar boogie. Nice job on the Freddie King tune "Sidetracked," too. Big guitar sound, expressive voice, and strong songwriting characterize this winner from 1993.

LINK➤ *Tommy Castro — Exception to the Rule* — ***Blind Pig 5029***

Castro is a talented guitar player who's beginning to attract a following (for an eye-opening demonstration of his instrumental skill, check out "Me and My Guitar"). If you like this 1995 CD, try his 1997 followup, Can't Keep a Good Man Down *(Blind Pig 5041).*

Round Every Corner — Shanachie 9010

Five years later Davies maintains her blues integrity, but also sets her sights on adult rock radio play. "Sittin' & Cryin'" is a jaunty blues-folk tune with some unexpected ingredients: a dobro, played by Davies, and a honky-tonk piano from Jeremy Baum. Befitting its title, "Blue and Lonesome" is mostly a guitar and organ solo (Baum, again) for a rainy day, with a moaning vocal from Davies. Her songwriting peaks with "A.C. Strut." It's a tune about "a houseful of trouble" that's sung with an impressively confident attitude and features a really good guitar solo. This album is also notable for a refreshing renovation of CCR's "Who'll Stop the Rain?" Very appealing work.

LINK➤ *Coco Montoya — Just Let Go* — ***Blind Pig 5043***

Montoya and Davies worked together in John Mayall's band; both approach blues with an electric go-for-it attitude. Montoya's a good singer and an even better guitarist. Once you're done with this 1997 CD, head for 1995's Ya Think I'd Know Better *(5033), and* Gotta Mind to Travel *(5020).*

Reverend Gary Davis

Born and raised in Laurens, SC, a small town near Greenville, Davis taught himself to play guitar, and by his teens was performing blues and other popular music on street corners and community gatherings. He moved to Durham, NC, in the 1930s; by the 1940s, he had traveled to NYC and was living in Harlem. Throughout the 1930s, he played more and more religious music, and he eventually became a preacher. But his extraordinary guitar playing made him a hero of the budding folk and blues revival of the 1950s and 1960s, and he became a regular at folk coffeehouses and at festivals (Newport and Mariposa, among others). During this time, he also recorded regularly. Davis strongly influenced many folk and rock guitar players, notably David Bromberg, Bob Dylan, and Jorma Kaukonen of Jefferson Airplane. Davis died of a heart attack on his way to a concert in southern New Jersey in 1972.

The Complete Early Recordings of Reverend Gary Davis **Yazoo 2011**

Most of these gospel blues were recorded in 1935. Through the static of rare old recordings, Davis's voice shrieks and strains for the high notes and grumbles through lower ones. Try to get past the gruff voice. His heartfelt devotion comes in many forms: the simplicity of "I Saw the Light," the toe-tapping musicality of "Twelve Gates to the City," and the pure gospel of "I Can't Bear My Burden by Myself." The guitar's distinctive light touch on "The Angel's Message to Me" balances Davis's gruff singing and gets under the skin. On "Cross and Evil Woman Blues," his unusual guitar melody is especially uplifting. "The Angel's Message to Me" is a classic.

LINK➤ *Ry Cooder — Boomer's Story* ***Reprise 26398***

Although this 1972 album is about as close as Cooder came to recording strictly blues, it does reflect time spent learning from his teacher, Rev. Davis. This is especially clear on "Cherry Ball Blues" and "Maria Elena," two numbers that feature his acoustic guitar.

Pure Religion and Bad Company
Smithsonian Folkways 40035

If you're at all curious about Davis's splendid reputation as a guitar player, this 1957 album supplies the evidence. He performs several exquisite unaccompanied guitar solos; his finger-picking and use of ragtime shimmer on "Hesitation Blues." His sense of time makes "Buck Dance" the envy of many guitar players. "I Didn't Want to Join the Band" is even more stunning. Then he turns on a dime, and takes the part of a man on death row, singing "Bad Company (Brought Me Here)." Ultimately, Davis was in the business of saving souls, and on "Pure Religion," his passion comes through both voice and on guitar (his singing partner here). Terrific album!

LINK➤ *Various Artists — Wade in the Water* ***Smithsonian Folkways 40076***

A spectacular collection of early gospel music on four CDs, with considerable space given to the Fisk Jubilee Singers (the group that began the tradition of traveling gospel choruses), and newer ensembles like Sweet Honey in the Rock.

Blues & Ragtime **Shanachie 97024**

Sheet music is provided for five songs on this 1960s collection—a kind of testament to Davis's influence as a guitar player. The instrumentals are a particular delight; personal favorites include "Walkin' Dog Blues," "Buck Rag," and "Cincinnati Flow Rag." Davis is also presented in some less formal live settings, and it's marvelous to hear the audience laugh at his clever lyrics and stylings. The album includes an especially clean version of "Cocaine Blues" and a fine live rendition of "Baby Let Me Lay It On You" (later cleaned up by the folkies as "Baby Let Me Follow You Down"). A handsome, varied, well-recorded collection of performances from 1962 to 1966.

LINK➤ *Blues Blue, Blues White: Bluesville Years, Vol. 7 Prestige (Fantasy) 9915*

Davis's impact on the 1960s folk revolution was enormous. Here's Dave Van Ronk laying down a bluesy "Fixin' to Die," Eric von Schmidt doing "Gulf Coast Blues," Tracy Nelson's "Ramblin' Man," and Geoff Muldaur's "Motherless Chile Blues."

From Blues to Gospel **Biograph 123**

A magnificent recording of 12-string Bozo guitar, perfectly engineered and regal in its presentation. Made in NYC in 1971, the intricate instrumental "Crow Jane" explains Davis's spellbinding influence on generations of acoustic guitarists. "Talk on the Corner," a century-old blues, contains some of the finest blues guitar on record. Davis is also facile on harmonica, and "Lost John" recalls the relationship of blues to field hollers. Davis's voice has mellowed some, making "Cocaine Blues" both effective and chilling. The most satisfying material is gospel blues: a tired old voice breathing fire into "Samson and Delilah" (also known as "If I Had My Way"). A superb album, this is the place to start on Reverend Davis.

LINK➤ *Randy Newman — 12 Songs* *Reprise 27449*

Newman likely borrowed some vocal styling and phrasing from Davis. Compare, for example, Davis's "Talk on the Corner" with Newman's "Under the Harlem Moon" or "Rosemary." Other Newman classics include "Yellow Man" and "Mama Told Me Not to Come."

O, Glory: The Apostolic Studio Sessions **Genes 9908**

This is a superb album, a labor of love for producer John Townley, who had been Davis's student. The sound quality is excellent and the material is varied. Harmonica player Larry Johnson helps brew up a storm on "Sun Goin' Down," and paints with quiet elegance on "Lo, I'll Be With You Always." Davis plays the 5-string banjo on "Out on the Ocean Sailing," and leads the Apostolic Family Chorus as singer and pianist on "God Will Take Care of You" (he'd never recorded on banjo or piano before). "Right Now" begins with a fine Johnson harmonica solo, then becomes an old-time gospel song with hand claps and fervent vocals from the Apostolic Family with Sister Annie Davis. Very highly recommended!

LINK➤ *Anthology of American Folk Music* *Smithsonian Folkways 902*

It's surprising that Davis wasn't included in this 6-CD overview of American traditional music, but his music fits somewhere between Blind Lemon Jefferson and Mississippi John Hurt. This set, edited by Harry Smith, turned musicians on to folk music in 1952.

Larry Davis

Stevie Ray Vaughan fans know Larry "Arkansas" Davis as the author of "Texas Flood." Davis was paid $300 for the blues classic, a side he cut for Duke in 1958 with Fenton Robinson on lead guitar. Davis was 22 years old, and already a seven-year veteran who came up through Little Rock's blues scene. Davis first learned to play the drums, but his hard-working mother found the money for a tenor saxophone, piano, bass, and guitar. In the 1960s, Davis toured with Albert King and recorded for B.B. King's label, but a 1972 motorcycle accident and a subsequent stroke changed everything. Sidelined for a decade, Davis was encouraged by Albert King and B.B. King to try again. His 1982 album, *Funny Stuff* (Rooster Blues), won four W.C. Handy awards and critical acclaim. Davis moved to Los Angeles in 1987 and recorded several more albums before his death from cancer in 1994.

I Ain't Beggin' Nobody — Evidence 26016

Davis did two things extremely well: he sang soulful blues, and he played electric guitar. He found his audience by teaming up with Oliver Sain, who not only produced and engineered this album, but played saxes and keyboards as well. The title song is a midtempo R&B tune, written by Sain, about pride and self-esteem. The lyrics provide a nice hook: "I ain't no millionaire, but I got everything I need." There's a soft, slow-dance feeling to "Sneaking Around"; Davis's sweet tenor wraps around the words "so-o-o tired," and the moon shines brighter. "I'm Coming Home" starts with a good guitar solo, then shows what Davis's voice can do desperate homesickness. There's plenty more good material, too. From 1987.

LINK➤ *Larry Davis — Blues Knights* — ***Evidence 26042***

In fact, there are just four tracks by Larry Davis on this CD, and they're all good: "Giving Up on Love" is here in a different version, and Davis also does Jimmy Rogers's "That's All Right." Another six tracks are sung by Byther Smith, an underrated R&B performer.

Sooner or Later — Bullseye Blues 9511

Producer Ron Levy took a different approach in 1992, also with excellent results—and superior sound. Davis adds real meaning and bite to Robert Johnson's jailhouse song, "Penitentiary Blues." Davis's guitar is more economically used, with pianist James Rudy filling in gaps. The band finds a steady groove on Howlin' Wolf's "How Long?" Levy's organ anchors the arrangement. Levy's also active on "I'm Workin' on It," a bluesy R&B tune that makes good use of the Memphis Horns at just the right moments. Nice guitar work on "102nd Street Blues," and on Davis's signature instrumental, "Little Rock." Still, this is second to the simplicity of the Evidence set.

LINK➤ *Jimmy McCracklin — My Story* — ***Bullseye Blues (Rounder) 9508***

Another Ron Levy production involving a fine R&B vocalist, this album features a terrific "Tomorrow" (lyric: "you won't know 'til the time comes") with Irma Thomas singing duet. McCracklin wrote "The Thrill Is Gone" and was a top 1950s–1960s vocalist. He shines.

Floyd Dixon

Dixon was a popular R&B musician in the 1940s and early 1950s; he became known to contemporary audiences when his hit "Hey Bartender" was featured in the motion picture *The Blues Brothers.* Dixon was born in Marshall, TX, in 1928 (according to his own song lyric, it was "204 miles from Houston, 39 miles from Shreveport, Louisiana, and 153 miles from Dallas"). When Dixon was a teenager, his family moved to L.A. While in high school, he befriended local singer Charles Brown and migrated toward the city's active Central Avenue scene. By age 18, Dixon was recording R&B sides for L.A.-based Modern Records. By 1949, he was charting top 20 hits (and working in a sauerkraut factory by day). The hits kept coming for Modern, then Aladdin, then Specialty and other labels. Dixon's career peaked in the early 1950s, although he steadily toured (one-night stands, mostly) through the 1970s. He recorded a comeback album in 1990.

The Complete Aladdin Recordings — Capitol 36923

This 2-CD set covers sides made for Aladdin from 1949 until 1952 (actually, some of the 1949 material was made in Texas for Peacock). It's all very appealing, lots of fun, well recorded, and chock-full of hits. Start with the comic jump blues "Let's Dance," complete with Sammy Benskin's hot guitar, Bill Ellis's hotter tenor sax, and the line "don't be a square from Delaware." The two big hits are "Telephone Blues" and "Call Operator 210"; both begin as novelty songs (with telephone sound effects), then become very respectable slow, lonely piano blues. Dixon is a gifted, undervalued songwriter and an entertaining performer who makes two CDs go by very quickly. Great stuff!

LINK➤ *Amos Milburn — Blues, Barrelhouse & Boogie Woogie: The Best of Amos Milburn 1946–1955* — ***Capitol 36879***

Dixon fans are bound to enjoy the free-spirited piano antics of Milburn (though a 3-CD set may seem a formidable investment). Milburn essentially updates Fats Waller's formula, adds a dash of blues, and pulls it off. He's a great pianist with an interesting repertoire.

Marshall, Texas Is My Home — Specialty 7011

These 22 songs were cut (mostly) for Specialty from 1953 through 1957. "Hard Living Alone" and "Old Memories" belong to a favorite Dixon genre—an emotionally wounded man at his piano with a bass and a sax discreetly in the background. But he also knows how to have fun, as on the up-tempo "Hole in the Wall" and "Nose Trouble" (as in "see how nosey you been"). Dixon has a great time with "Hey Bartender" ("draw one, draw two, draw three more glasses of beer"), sharing the lead with a tenor saxophone at the lowest end of its range. Still, the Aladdin set is the better starting point.

LINK➤ *Floyd Dixon — Wake Up and Live!* — ***Alligator 4841***

Big-sounding comeback, circa 1990, starts with a hopping "Hey Bartender" and gets to the optimistic heart of the matter with the title cut. The master has not lost his touch—his voice possesses plenty of character, and his piano playing has matured beautifully.

Dixon grew up in Vicksburg, MS, and sang in a gospel group as a child. He started boxing as a teenager, but a disagreement in the commissioner's office ended the heavyweight's career after a few bouts. By 1939, at age 24, Dixon was living in Chicago, playing bass at local clubs. A conscientious objector, he was jailed for several years because he would not serve in the military. After WW II, Dixon performed with the Big Three Trio; he took a job as a composer at the new Chess Records in 1948. Over the next two decades, Dixon wrote many of the label's best hits. He also played bass and produced. (His brief stint with Cobra launched Chicago's West Side sound.) Dixon toured through much of the 1970s, recording when he could and appearing at festivals and special events as a blues ambassador. He died in Burbank, CA in 1992.

The Chess Box — Chess 16500

This 2-CD Chess Box differs from others in the series because Willie Dixon's contribution to the label was not only as a performer—he was a producer and a songwriter as well. That's why the first song on this set is performed by Little Walter. And yet, "My Babe" is as much associated with Dixon as anyone else from the era. Similarly, Dixon's "Seventh Son," another 1955 classic, is listed under the name of a somewhat-forgotten Willie Mabon. Howlin' Wolf gets the credit for what became a signature song, "Spoonful." Wolf also had hits with Dixon's "Back Door Man" and "Little Red Rooster." To put all of this another way, nobody has contributed more important songs to the blues repertoire than Willie Dixon. The list continues: "Hoochie Coochie Man" by Muddy Waters, "Wang Dang Doodle" by Koko Taylor, and many more recorded either in the mid-1950s or early 1960s. Dixon was also a formidable performer with a dark chocolate voice, a bit like Roosevelt Sykes's. Here, Dixon, always one to take chances with his performances, sings lead on "Pain on My Heart" and "29 Ways." On "Walkin' Blues," Fred Below lays out a footstep-like percussion track, Lafayette Leake strides and glides along the keyboard, and Dixon casually strolls through his vocal. He's not less predictable on the eerie, acoustic tune "Weak Brain, Narrow Mind." It's a folk song, not Chicago blues, and Dixon's performance is excellent.

LINK➤ *Various Artists — Chess Blues* — ***Chess (MCA) 9340***

Two decades after they left Poland, the Chez brothers (or Chess brothers) started Aristocrat, their first label. Dixon showed up about five years later and shaped the vast majority of their successful recordings. A wonderful 4-CD anthology of 1950s & 1960s blues.

The Big Three Trio — Columbia 46216

Shortly after WW II, Dixon and pianist Leonard Caston put together the Big Three Trio with guitar player Bernardo Dennis. "We were pretty much playin' what the peoples wanted to hear," Dixon explained. This CD collects various jump blues, instrumentals, and novelties. Caston's boogie-woogie piano is the group's biggest selling point. The harmonizing vocals on "I Ain't Gonna Be Your Monkey Man," with Ollie Crawford replacing Dennis, sound similar to the Mills Brothers but without the satin sheen. On that song, Crawford suggests traces of what would become Chicago's blues. Mostly, however, this album is pop, not blues. The instrumental "Big 3 Stomp" also shows some of Dixon's bass chops.

LINK➤ *Various Artists — The Doo-Wop Box* **Rhino 71463**

Groups like the Big Three and the Ink Spots (who were similar) laid the groundwork for the 1950s explosion of a capella and harmonizing groups. This is the treasure trove—101 of the best, mostly from 1948–57.

The Original Wang Dang Doodle: The Chess Recordings and More **Chess 9353**

Here's a more focused look at Dixon the performer than the Chess Box provides. There's a bit of duplication—both "Walking the Blues" and "Weak Brain, Narrow Mind" are repeated here—but that's no impediment. Dixon's enthusiastic jump blues and Harold Ashby's honking tenor sax hook are nothing short of fantastic. "Crazy for My Baby" merges jump with Chicago blues; it's a good-hearted romp with a solid beat and better rhythm. Al Duncan provides Caribbean-style percussion behind "Twenty-Nine Ways to Baby's Door," which comes complete with Dixon's big-voiced vocal and backup singers. There's a jazzy combo number with pianist Lafayette Leake from 1962 called "Wrinkles," plus three twilight numbers from 1981, 1989, 1990.

LINK➤ *Bo Diddley — His Best* **Chess (MCA) 9373**

Like Dixon, Bo Diddley had a fundamental effect on rock 'n' roll. These 20 tracks contain riffs and rhythms heard throughout rock's history. Diddleyl's vocal style is also incredibly cool; the way he phrases "I'm a Man" and "Who Do You Love?" are inimitable.

I Am the Blues **SONY 53627**

This 1970 Columbia (now Sony) collection finds singer-bassist Dixon reviewing some of his greatest songs with Walter "Shakey" Horton (harmonica), Sunnyland Slim or Lafeyette Leake (piano), Johnny Shines (guitar), and Clifton James (drums). This solid Chicago ensemble runs through a slightly slowed-down "Back Door Man," a boogying "Seventh Son," a version of "Spoonful" with a meaty rhythm package, and so on through the catalog. The session never soars, and the mix could have made Dixon's voice more prominent, but this is certainly worth a listen. The other songs include "I'm Your Hoochie Coochie Man," "I Ain't Superstitious," "The Little Red Rooster," and "I Can't Quit You, Baby."

LINK➤ *Various Artists — The Chess Blues-Rock Songbook* **Chess (MCA) 9389**

A 2-CD distillation of the Chess box, this was issued for the company's 50th anniversary. A handy rundown on Dixon's world, this collection contains 36 songs, most of which are well known: "Hoochie Coochie Man," "Wang Dang Doodle," "My Babe," The Seventh Son," and "Walking by Myself," among others.

Champion Jack Dupree

Dupree was born around 1909 in New Orleans. An orphan whose parents died when their store burned down, Dupree was brought up in the Colored Home for Waifs (where Louis Armstrong was also raised). There, he learned piano. Dupree honed his musical skills in bordellos and speakeasies, hoboed through the U.S., and eventually zeroed in on the area around Chicago, Indianapolis, and Detroit, working short-term jobs (cook, porter, etc.). He also boxed (hence "Champion Jack") and won Golden Glove awards and State Championships. But he was never far from the music scene, hanging around Tampa Red's Chicago apartment, recording for producer Lester Melrose, and playing gigs. After WWII (he was a POW for two years), Dupree became a full-time musician; he recorded over 30 albums (including several with John Mayall and other British blues friends) and toured. In time, Dupree moved to Europe; he died in Germany in 1992.

New Orleans Barrelhouse Boogie — Columbia 52834

On these 1940–41 sides for OKeh, Dupree is so facile with his piano that it sometimes sounds as if he's playing the guitar. Building from a base not dissimilar from Fats Waller and boogie-woogie pianists popular at the time, Dupree applies a manly vocal on top of an endlessly creative stream of accompaniment ideas. He's a very good storyteller. The combination comes together perfectly on "Gamblin' Man Blues." Dupree was enormously versatile, capable of creating a mood with just a few keyboard strokes. Two fine examples are "Angola Blues," a frightening story about the notorious prison, and the famed "Junker Blues," with its dubious honesty of a drug-free singer.

LINK➤ *Juke Joint Jump: A Boogie Woogie Celebration* — ***Legacy 64988***

Dupree contributes "Dupree Shake Dance" to a sampler featuring well-known pianists (Jimmy Yancey, Art Tatum) and lesser knowns (Charlie Spand, Freddie Slack). Highlight: "Boogie Woogie Prayer" by Pete Johnson, Albert Ammons, and Meade "Lux" Lewis.

Blues From the Gutter — Atlantic 82434

The best among dozens of albums Dupree recorded over more than five decades, this 1958 album was produced by Jerry Wexler. It was clearly an important project: new stereo technology was used to make it sound great. The band sizzles, and Dupree is at the top of his game as an aggressive, imaginative pianist. His rough-and-tumble voice also sounds terrific. He makes the likes of "Frankie and Johnny" and "Stack-o-Lee" seem so easy, but this album's heart is dark with the grime of city life. Dupree recaps "Junker's Blues" and also explores "T.B. Blues" and "Can't Kick the Habit." In addition, there's "Bad Blood" and "Evil Woman." This is Dupree in a nasty mood.

LINK➤ *Champion Jack Dupree — Back Home in New Orleans* — ***Bullseye Blues 9502***

Celebrating his 80th year, Dupree returned home. The spirit is certainly willing here, and only a small concession need be made for his aging fingers and voice. A strong band more than compensates for the slight weaknesses, making this 1990 album worth a listen.

Fird Eaglin, Jr. was born in New Orleans in either 1936 or 1937. Before he was two years old, he was diagnosed with a brain tumor and glaucoma; he was hospitalized until age four. By then, Eaglin was blind, but healthier. His father, an amateur harmonica player, gave his six-year old son a guitar, and soon, they were recording acetate discs for fun. Eaglin also performed at local churches, and won a $200 First Prize at age 11 in a talent contest. By age 14, he'd dropped out of a local school for the blind, and soon joined Allen Toussaint in the legendary Flamingoes. Finding the group's strict rules restrictive, he left to free-lance, and perform for tourists on French Quarter streets, and in 1960, signed with Imperial, weathering the dry spells over the decades. He currently records for Black Top.

The Complete Imperial Recordings — Capitol 33918

Eaglin's approach to R&B was light and melodic, but always with a beat and a hook. His knack for commercial songs somehow didn't result in national hits, but the performances certainly weren't the reason why. The bouncy melody and tasty guitar hook on "Yours Truly" can't help but bring a smile to one's face. Eaglin's arrangements are immaculate, but simple: "C.C. Rider" features guitar, bass, and drums with every note in its proper place. When Eaglin says he's "Goin' to the River" to commit suicide, he's credible—even with a tolling bass, a background chorus, and other accoutrements. "I'm Slippin' In" does it with horns; it's a slinky, funky tune with broad appeal. Excellent!

LINK➤ *Snooks Eaglin — Country Boy in New Orleans* — ***Arhoolie 348***

Slightly hoarse, unassuming and accompanied almost exclusively by his own quiet acoustic guitar, it's hard to believe that this is the same man who rocked New Orleans R&B clubs a few years later. Never mind that! This is 60 minutes of superlative country blues, worthy on its own merit.

Soul's Edge — Black Top 1112

This is the most exciting of Eaglin's handful of albums for Black Top Records, a New Orleans label that keeps the blues heritage alive and flourishing. On 1989's *Out of Nowhere*, 1992's *Teasin' You* (1072), and on this 1995 album, Eaglin puts his heart and soul into a set of originals and R&B classics. There's a sentimental revision of Joe Simon's "Nine Pound Steel," an ashamed and downhearted prison blues. Fats Domino's "Josphine" is handled in a rocking style, and the ever-popular party song "Thrill on the Hill" also shines. Even with the gimmicky "Ling Ting Tong," Eaglin's the solid professional with an ultraslick backup band. Tidy performances, excellent engineering.

LINK➤ *Dalton Reed — Willing & Able* — ***Bullseye Blues***

A soul singer from the old school, Reed's 1991 album is sincere and romantic. The title song, a slow number featuring Sammy Berfect's Hammond B-3 organ, is silky smooth. Michael Toles shapes the album's sound with some very capable electric guitar performances.

Ronald Earl Horvath was born into a middle-class family in Queens, NY, in 1953. He went to Boston University and majored in special education. In 1975, Earl attended a Muddy Waters concert. It changed his life. He completely devoted himself to learning blues guitar—a hobby picked up a few years earlier that quickly became an obsession. Earl's dedication paid off. After backing up various Boston blues bands, he found a spot in the house band at Cambridge's Speakeasy, a leading club. By 1979, Earl's skills were formidable. He replaced Duke Robillard in the hard-working Roomful of Blues. Earl stayed until 1987, but also spent time building his own band, the Broadcasters. For over 10 years, Ronnie Earl and the Broadcasters have been one of the most popular blues bands in the U.S., and Earl is widely regarded as one of the decade's top blues guitarists.

I Like It When It Rains — Antone's 2

Recorded in 1988, this is Ronnie Earl's best CD. In some stores, you'll still find the album with its original label; in others, it may be a Discovery release. The songs are quite different from one another. "Ridin' with Ronnie" is a fast-paced electric blues romp. "Linda" is a tender number accompanied by Ron Levy's organ with Earl's guitar glimmering in several long solos. Earl switches over to a National Steel for some gleaming slide guitar work. He performs the title track as a solo with minimal accompaniment. "Down on Guadalupe" features the formidable Jerry Portnoy on harmonica. Their version of "Sittin' on Top of the World" is sweet and gentle.

LINK➤ *Johny Littlejohn — Chicago Blues Stars* — ***Arhoolie 1043***

John Fuchness's slide guitar centers this 1969 album in a style that recalls any number of Chicago blues favorites. Produced by Chris Strachwitz and Willie Dixon, highlights include "Kiddeo" and "Nowhere to Lay My Head." Good rocking band, too.

Test of Time — Black Top 1082

The 1980s albums that Earl recorded with the Broadcasters for Black Top contain some work that's fine and some that's lackluster. This one CD collects the best material from *Deep Blues* (Black Top 1033), *Soul Searchin'* (1042), *Peace of Mind* (1060) and 1991's *Surrounded by Love* (1069). The release dates are deceptive; "I Smell Trouble," one of several songs from 1982, has Earl playing a stinging guitar as he moves through consistently interesing improvisations. "Narcolepsy" is a wide-awake boogie led by organist Anthony B.B. Geraci, with Earl on guitar. The road band experience rocks the house on Earl Hooker's "Off the Hook." Ditto for "I Want to Shout About It."

LINK➤ *Ronnie Earl — Grateful Heart: Blues and Ballads* — ***Bullseye Blues 9565***

A reverential mood on John Coltrane's "Alabama" begins a 1996 series of tributes. Frequently pleasant, sometimes light, Earl and keyboardist Bruce Katz salute Carlos Santana, Duane Allman, Vietnam veterans, and others. Big contributions from David "Fathead" Newman on saxophone.

One of at least ten children of a western Tennessee farm family, John Adam Estes was born in 1904. He grew up without much education and lost the sight in one eye after a baseball accident. By the early 1950s, he was totally blind. Whether the droopy eye or a propensity to nap provided the nickname remains a question. As a young teen, Estes learned guitar from local musicians. He teamed up with 11-year-old Yank Rachell; eventually he formed the Memphis Jug Band (whose recordings survive) and a trio with Jab Jones on piano and Rachell playing mandolin, while Estes sang and played guitar. Estes recorded regularly through the 1930s, sometimes with harpist Hammie Nixon. He mostly stayed around the Brownsville area, visiting Memphis during harvest time and playing for handouts. Estes benefited from the early 1960s rediscovery of blues musicians: he recorded and toured the club and festival circuit (sometimes with Nixon) during the early 1970s. Estes died in Brownsville in 1977.

I Ain't Gonna Be Worried No More — Yazoo 2004

These delightful recordings are pure country blues enriched by enormously talented sidemen. Yank Ranchell's mandolin and Jab Jones's piano boogie bass line on "Milk Cow Blues" support Estes's storytelling. Hammie Nixon's outstanding work on harmonica (some of the finest ever recorded) makes "Someday Baby" a classic. "Drop Down Mama" has equally fine work from both Estes and Nixon. Estes was also known for writing about specific people and places in his life. The catchy "Lawyer Clark Blues" is a very positive song about a protective local attorney. "Floating Bridge" reports on a Kentucky accident in which Nixon saved the life of Estes and his relatives.

LINK➤ *Sleepy John Estes — Brownsville Blues* **Delmark 613**

From 1965, a revival of songs about Estes's hometown, including "Lawyer Clark," "Vassie Williams," "Pat Mann's Store," and some commentary, as in "Government Money." Estes's guitar work is, as always, fairly simple.

The Legend of Sleepy John Estes — Delmark 603

Delmark recorded several albums with Estes and Nixon in the 1960s, and all are worth owning: *Broke and Hungry* (608), *In Europe* (611), and especially *Brownsville Blues* (613). This 1962 release begins with a heartrending harmonica solo from Nixon, with Knocky Parker (a British blues piano player) successfully filling the old roles of Rachell and Jones. It's powerful blues, perfectly executed on "Rats in My Kitchen," a new composition, and on classics, such as "Drop Down Mama, that have become standard blues repertoire for many musicians. "Diving Duck Blues" is an old Estes favorite with a catchy harmonica and bass line. On this album, Estes's singing is dark, emotional, and clearer than on subsequent releases.

LINK➤ *Various Artists — East Coast Blues: 1926-1935* ***Yazoo 1013***

The country ragtime players on this CD are generally less well known than on other Yazoo sets. Willie Walker, for example, came from South Carolina. William Moore represents Virginia. Compare this collection to blues from other regions to hear stylistic differences.

Fabulous Thunderbirds

The Fabulous Thunderbirds worked their way from a Texas bar band to become top blues stars. Guitar player Jimmie Vaughan (Stevie Ray's brother) and harmonica player Kim Wilson started the band in 1974, struggled for a while, and eventually became the house band at Austin's popular Antone's blues club. Music journalists revered the band and wrote about them often; Chrysalis released several well-regarded albums (which sold poorly). Still, the T-Birds' cachet led to early 1980s tours opening for the Rolling Stones and for Eric Clapton. A few years later, the band was dropped by Chrysalis but picked up by Epic, where it scored a top ten pop hit with "Tuff Enuf"; two more popular albums followed. Vaughan left the group before1990; he was replaced by Duke Robillard (one of several Roomful of Blues alumni in the T-Birds). The group continues to record and perform, but without the loyal fan following of the 1980s.

The Essential Fabulous Thunderbirds **Chrysalis 21851**

These 20 tracks came from two very highly regarded albums released by Chysalis—1979's *The Fabulous Thunderbirds* (21250) and 1980's *What's the Word* (21287), as well as from two also-rans, 1981's *Butt Rockin'* and 1982's *T-Bird Rhythm*. This is a tight, capable, stylish band of blues-rockers. Kim Wilson's voice is clear, focused, and just slightly shady. The contrast between Wilson's smooth delivery and the jagged glass particles of Jimmy Vaughan's guitar on "Full-Time Lover" is sublime. This is as good as it gets. The band borrows liberally from old rock 'n' roll, Texas blues, and swamp blues. "Running Shoes," with its mucky rhythm, is the T-Birds at their down-and-dirty best. Good stuff.

LINK➤ *Jimmie Vaughan — Strange Pleasure* ***Epic 52702***

Nile Rodgers produced this 1995 effort, the first for Vaughan as a solo. Lou Ann Barton and Dr. John are among the guests. Dr. John also cowrote several tunes ("Two Wings" and "Love the World"). No big surprises, but certainly it's entertaining, satisfying work by a top professional.

Tuff Enuff **CBS 40304**

Dave Edmunds produced this 1986 album; it's the one that transformed the T-Birds from a little-known Austin band to the darlings of mid-1980s MTV-based rocking blues. It's a good album—slick work from a band always known for its tight, sharp arrangements. More commercial, too. "Tuff Enuff" was the big hit, with a heavy rotation on MTV; a remake of Sam & Dave's "Wrap It Up" was the follow-up. Wilson's 1950s-style "True Love" is clever and stylish, and "Two Time My Own" is a soulful Wilson original inspired by Memphis soul. Wilson's harp gets its workout on the fast-paced jump "I Don't Care" and on the closer, "Down at Antone's," which is similar.

LINK➤ *Fabulous Thunderbirds — Hot Stuff: The Greatest Hits* ***CBS 53007***

Recaps 1986 through 1991. The best tracks by far come from Tuff Enuff, but even the so-so material by the T-Birds outshines the work of many other bands. "Stand Back" was a 1988 hit, and "Powerful Stuff" was in the soundtrack of Cocktail, *a Tom Cruise film.*

Fuller came from Wadesboro, NC, and in the 1930s, he was a recording star. Born in 1907, he learned guitar as a child; after losing his sight as a teenager, Fuller earned a living by performing on the streets. He never gave up that way of working. Even when he was central to the Piedmont blues scene, Fuller still earned most of his money by picking up change tossed by tobacco factory workers. Fortunately, in 1935, Durham record store owner J.B. Long heard Fuller play and arranged a contract with ARC Records. Long stayed on as Fuller's producer-manager. Fuller became very influential (his influence can still be heard in music from Virginia and North Carolina) and encouraged other musicians to record. Sadly, his fast street life took its toll on his health, and he died from problems related to kidney disease at age 33.

Truckin' My Blues Away — Yazoo 1060

Fuller's toe-tapping shuffle inspired the Grateful Dead, The Band, and lots of other folk and rock bands. The title song, with Fuller's spirited "Keep on truckin' baby, truckin' my blues away," is complemented with a catchy percussion track that would fit into any contemporary repertoire. Fuller also does some world-class scat singing on this song and on "Jivin' Woman Blues," another upbeat number. "Walking My Troubles Away" is essentially a slower, sadder version of "Truckin'," one of several down-tempo songs handled with flair. Fuller also gets into his share of sexual material ("Sweet Honey Hole" and "I Crave My Pigmeat"). On "Meat Shakin' Woman," a song about an overweight lady friend, Fuller's guitar work is built on a Blind Lemon Jefferson conception.

LINK➤ *Various Artists — String Dazzlers* **Columbia/Legacy 47060**
Country blues guitar is the emphasis, and although Fuller isn't included, the CD provides meaningful context. Blind Willie McTell performs "Georgia Rag," Tampa Red does "Denver Blues," and Casey Bill Weldon plays "Guitar Swing." Lots more good material.

East Coast Piedmont Style — Columbia 46777

This collection begins with the other well-known Fuller tune, "Rag Mama Rag" (a 1970 hit for The Band). It's a shuffling song with washboard percussion (played by Bull City Red) and terrific guitar accompaniment from Fuller and Reverend Gary Davis. It's tough not to sing (and dance) along with the romping stop-and-start rhythm of "Baby You Got to Change Your Mind" (same musicians, same 1935 session). "I'm Climbing on Top of the Hill" is one of Fuller's finest melodies. The sexual "I'm a Rattlesnakin' Daddy" is another strong melody. Good sound, too. Start here, but quickly move on to the Yazoo album (which duplicates just a few tracks). Highest possible recommendation!

LINK➤ *Etta Baker — One-Dime Blues* ***Rounder 2112***
A personal favorite, these 1988 and 1990 sessions present an absolutely crystal-clear performance of finger-picked blues and other traditional music. The 75-year-old Baker transmits a wonderfully calming wisdom along with her instrumental work. Absolutely delightful.

Lowell Fulson

Fulson was born in Tulsa, OK, in 1921, the son of black and Choctaw parents. As a teenager, he moved away from the gospel music of his youth and into the blues. He befriended blues singer Texas Alexander and played behind him in the early 1940s. Time in the service led to a business relationship with Bob Geddins, an Oakland, CA, producer who owned several small labels. Before long Fulson was recording R&B hits for Geddins, including "Everyday I Have the Blues" and "Blue Shadows." Fulson then signed with Chess, where his own composition "Reconsider Me" was one of many hits over nearly a decade. By 1964, he was signed to Kent; the blues scene was changing, but Fulson continued to record and scored the occasional top 10 R&B hit, like 1967's "Tramp." Clubs and festivals provided work in the 1970s and 1980s. A 1991 contract with Rounder's Bullseye Blues helped keep his name alive.

My First Recordings — **Arhoolie 443**

The first half of this collection emphasizes Fulson's earlier years, when he was a country blues guitar player with a slightly nasal, slightly mumbly vocal. His performance is a model of moderation, with some bold strokes on guitar. On "River Blues," "The Blues Is Killing Me," and many others, Fulson's a poor man in a roadside joint, fortunate to find electricity for his guitar. The story changes completely with "San Francisco Blues," a modified jump/R&B tune that makes only passing reference to Fulson's roots. It's sophisticated city blues, suitable for a classy uptown lounge. "Trouble Blues" makes the connection between Fulson's old and new worlds. From 1946–51.

LINK➤ *Lowell Fulson — San Francisco Blues* — ***Black Lion 760176***

On these 16 songs, the emphasis is on piano-bass-guitar and Fulson's slick singing voice. He's transformed into an R&B singer with honest blues roots and a clever repertoire that includes "Television Blues" (which allows him to "see every place my baby goes").

The Complete Chess Masters — **Chess (MCA) 93942**

This 2-CD set finds Fulson at his R&B peak. It's amazing how far this man had come. "Reconsider Baby," from 1954, features a big, tight horn section; extremely articulate singing; stylish piano comping in the background; and Fulson's signature guitar playing its fat sound for extended solos. A baritone saxophone's dark strains richly complement Fulson's voice on "Loving You," and the addition of his R&B approach is a handsome complement to Willie Dixon's standard Chicago blues setting of "Do Me Right." With screaming saxes and echo-chamber vocals, 1960's "Blue Shadows" is Fulson's confident R&B at its best. Part of the Chess 50th Anniversary collection.

LINK➤ *Pee Wee Crayton — The Complete Aladdin and Imperial Recordings* — ***Capitol 36292***

Beautiful ballad work from the early 1950s. Crayton's guitar is pungent, but his voice is sweet and sentimental. He's also a talented songwriter. It all works especially well on "When It Rains, It Pours," and the free-flowing "I Need Your Love." Very entertaining.

Anson Funderburgh

Born in 1954, Plano, TX, native Funderburgh has been playing the blues guitar since he was around 8 years old. While a teenager in the 1960s, he spent many hours studying blues records and copying what he heard; when he was old enough to get by the front door, he hung around Dallas's blues clubs and picked up all he could from Albert Collins, Jimmy Reed, and others. After a spell with the Fabulous Thunderbirds, Funderburgh and vocalist/harmonic player Darrell Nulisch formed the Rockets in 1978. The group signed with Black Top, a new label in New Orleans, in 1981. Nulisch left in 1986 to join a local band (he later played for Ronnie Earl and the Broadcasters) and was replaced by Sam Myers, a veteran Chicago blues harmonica player. During the 1990s, the band steadily gained momentum, moving up from small clubs to festivals and medium-sized venues.

Thru the Years: A Retrospective **Black Top 1077**

Covering a decade from 1981 to 1991, here's the musical story of a top contemporary blues band. Early on, it's Darrell Nulisch singing lead on Earl King's "Come On" and Little Milton's "The Blues Seem to Follow Me." The latter song follows a solid Chicago tradition, complete with a Chess-style arrangement and a harmonica solo. Funderburgh's guitar makes it clear that this is not a cover band. Myers comes in for "My Heart Cries Out for You," which juxtaposes his Chicago experience against a more modern guitar solo from Funderburgh. "Meanstreak," from the late 1980s, has a cleaner sound with horns. Plenty of imaginative musicianship and solid craftsmanship here.

LINK➤ *Sam Myers — My Love Is Here to Stay* ***Black Top 1032***

Rather than Myers sharing billing with Funderburgh, this 1986 effort places Myers's name first. His powerful voice is out in front, sometimes recapping successes from years back. Myers's harmonica is, of course, a primary asset. Songs include "Poor Little Angel Chilld" and "True Love."

Live at the Grand Emporium **Black Top 1111**

A supportive Kansas City crowd, a good sound system, and a set of really fine live music make this Funderburgh album one of the best of the 1990s. "Sidetracked" is mostly an opportunity for Funderburgh to show his stuff on electric guitar; it's a six-minute solo that rocks and never goes stale, with an extended break for Carl "Sonny" Leyland's piano. (Leyland, in fact, plays a big role throughout the concert.) Sam Myers comes out for a relaxed version of B.B. King's "Understand," a vocal. The band is quite versatile, but it sounds best when shifting from vocal to harmonica to lead guitar, as on the upbeat "It's You." Excellent fidelity, too.

LINK➤ *Smokey Wilson — Smoke 'n' Fire* ***Bullseye Blues 9534***

With cameos from older blues heroes like Larry Davis and Jimmy McCracklin, Wilson is a jangling guitar player with a coarse, lowdown voice that's an interesting blend of Mississippi freedom and L.A. street savvy. Harsh by design, this is honest 1993 city blues.

A leading student, teacher, and advocate of finger-picked guitar, Grossman's influence runs deep. In 1959, at age 15, he started traveling to a particularly nasty Harlem neighborhood to take lessons from Reverend Gary Davis. At age 20, Grossman befriended Rory Block, and the two learned together. He also formed the Even Dozen Jug Band with John Sebastian, David Grisman, Maria Muldaur, and other notables. Grossman also wrote a series of instructional guitar books and created an instructional record. This path eventually led to a full-scale publishing program involving videos, more books, and a school. Among many other projects, Kicking Mule Records and accompanying tours kept Grossman busy in the 1970s. In the early 1980s, he toured with John Renbourn. By the mid-1980s, Grossman was working on new audio and video product lines for Shanachie. Throughout the 1990s, the Guitar Workshop and Vestapol Video's line of performance tapes have been occupying Grossman's time.

How to Play Blues Guitar — Shanachie 98001/2

Grossman is one of the best guitar teachers on the planet and a great advocate of country blues. To encourage students to mimic the best, Grossman put together a remarkable collection of acoustic blues based on classic styles, and then explained how to play each one. The disc opens with Son House singing "Yonder Comes the Blues." Grossman's guitar accompaniment is in the style of Charlie Patton. Mississippi John Hurt's style glistens on "Mississippi Blues #3," which is performed here by Grossman, slide guitarist Sam Mitchell, and singer Jo Ann Kelly. For education and for just plain listening, this is a remarkable collection of wonderful performances; the recording is demonstration quality.

LINK➤ *John Renborn — A Maid in Bedlam* **_Shanachie 79004_**

Founder of the British folk group Pentangle and Grossman's partnerfor several years, Renbourn is known for his association with classic British folk music. This 1977 album samples his favored genre and also features former Pentangle vocalist Jacqui McShee.

Shake That Thing: Fingerpicking Country Blues Guitar — Shanachie 97027

Grossman's first solo album in a decade is a total delight. It's for lovers of country blues guitar, as pure and bracing as water from a mountain stream. In his enthusiastic, well-written liner notes Grossman carefully credits every influence for each of the 17 songs. "Yazoo Strut" combines touches of Lonnie Johnson, Tommy Johnson, and Mississippi John Hurt. "Candyman" is associated with Reverend Gary Davis and many others. "Monkey Wrench Rag" makes use of ideas from Lightnin' Hopkins, Lil Son Jackson, and Mance Lipscomb. "Death Come Creeping," one of the first songs Grossman teaches new students, will be familiar to Charlie Patton and Lipscomb fans, perhaps under different titles. From 1998.

LINK➤ *Stefan Grossman — Yazoo Basin Boogie* **_Shanachie 97013_**

The emphasis on these early 1970s recordings is old-time music, and once again, Grossman's liner notes are educational. This is, in fact, a collection of work from Grossman's own Transatlantic Records. Some songs are originals, others, such as "Roberta," are classics.

Louisiana-born George Guy got started in Baton Rouge blues clubs, then moved to Chicago in 1957 at age 22. He was quickly accepted by the scene's best blues musicians, including Muddy Waters, Otis Rush, and Magic Sam. Guy's growing notoriety led to a recording deal with Cobra Records and then, in 1960, with Chess. While at Chess he also became a very popular session guitar player behind Muddy Waters and other top Chess artists. After seven very productive years, Guy went to Vanguard and then a series of other labels. He also joined forces with Junior Wells, and the two toured and recorded during the 1970s. At the time, Guy also became popular with rock audiences, but his fame faded. He didn't record very much during the 1980s and lived off club dates. In 1989, Guy's life changed. He opened a Chicago blues club (Buddy Guy's Legends), signed with Silvertone Records, promoted his work on national talk shows, and won fame.

The Complete Chess Studio Recordings

MCA 9337

Pound for pound, this is the best Buddy Guy release. It's a 2-CD set with 47 tracks recorded between 1960 and 1967 (half have not been released before). The most satisfying material puts Guy next to a happening horn section (two tenor saxophones and one baritone) for 1961's "Watch Yourself" and the harder "Let Me Love You Baby," a Willie Dixon tune cut in 1960. On both tracks, Otis Spann plays piano and Fred Below's the drummer. Junior Wells's harmonica is the melancholy foundation of "Ten Years Ago," from the same era. This is all seminal blues, among the best ever recorded—it gets under the skin and stays there forever. Two 1962 tracks add a girl group; it's not primo, but it's fun. Nice organ from Lafayette Leake, too, on those cuts and on the deeply felt "When My Left Eye Jumps," notable for Guy's astonishing guitar solos and flawless blending with the horns (easily the best song on this album). Guy's 1950s-ish salute to *American Bandstand* also provides the opportunity to play like Chuck Berry, which he does perfectly. On CD2, "Worried Mind" is a warm, moody piece with fine Leake piano accompaniment; the popular Art Blakey jazz signature piece "Moanin'" (written by Bobby Timmons) gets a snappy R&B treatment (with a great bass solo from Jack Meyers), but things really take off with "Crazy Love (Crazy Music)" and several other cuts from 1965, particularly those released on *Left My Blues in San Francisco* (Chess 31265). The cluster of unreleased material that completes CD2 is less distinguished.

LINK➤ *Buddy Guy — I Was Walking Through the Woods* **_Chess 9315_**

The album's title is the first line of "First Time I Met the Blues," one of many superb Guy tunes from the early 1960s featured here; others include "Watch Yourself," "Stone Crazy," "Ten Years Ago," and "Let Me Love You, Baby." Very highly recommended.

The Very Best of Buddy Guy — Rhino 70280

For context and for a quick-and-easy overview of 25 years (1957–82), it makes sense to begin with this single CD collection. It starts with the 1960 tune that established Guy as a serious, intense musician, "First Time I Met the Blues." It's one of four Chess singles. The stinging pierce of Guy's guitar, matched with his desperate vocal, makes "This Is the End" not only his best work for the Artistic label, but one of his all-time best tracks. "Hello San Francisco," with its delicate lines, nicely represents Guy's Vanguard era, but there's only one song with his longtime collaborator, Junior Wells. Some interesting collectible material is included.

LINK➤ *Various Artists — Blues Masters Vol. 2: Postwar Chicago Blues* — ***Rhino 71122***

Buddy Guy's 1958 recording of "First Time I Met the Blues" and Earl Hooker's "Blue Guitar" are among the later tracks on this chronological survey. The earlier ones include Jimmy Rogers's "That's All Right" and Johnny Shines's "Evening Sun," both from the early 1950s.

Buddy Guy and Junior Wells: Live in Montreux — Evidence 26002

Guy and Wells made several albums together, but this 1977 concert (plus some unreleased tracks) emerges as the best. The band is particularly good on blues classics like "Messin' with the Kid," "Got My Mojo Working" (with a great rhythmic harmonica from Wells) and Sonny Boy Williamson's "Help Me." Guy and Wells are not at all shy about taking long solos and showing off onstage; Guy is famous for exciting live performances, and some of that energy comes through here. And don't discount the unreleased material—Andrew "Big Voice" Odom is gutsy and intense on "I Don't Know," and Eddy Clearwater gets the crowd clapping along with "Hoochie Coochie Man."

LINK➤ *Buddy Guy & Junior Wells — Play the Blues* — ***Rhino 70299***

This popular 1972 album features Eric Clapton, Dr. John, and members of the J. Geils Band, but it's seriously overcooked. Wells's work on "My Baby, She Left Me" is impressive.

And Junior Wells Play the Blues — Atlantic 70299

When Buddy Guy sings "Don't Leave Me," his vocal is expressive with all the right touches, and his guitar's accompaniment flows like crystal-clear water. And when Junior Wells opens "Give Me My Coat and Shoes," his harmonica sends shivers down the spine, an alchemy he repeats on the album's best song, "Rollin' and Tumblin'." When they're good, as they are on country blues, Muddy Waters's "My Home's in the Delta," and three John Lee Hooker songs, this is a terrific experience. Strangely, these moments never gel into a dramatic, coherent whole. Pacing and too many same-sounding songs are the reasons why. Recorded in Paris in 1981; released in the U.S. in 1991.

LINK➤ *Various Artists — Chicago Blues Harmonica* — ***Paula 7***

A sweet harmonica performance by Baby Face Leroy begins this 1949–56 collection. There's a good amount of Snooky Prior, two tracks by Louie Myers and the Aces, and a ripping "When I Find My Baby" from Arbee Stidham. Sonny Boy Williamson, too.

A Man and the Blues **Vanguard 79272**

The title tune is likely to sound familiar; it's quintessential Buddy Guy, with long, sad sliding notes that easily drift off into an improvisation by horns and piano (Spann, again) that brings on the sad and hopeless night. The cut is 6 minutes and 17 seconds of perfection and ecstasy. The band has some R&B fun with Berry Gordy's "Money (That's What I Want)" and even does a credible job with nursery rhymes, successfully transforming both "Mary Had a Little Lamb" and "A-Tisket, A-Tasket" into Chicago blues. On the serious side, Mercy Dee's "One Room Country Shack" is profoundly depressing, an emotion expressed with dignity on Guy's guitar. He also sings the song beautifully.

LINK➤ *Various Artists — In the Key of Blues: Bluesville Years, Vol. 4* ***Prestige 9908***

Mercy Dee Walton's "One Room Country Shack" leads off this Bluesville collection (1959-61). This is superior stuff: Little Brother Montgomery's "Vicksburg Blues" (plus three more), four from Roosevelt Sykes, and four by Curtis Jones, notably "Weekend Blues."

Drinkin' TNT 'n' Smokin' Dynamite **Blind Pig 71182**

Jointly credited to Buddy Guy and Junior Wells, this 1974 concert date was recorded live at the Montreux Jazz Festival, but it wasn't mixed until six years later. It's a whole lot of fun, mainly because the band combines classic blues players (Guy, Wells, and pianist Pinetop Perkins) with a rhythm section from the rock world (bassist Bill Wyman, rhythm guitarist Terry Taylor, and drummer Dallas Taylor). There's plenty of show-off guitar work, as on "How Can One Woman Be So Mean?" and "Everything Gonna Be Allright." "Messing with the Kid" and "Hoodoo Man Blues" feature some surprisingly tight playing for what amounted to a pickup band.

LINK➤ *Ronnie Earl — Eye to Eye* ***AudioQuest 1043***

Pinetop Perkins's project list is miles long. Here, he's back with three Muddy Waters alumni, running blues classics with Earl as lead guitarist. The song list includes material by Little Willie John ("Country Girl"), Memphis Slim ("How Long?"), several by Roosevelt Sykes, and so on.

Damn Right I've Got the Blues **Silvertone 1462**

Full-throttle electric blues with a massive footprint. Every song gets the rocking treatment, the feeling is the middle of a Saturday night, the band is hot, Guy's lead guitar is tempered steel, and subtlety is reserved for well past midnight. "Early in the Morning" is rambunctious and star-studded (with Eric Clapton and Jeff Beck). On many songs, such as "Mustang Sally" and the title number, the big sounds cut hard and feel right. Equally powerful is "Too Broke to Spend the Night" (about a father afraid to go home) with its relentlessly emotional guitar runs. But the 3 A.M. blues is a Guy trump card, and "Black Night" is one of his best. From 1991.

LINK➤ *Various Artists — Legends of Guitar: Electric Blues Vol. 1* ***Rhino 70716***

How good is Buddy Guy? Compare his work to these 17 top electric guitar players selected by Guitar Player *magazine. Contenders include Howlin' Wolf, T-Bone Walker, B.B. King, Guitar Slim, Earl Hooker, Hound Dog Taylor, and others, each contributing one song.*

For six sweet years, from 1946 until 1952, the exuberant R&B singer Wynonie Harris was one of the hottest acts on L.A.'s famed Central Avenue. In 1952 alone, Harris scored a dozen hit records. Over the next two years, Harris's star faded as the public lost interest in his music. Born in Nebraska in 1915, Harris hung out in Kansas City, where he studied Joe Turner's technique. In Chicago, he became a nightclub emcee; he joined Lucky Millinder's big band as lead vocalist in 1944 and had a few hits with the band (including "Who Threw Whiskey in the Well?"), before landing in L.A. in 1945. Harris signed with King Records in 1947 and recorded hit after hit, including many jump blues with lyrics about sex and drinking. When tastes changed from R&B to rock, Harris's career fell apart. He made several unsuccessful comeback attempts, and he died of cancer in 1969.

Everybody Boogie **Delmark 683**

Four 1945 recording sessions for the Apollo label resulted in an interesting blend of big band, early bebop, and jump blues. Mostly, Harris sings out as if all of his accompaniment was jump blues. He has a grand old time with his double-entendre lyrics, as in "Somebody Changed the Lock on My Door." Harris sings about the rough-and-tumble love affairs that were so much a part of his real life. Few blues singers would include a lyric like, "You want to pull your knife and cut me 'cause I won't let you tell me what to do." A rueful muted trumpet drives the message home.

LINK➤ ***Various Artists — Blues Masters Vol. 14: More Jump Blues Rhino 71133***
Highlights include Professor Longhair's "Ball the Wall," Piano Red's "Jump Man Jump" with its tinkling piano sound, Little Richard singing "Little Richard's Boogie" with Johnny Otis's band, plus Bobby Charles inimitable "Later Alligator." Lots more. Loads of fun.

Bloodshot Eyes: The Best of Wynonie Harris
Rhino 71544

A fascinating mix. This 1947–54 collection begins with "Good Rockin' Tonight," a partying romp that's less about dancing and more about sex. And when Harris sings "All She Wants to Do Is Rock," from 1949, his meaning is undeniably clear. But he digs deeper. In 1951's "Bloodshot Eyes," he admonishes an old flame after she's been beaten up on a drunken spree; it sounds like jump blues, but the attitude is nasty, direct, and angry. It was a big hit, the followup to 1950's "Good Morning, Judge" ("I didn't know her pop was a city cop and she was just 16"). All wrapped up in just-for-fun jump blues.

LINK➤ ***Various Artists — Blues Masters, Vol. 5: Jump Blues Classics Rhino 71125***
The best jump anthology, bar none. Harris contributes "Good Rockin' Tonight," but things get hotter with Bullmouse Jackson and His Buffalo Bearcats ("Why Don't You Haul Off and Love Me?"), Clarence Brown ("Rock My Blues Away"), and Jackie Brentson ("In My Real Gone Rocket").

Michael Hill's Blues Mob

Michael Hill grew up in the South Bronx, one of NYC's toughest areas. Coming of age in the late 1960's, he was greatly influenced by Jimi Hendrix and other leading guitar players, including Buddy Guy, B.B. King, and Carlos Santana. Hill admired Bob Marley for his ability to express social concerns in music. Authors Toni Morrison and James Baldwin also inspired his songwriting. Hill built his career by working a day job and picking up session work at night. He played with Little Richard, B.B. King, and Bobby Womack, among others. Hill appeared on a Shanachie tribute album for Curtis Mayfield. He also played in a NYC band called Dadahdoodahda with Vernon Reid (later of Living Color). Hill's break came in 1993, when *Guitar Player* editor Jas Obrecht called Alligator president Bruce Iglauer to tell him about Hill. An Alligator contract followed, along with critically acclaimed albums and touring.

Bloodlines **Alligator 4821**

Here's the future of urban blues: thick, complex sounds; articulate, well-considered lyrics; real meat and real meaning. That's the essence of "Can't Recall a Time," a tight, smart taste of street-corner philosophy, embodied in lyrics such as "Can't recall a time so many children had the blues," and "Can't recall a time so many elders lived in fear." These are accentuated with direct hits of electricity from Hill's stun-gun guitar. The group explains itself in "Why We Play the Blues": tell real urban stories and do something good for the soul at the same time. This no-nonsense approach to contemporary blues gets the city's grit right. "Evil in the Air," a song where several murders are planned, gets the city's tension right, too.

LINK➤ *Various Artists — The Roots of Rap* ***Yazoo 2018***

Urban music and issues have been linked for a century or more. Here's a look at talking blues (the connection to rap is hopeful at best). Highlight is Blind Willie Johnson singing "If I Had My Way I'd Tear This Building Down." An interesting mix of musical history.

Have Mercy! **Alligator 4845**

Hill and company are still at their best with an issue at the heart of a song. The best work on this album is "Grandmother's Blues," about a police killing of a defenseless older woman in New York City. It's harsh, not only in its lyrics, but in its severe instrumentation. "Backyard in Brooklyn" tries to move from the mean streets to a safe haven; it's a kind of urban love song that's similar in spirit to "Up on the Roof." As on the first album, the group rocks but it's reflective: "Bluestime in America," "Women Make the World Go 'Round," and so on. Michael Hill's lead guitar cuts clean, with keen timing.

LINK➤ *Various Artists — The Alligator Records' 25th Anniversary Collection* ***Alligator 110/111***

An ultimate Alligator sampler, with "Can't Recall a Time" from the Michael Hill group. Liner notes from label founder and modern blues pioneer Bruce Iglauer tell the story of how Alligator breathed life into a rapidly aging form of American music.

Like many of Chicago's best, Earl Hooker was born and raised in Mississippi. His home was the Delta town of Clarksdale. Hooker's family moved to Chicago in the early 1940s, when he was about 11 years old. He attended school, performed on street corners, and befriended slide guitar player Robert Nighthawk, a friendship that led to gigs around Chicago. In 1947, Hooker was hired by Ike Turner to play guitar with his touring band. After a few years of road work (much of it in the South), Hooker returned to Chicago, where he became popular in the area's clubs; he worked regularly through the 1960s, occasionally recording, occasionally traveling (he did a European tour in 1965), and enjoying somewhat legendary status among rock guitar players. (Incidentally, Earl Hooker was blues great John Lee Hooker's cousin.) Earl Hooker died of tuberculosis at age 40, a fine slide guitar player who never became famous.

Two Bugs & A Roach **Arhoolie 324**

On this 1968 title track, Hooker lays down one of his finer electric guitar tracks, but he also chats on top of the music with Andrew "B.B." Odom throughout the instrumental. Their conversation enhances the song. "Two Bugs" is code for tuberculosis (T.B.), a disease that haunted Hooker, then killed him. The purity, slight twang, and utter confidence of Hooker's picking has no better showplace than "Wah Wah Blues," a kind of musical conversation with Joe Willie Perkins's organ. The walking blues "Off the Hook," nicely recorded in 1968 to show off Hooker's sparkle, comes from the same session as the intensely soulful "You Don't Love Me." Some 1950s material is included, too.

LINK➤ *Andrew "B.B." Odom — Going to California Flying Fish (Rounder) 70587*
Recorded in 1991—the same year he died—the big-voiced blues vocalist recorded this album with the Gold Tops (Steve Freund is especially good on lead guitar). Some familiar tunes, like "Rock Me Baby," are balanced with several impressive Odom originals, such as "Come to Me."

Blue Guitar **Paula 18**

Recorded for the Age and Chief labels in the early 1960s, Hooker's guitar is sometimes lost in so-so mixes. Still, there isn't much Hooker material available on CD, and there are many spots here that present the guitarist at his best. "Calling All Blues" is one of those tracks, and so is "Blues in D Natural." The latter is a duet with an organ that's not brilliantly recorded, but take the time to follow Hooker's lines. Ditto for the up-tempo "Off the Hook" with its dopey ice-rink organ arrangement. Hooker is often the more-than-capable session guitarist behind Lillian Offitt ("Will My Man Be Home Tonight") and others.

LINK➤ *Various Artists — Legends of Guitar: Electric Blues, Vol. 2 Rhino 70564*
Volume 2 in Rhino's series presents Mike Bloomfield, Peter Green, Magic Sam, Freddie King, Snooks Eaglin, and Buddy Guy. These are among the top blues guitar sides of the second half of this century. And some might argue that Hooker was better than them all!

Born in Clarksdale, MI, in 1920, Hooker got his musical education by singing in church and from his stepfather Will Moore and friends Charlie Patton and Blind Lemon Jefferson. Around age 15, he left home for Memphis, then moved to Cincinnati, where he had little impact. In 1943, Hooker tried Detroit; he worked as a janitor and performed where he could. He recorded "Boogie Chillun" in 1948; it became a number one R&B single, and Hooker feverishly recorded more tracks for other labels under assumed names like John Lee Booker, Texas Slim, Delta John, and Birmingham Sam. In time he settled down with Vee Jay, where his recordings entranced a young generation of British blues musicians such as John Mayall and Eric Clapton. This eventually led to European tours, gigs at rock clubs—and fame. By the late 1970s, Hooker's ride was over, but a recording with disciples Bonnie Raitt, Robert Cray, and others won the 1989 Grammy for blues. This led to a 1990 tribute concert at Madison Square Garden and a major label deal.

Boogie Chillun **Fantasy 24706**

Hooker fans will also want to get his *Alone* album (Tomato 70387), but this 1962 set should satisfy more casual listeners. Hooker plays electric guitar and sings in that rough, gruff voice, making dramatic use of space and time on "I Just Can't Hold On Much Longer" and "T.B. Is Killing Me." The approach is sparse and pungent, hard as nails. And yet, Hooker has a certain dark romance, a sexy side that comes out on "Night Time Is the Right Time" and "I Want to Get Married" (he's scared to take the chance). When he performs "I Got the Key to the Highway," he makes magic seem so darned easy.

LINK➤ *Willie Cobbs — Down to Earth* ***Rooster Blues 2628***

Cobbs, who hails from Arkansas, made his way to Chicago in the late 1940s and became a Jimmy Reed soundalike. He returned to the South, where he had a small-time career. Cobbs had a hit in 1960 with "You Don't Love Me." His easy, enthusiastic style makes this 1994 album a pleasure.

The Ultimate Collection: 1948–1990 **Rhino 70572**

This essential Rhino 2-CD collection does a good job with two key periods—Hooker's work for Modern in the late 1940s and early 1950s, and his Vee-Jay recordings of the following decade. It starts with a tasty and rare 1961 cut, "Teachin' the Blues," a talking blues that explains Hooker's music and his early influences. Then it's back to 1948 and his first hit record for Modern, "Boogie Chillen'." It's an autobiographical song about his early years that has an unusually powerful repeating rhythm. That same year's "Sally Mae" contains the growling nasal intonation that makes Hooker's voice sound so angry. And there aren't many lowdown dirty blues that can go down lower than the bass-riden "Crawlin' King Snake" from 1949. "Huckle-Up Baby," which shares themes with several other hit tunes, scored for Hooker in 1950. Of the half-dozen Vee-Jay songs, "Dimples" (about an eye-catching woman) is aggressive, even somewhat predatory. "Big Legs, Tight Skirt," recorded a decade later in 1966, is no less lascivious, but 1962's "Boom Boom" is the sexist classic. In any case, by the mid-1960s, Hooker was one of the better-known names in urban blues, one who served it up in man-sized doses. Later in the 1960s, he recorded one of his best albums, *Urban Blues* (for ABC Bluesway; long out of print), represented here by "Back Biters and Syndicators" and "Think Twice Before You Go." Of the later work, there are two cuts from Hooker 'n Heat and a few from other albums, but no clear focus.

LINK➤ *Various Artists — Rediscovered Blues* **Capitol 29376**

An interesting assemblage of blues greats. The first six tracks were performed by Lightin' Hopkins, Sonny Terry, Brownie McGhee, and Big Joe Williams in a 1960 "Summit Meeting." A dozen tracks by McGhee and Terry, plus seventeen by Williams, complete the 2-CD set.

The Legendary Modern Recordings: 1948–1954 — Flair 39658

Although some of these songs are available on other anthologies, it's probably fair to call any blues library without this CD incomplete. In addition to the well-known hits like 1948's "Boogie Chillen" and 1949's "Crawling Kingsnake," Hooker excels on 1951's romping "Women in My Life" (with a very different guitar style and a unique rhythm) as well as on the updated boogie of the same year's "Queen Bee." There's a bigger sound (and some vocal double-tracking) on 1953's "Rock House Boogie"—the technique is so poorly executed that it's almost funny. "Need Somebody," also from 1953 but sounding newer, explores a more sophisticated style that would be adopted by Cream nearly 15 years later.

LINK➤ *John Lee Hooker — Alternative Boogie: Early Studio Recordings 1948–1952* **Capitol 33912**

At first, three CDs filled with material released under phony names might seem interesting only to collectors, but the first few tracks alone quickly melt down that position. This is a trove of superb blues, wonderful guitar, and good songwriting. It's well worth owning.

Plays and Sings the Blues — Chess 9199

Hooker did a whole lot of recording in the postwar years, but this 1952 album is among his best work. His lyrics rip across his desperate, knowing guitar line, claim two wounded souls, and become the essence of "I'm Wandering." Few contemporary musicians so completely inhabit the heart of the blues. Hooker rocks out in his most threatening voice on "Mad Man Blues"; he then runs tender on "Worried Life Blues" and "Dreamin' Blues." Hooker's version of "I Need Some Money" is more of a pop-blues, but with lots of style (and handsome licks). A defining work in urban blues.

LINK➤ *Z.Z. Top — Greatest Hits* **Warner Bros. 26846**

"La Grange," the song that made the band nationally famous, is based on musical ideas from "Boogie Chillen." The band combines hard-core Texas electric blues, a good sense of humor, and very fine guitar work from Billy Gibbons. Bassist Dusty Hill and drummer Frank Beard complete the band.

Get Back Home . . . **Evidence 26004**

These recordings, made in 1969 in Paris, present Hooker accompanied only by his electric guitar—an intriguing setup. This spare approach is chilling on "T.B. Is Killing Me," but somehow, the same man plus machine combination becomes a party on "Get Back Home in the U.S.A." This song also reveals Hooker's knack for repeating a relatively simple musical idea while maintaining the listener's riveted interest. Mostly this is a guitar lover's album—without other instruments, Hooker's guitar shines—and a study in the persuasive power of a commanding entertainer. Listen (attend to every word) as Hooker quietly dominates the room on "Sittin' Here Thinkin.'" The man's got magic. Highly recommended.

LINK➤ *Various Artists — American Folk-Blues Festival Highlights '62-'65*
Evidence 26087

Seventeen live tracks featuring Lightnin' Hopkins, Fred McDowell, T-Bone Walker, Sonny Boy Williamson, Buddy Guy, and other top blues performers. The Folk-Blues Festival was a European traveling show featuring the best in blues.

Hooker 'n Heat: Canned Heat & John Lee Hooker

Mobile Fidelity 2-676

Recorded in 1970, this is one of the only successful collaborations between an authentic black bluesman and a group of adoring white blues-rockers. While Hooker growls, soothes, and seethes with world-class vocals and a searing lead guitar, Canned Heat delivers the goods, mostly as a backup band. In time, they learn to work as a single unit, and as a result, "Whiskey and Wimmen" turns out to be one of the 2-CD set's best. Alan Wilson's harmonica is superb both here as well as on the stop-and-start "Let's Make It," the album's best tune. Kudos to Henry Vestine, whose lead guitar is featured on several tracks. Overall, the second CD is much stronger than the first.

LINK➤ *Canned Heat — Uncanned!: Best of Canned Heat* ***EMI America 29165***

The song list on this 2-CD anthology is amazing. It seems to cover every significant electric blues song, plus "Wooly Bully" and a Levi's commercial! Canned Heat was the point where hippie culture met the blues, and the combination, although dated, is a whole lot of fun.

Mr. Lucky **Virgin 86237**

Hooker got lucky in the 1990s as major labels jumped on a blues revival bandwagon. He was soon in the studio, surrounded by stars, and recorded several appealing albums (though nowhere near the quality of his best for Modern, Chess, or Vee-Jay). The best of this recent batch is 1991's Mr. Lucky, which features Albert Collins, Van Morrison, Keith Richards, and others. The earlier Grammy-winning *The Healer* (Chameleon 74808) is supported by Bonnie Raitt, Carlos Santana, and Robert Cray. Hooker does the job, but never really digs in. At this point in his career, the difference between a star-studded album and a Pepsi commercial becomes a marketing blur.

LINK➤ *George "Wild Child" Butler — These Mean Old Blues*
Bullseye Blues 9518

Butler's got the same nasty, leering personna as John Lee Hooker, and the same kind of deep, dangerous voice. Like Hooker, Butler sounds best with a very pronounced rhythm section (evidence: "Give Me an Answer). From 1991. Try also 1994's Stranger *(9539).*

Lightnin' Hopkins

Sam Hopkins was born and raised in Centerville, TX, a small town north of Houston. By age 8, in 1920, he played his homemade cigar box guitar with his idol, Blind Lemon Jefferson. The same year, Hopkins left home to hobo and supported himself for the next 20 years with part-time farm work, street and party performances (with cousin Texas Alexander), and by scamming farm hands with cardsharping. By the mid-1940s, Hopkins left his own farm for Houston's growing music scene. After a few hits, he cut short his career and returned to the streets of Houston. A 1959 rediscovery led to two decades in the big time. In the early 1960s, Hopkins was a central figure on the NYC folk scene. He played Carnegie Hall, recorded with Pete Seeger and Joan Baez, and performed at U.S. folk festivals, colleges, and coffeehouses. In addition to a tour of Europe, Hopkins was featured in several documentaries. Cancer ended his life in 1982.

Mojo Hand: The Lightnin' Hopkins Anthology — Rhino 71226

Since Hopkins recorded for so many labels, this type of anthology is essential to make sense of his career. As usual, Rhino starts the 2-CD set with a single song that represents the artist at his best; this time, it's a singing and talking piece of extraordinary recorded quality entitled "Blues with a Feeling." Then the story begins with pair of songs from 1946–47, "Katie Mae Blues" (his first hit) and "Play with Your Poodle," both released on Aladdin. Assorted Gold Star recordings include the folky "Baby Please Don't Go," and down-home "Mad with You" with some tidy guitar. L.C. Williams provides percussion by tap-dancing through 1949's "Lightnin' Boogie," and because Hopkins's sound is so often just voice and guitar, his 1953 Decca single "I'm Wild About You, Baby," with bass and drums, is striking. At first, it sounds a little overproduced, then seems nicely rounded-out and complete. From the mid-1950s, there are a handful of songs released by Herald, including a very electric "Lightnin' Don't Feel Well," and a rocked-out "Movin' On Out Boogie." Sonny Terry and Brownie McGhee are comfortable partners on 1960's World Pacific recording "Wimmen From Coast to Coast" (Terry's harmonica is particularly good). Next come some Verve/Folkways recordings, and a nice batch from Hopkins's 1960s Prestige work. Hopkins plays a ballpark organ (not too well, either) on 1969's "Los Angeles Boogie." Among later cuts for small labels, "Mr. Charlie" is a charmer.

LINK➤ *Juke Boy Bonner — Life Gave Me a Dirty Deal* — ***Arhoolie 375***

Bonner's health problems prevented him from enjoying the attention lavished on his peers during the 1960s, but he did write poetry that became lyrics during his hospital stays (due to stomach illness). He sings here with just electric guitar and harmonica, simply and effectively.

Complete Aladdin Recordings **EMI 96843**

It's easy to lose sight of how much time has passed (more than 50 years) since Hopkins recorded his first commercial tracks. The first batch was recorded in 1946 in Los Angeles with pianist Wilson "Thunder" Smith and a drummer. The output of that first session included "Katie May," a solid hit (which Hopkins never repeated) and the jaunty "Feel So Bad." Two other songs from that session—"Can't Do Like You Used To" and "West Coast Blues"—are sung by Thunder Smith; the pair was billed as Thunder & Lightnin', which is how Hopkins got his nickname. (Both songs are piano blues, in which Hopkins plays a minor role.) "Big Mama," from their 1947 session, is also a Smith concoction, but most of the work is more like "Thinkin' and Worryin," with its odd-shaped sense of time, sharply sculpted guitar lines, deep-voiced nasal vocal, and darkening mood. The other recordings were made on several occasions in Houston, with Hopkins alone on guitar. "Lightnin's Boogie" presages Chuck Berry in its fast-footed guitar, specialty riffs, and even its use of tempos. From the 1948 session, "Abilene" is another testament to versatility; it's a bit like Mississippi John Hurt's work. The R&B top 5 hit "Shotgun Blues" is one of the best songs Hopkins ever recorded; it's a story about deciding not to kill someone. His guitar work deserves a special mention here. In all, a 2-CD set worth owning, and if the songs sound a bit similar at first, they certainly won't sound that way at last.

LINK➤ *Various Artists — The Gold Star Sessions* *Arhoolie 352*
Hopkins plays piano on many of these 1947–51 tracks. Ten are by an underappreciated Texas acoustic blues singer named Melvin "Lil' Son" Jackson. His guitar style is rhythmic, and his voice is low, slightly hoarse, and easy to enjoy.

The Gold Star Sessions, Vol. 1 **Arhoolie 330**

Hopkins recorded enough tracks for the Texas-based Gold Star label to fill two Arhoolie CDs. Gold Star released the songs in the South and simultaneously leased many masters to Modern, whose distribution was wider. "Baby, Please Don't Go" became a signature tune for Hopkins, and a good guitar demo piece. "Going Home Blues" is a biographical piece wallowing in self-pity. "Tim Moore's Farm" is sung in the voice of a field hand protesting treatment by a local (Grime County, TX) farmer. On both songs, Hopkins uses his guitar to set the mood, frame the meaning of words, and simply show off. "Zolo Go" is a song about zydeco music. Highly recommended.

LINK➤ *Lightnin' Hopkins — The Gold Star Sessions, Vol. 2* *Arhoolie 337*
Hopkins redeems himself with the gospel-tinged "Hammond Boogie," but mostly follows his tried-and-true formula of acoustic blues. Generally, the choice of material is not as strong as on Vol. 1, and the recording quality is not always refined. Still, it's worth hearing.

The Herald Recordings: 1954 — Collectables 5121

It's 1954, and Lightnin' Hopkins is coming dangerously close to playing rock. His guitar is very heavily amplified, and the antics would be copied by rockers many years down the line. The sound isn't perfect, but it's close enough for early rock 'n' roll, and when he wails, as he does on "Hear Me Talkin'," or handles a sexy slow rhythm as on "Flash Lightnin'," he lights up the house. The remake of his popular "My Little Kewpie Doll" reveals why this is ultimately blues, not 1950s rock—it's too rough and too tasty. Plenty of straight-ahead blues guitar here, too. There's more good Herald material on the Rhino anthology.

LINK➤ *Junior Kimbrough — All Night Long* ***Epitaph 80300***

Delta musician Kimbrough was discovered by Robert Palmer during the making of the extraordinary blues documentary, Deep Blues. *This 1992 album is no-nonsense juke joint blues, the real thing that formed the basis for Chicago and Texas blues.*

Lightnin' Hopkins — Smithsonian Folkways 40019

It's almost as if Hopkins wanted to make this music for posterity—he's careful about his articulation, polite, good-humored, and very polished on his guitar. In fact, blues historian Samuel Charters recorded this 1959 album in Hopkins's shabby rented room in Houston, moving a hand-held microphone from Hopkins's guitar to his mouth, hoping to capture it all . Not only are these country blues well recorded, they're delightful, especially when recalling the spirit of Blind Lemon Jefferson ("See That My Grave Is Kept Clean," some spoken reminiscences). "Come Go Home with Me" is typically downbeat, and whistle-clean—a pristine example of Texas country blues. While not flashy, the album is nevertheless remarkable.

LINK➤ *Texas Alexander — Complete Recorded Works, Vols. 1-3* ***Document 2001-3***

Re-issues of work for OKeh and Vocalion: the first volume covers Alexanders's first year, the second presents music through 1930, and the remainder of his work fills the last disc. Alexander sang accompanied by another musician's guitar; Hopkins and Lowell Fulson were among his partners.

The Complete Prestige/Bluesville Recordings — Prestige 4406

Beginning with the very first track, "Rocky Mountain," recorded in 1960, it's clear that Hopkins properly recorded in stereo sounds much better than Hopkins in dullish mono. The track begins a 7-CD, four-year retrospective of Hopkins at his very best. Admittedly, a full day's listening represents a solid investment of time and money, but this is mighty fine blues—originally released on 12 albums (plus more material that was never released). Just about every song is appealing and quite personal, but Arthur Crudup's "Mean Old Frisco" crystalizes that sense of fog-bound loneliness beautifully. From the same session, "Shinin' Moon" provides the singer with just enough light to see his love asleep; it's evocative of a quiet Texas night, pure and natural. Hopkins also recaps most of his old hits, such as "Katie Mae," and country blues standards such as "Good Morning, Little School Girl." Because he's in prime form on excellent recordings, these are the versions to own. "DC-7," a song about flying on an airplane, is one of several improvisations. Hopkins celebrated the first American orbital space flight with "Happy Blues for John Glenn," notable for the inspired lyric "he did it just for fun!" This childlike enthusiasm is reflective of the real-life childishness of Hopkins's behavior, which was angrily reported on the liner notes of 1962's *Smokes Like Lightning* (and reprinted in the liner notes accompanying this set). The next year's concert at Swarthmore College is yet another opportunity to hear the likes of "Baby Please Don't Go," "Mojo Hand," "Short Haired Woman," and "Mean Old Frisco." The loose folk festival atmosphere is comfortable, the music's fine and familiar, and so it gets added to a growing stack of Hopkins CDs. *Hootin' the Blues*, a 1962 live album recorded in a Philadelphia coffeehouse, is also included in its entirety. As before, Hopkins's style is friendly, personal, and engaging. In general, the earlier material and live albums are best, and the later ones are somewhat sloppy (1964's *Soul Blues*, for example, distorts Hopkins's guitar). All told, this large box is a superb presentation of a classic American artist, and if it includes a little too much music, this is a sin that can certainly be forgiven.

LINK➤ *R.L. Burnside — Too Bad Jim* **_Epitaph 80307_**
Burnside, along with Junior Kimbrough, keeps the Mississippi Delta juke joint tradition alive. The sound, created by his Sound Machine band, is meaty, raw, and honest. Burnside's in his seventies, but didn't take music seriously until about ten years ago. Try also Bad Luck City *(Fat Possum 1001).*

Double Blues

Fantasy 24702

For those unwilling to spend the time or money on the big box, here are two representative 1964 albums on a single CD. "Lonesome Graveyard" explores feelings and images related to a local cemetery, from creepy to the comforting idea of final rest. And deep in the background, there's the understated bassist Leonard Gaskin and drummer Herbie Lovelle. Willie Dixon's "My Babe" gets an unusual and very spirited acoustic reading, showing how much guitar Hopkins could play. He plays a very expressive electric guitar on "I Was Standing on Highway 75," combining acoustic and electric technique to make weary magic. For those new to Hopkins, this is a good place to start.

LINK➤ *Lightnin' Hopkins — Texas Blues* **_Arhoolie 302_**
An intense close to a stunning career. "Come on Baby" wrings sheer misery from an electric guitar, as Hopkins sings about "the meanest mens I'd ever seen." The guitar turns up the dry heat on the dangerous "Bud Russell Blues," about a 1910 tough guy who mistreated men and women.

House was born in Clarksdale, MS, in 1902; his family relocated to New Orleans around 1905. By age 20, House was a Baptist pastor; he took up the guitar five years later, when women and liquor changed his ways. With longtime friend Willie Brown, House played at picnics, parties, and juke joints. He mostly avoided trouble, but in 1928, he shot and killed a man. Although House claimed self-defense, he served about a year at the notorious Parchman Farm. Through 1929 and the early 1930s House toured and recorded with Brown, Charlie Patton, and Robert Johnson. In 1941, Alan Lomax recorded House for the Library of Congress. House moved to Rochester, NY, in 1943 for a nonmusic job; he was rediscovered there in 1964. He played the Newport Folk Festival, Carnegie Hall, and also the U.S. and European festival circuits. He performed through the early 1970s, moved to Detroit in 1976, and died there in 1988.

Delta Blues — Biograph 118

Alan Lomax recorded Son House at two sessions for the Library of Congress. The first was held at Clack's Store near Lake Cormorant, MS, in August 1941; the other songs were recorded in nearby Robinsonville the following July. The dynamic range of the acetate originals was limited, but the sound is free from surface noise. Mostly, House performs alone—his droning, slightly mumbly singing voice adroitly accompanied by a guitar style that bounces from rhythmic to melodic. He's got a knack for melody and memorable hooks; the patriotic "American Defense" and the hum-along "Walking Blues" are two of many fine examples. This is the real thing—don't miss it.

LINK➤ *Various Artists — Roots of Rhythm and Blues: A Tribute to the Robert Johnson Era* — ***Columbia 48584***

An extremely satisfying collection of old blues songs, performed live at the 1991 Folklife Festival in Washington, D.C. Performers include Johnny Shines, Jesse Mae Hemphill, David "Honeyboy" Edwards, Lonnie Pitchford, Cephas and Wiggins, and others. Enthusiastically recommended.

Father of the Delta Blues — Columbia 48867

These fine-sounding 1965 sessions yielded 16 master takes, plus 5 alternates, resulting in a 2-CD set. "Death Letter," which runs over seven minutes, is a frank story of what happens after a love has died. It invokes Judgment Day, loneliness after the sun goes down, the empty pillow the next morning, hearing her call his name, and so on. Two unaccompanied vocals, House's popular "Grinnin' in Your Face" and the gospel "John the Revelator" are among his most affecting songs. "Empire State Express" is a train song with a rolling rhythm, a duet between House and Al Wilson of Canned Heat. One of House's classic numbers, "Levee Camp Moan," features some spectacular extended expressions by Wilson on harmonica. It's about life working on the levee. "Preachin' Blues" employs a somewhat jangly guitar style (here's where House's steel-bodied National guitar sounds its best); like so many of House's songs, it gets right to the point: "I want to be a Baptist preacher so I won't have to work." Unlike most blues musicians, House sometimes wrote about contemporary times. His "American Defense" later became "President Kennedy." The song is warm, friendly, and sincere: "His memory still rings in my ears." Two previously unreleased songs complete the set. One is "Downhearted Blues," with an especially confident accompaniment; a bit of musical humming becomes a seven-minute morning-after reconsideration of a big night out and a shaky love affair. "Pony Blues" is the other unreleased song. Altogether, this is an essential blues album.

LINK➤ *Various Artists — Mississippi Moaners 1927-1942* **Yazoo 1009**
Son House in context. Washington White, whose moan is world class, performs a half-talking, half-singing "The New 'Frisco Train"; Joe Calicott is more of a shouter whose guitar seems an afterthought. Besides some famous names, there's the obscure Bobby Grant, Bud Walker, and others.

Delta Blues and Spirituals — Capitol 31830

House's monologue explaining "The B-L-U-E-S" begins this 1970 album. It's interesting, but quickly pales in comparison with his wonderfully resilient singing voice as it fights and slashes its way through every song. Wilson's harmonica assists on "I Want to Go Home on the Morning Train," but when House takes on "Death Letter Blues" or "Levee Camp Moan," his emotions are very close to the surface. The live audience's clapping provides the percussion for "Grinnin' in Your Face" and "John the Revelator," which is sung by the enthusiastic crowd. This probably isn't the best place to start. Dedicated to Wilson, who died weeks after the concert.

LINK➤ *Various Artists — The Beauty of the Blues* ***Columbia/Legacy 47465***
Truly, the blues can be quite beautiful. This particular collection is a more or less random sampling of Columbia's vaults, with some Robert Johnson, Bessie Smith, Blind Boy Fuller, and the usual suspects. Here, too, is Jazz Gillum, Buddy Woods, and Willie "Long Time" Smith.

Chester Arthur Burnett was born in West Point, MS, on June 10, 1910. His nickname came from boyhood mischief, and his harsh singing style came from Charlie Patton, a local musician. Burnett's brother-in-law, Sonny Boy Willamson II (Alex "Rice" Miller), helped him along on harmonica, and in the 1930s and 1940s, they played and traveled together (often with Robert Junior Lockwood). Burnett was also a farmer. He served in WWII, entertaining the troops in the Pacific Northwest. After the war, he settled in Memphis, TN, where he started playing electric blues. Burnett first recorded at age 41, got entangled in a contract dispute, and ended up with Chess Records, where he became famous. British blues musicians took his music very seriously; the Rolling Stones recorded several of his songs and invited him to join them on ABC-TV's *Shindig*. Burnett continued working through the early 1970s and died of cancer in 1976.

Howlin' Wolf/Moanin' in the Moonlight — Chess 5908

With 24 tracks, this could be a very inexpensive alternative to the full-scale Chess box. In the 1950s, Howlin' Wolf's albums were collections of singles. These two "albums" collect a remarkable number of Howlin' Wolf's best songs—and yet this is a budget-priced CD. The list of tracks includes "The Red Rooster," "Wang Dang Doodle," "Spoonful," "Smokestack Lightning," and the truly nasty "I Asked for Water (She Gave Me Gasoline)." This is relentlessly fine blues, mostly played with Chicago's hottest blues musicians. Howlin' Wolf is in absolute peak form, and if his voice doesn't send shivers up and down your spine, then Willie Johnson's guitar will do the job. You must have this CD!

LINK➤ *Various Artists — Paint It Blue: Songs of the Rolling Stones* *House of Blues 13152*

An interesting reverse angle. The Rolling Stones built their early career on songs by blues heroes. Now, blues stars perform "Tumblin' Dice" (Johnny Copeland), "(I Can't Get No) Satisfaction" (Junior Wells), "Under My Thumb" (Lucky Peterson), and so on.

Howling Wolf Rides Again — Flair 86295

An unindentified boogie-woogie pianist and Willie Johnson's electric guitar underplay a talking blues that begins this collection of 1951–52 Memphis recordings. The sound is rough, and Wolf's voice is rougher, but the raw edges somehow suit the music, making it sound more authentically troubled. "Crying at Daybreak" has some spooked-out howling, and "I Want Your Picture" is a dangerous juke-joint slow dance. While some of these songs ("I'm the Wolf," for example) are repeated elsewhere, most are not. "Driving this Highway" is one of Wolf's best road songs, with its thumping bass and drums, his voice grabbing the night, and the electric guitar sparking as the scene speeds by. It's a perfect construction.

LINK➤ *Various Artists — Living Chicago Blues, Vol. I* *Alligator 7701*

Excellent reintroduction of several important Chicago blues leaders. Eddie Shaw was Howlin' Wolf's long-time saxman; he does "Sitting on Top of the World" and other tunes. Carey Bell and Jimmy Johnson both get Alligator debuts here, as does lesser-known Left-Hand Frank.

The Real Folk Blues **Mobile Fidelity 645**

Once again, this is a bunch of singles, not a bona fide album. The music spans almost ten years, from 1957 through 1965. It's all in monaural sound, but Mobile Fidelity's magic makes the music sound more lifelike. This makes "Three Hundred Pounds of Joy," a rollicking hybrid of blues and R&B, into something truly entertaining—the paired saxophones leap out, and Hubert Sumlin's guitar rides above. Howlin' Wolf can almost be seen dancing as he sings, and digging down deep for those bass lines (on "look what you get"). The Chess box set repeats most of these tracks, but they simply sound better here. Wolf's voice sounds terrific!

LINK➤ *Roosevelt "Booba" Barnes — The Heartbroken Man Rooster Blues 2623*

Hardworking contemporary blues with a solid Delta core. Barnes pretty much stayed in Greenville, MS, and ran a club (Booba's Playboy Club). This 1990 album preceded a move to Chicago (the club burned down). One of Barnes's specialties: reworked Howlin' Wolf songs.

The London Howlin' Wolf Sessions **Chess 9297**

From the first few seconds, it's clear Eric Clapton and friends have a whole lot to say about Howlin' Wolf. Recorded after Cream and Blind Faith in 1970, the depth and intricacy of British blues brought the form to a very sophisticated level, and yet Howlin' Wolf's straightforward, no-B.S. vocals cut right through. The key players in this band are Clapton, Steve Winwood (piano and organ), Bill Wyman (bass), Charlie Watts (drums), and Hubert Sumlin (guitar). There's a nice mix of Howlin' Wolf standards ("Poor Boy," "Built for Comfort," "The Red Rooster") and surprise material, like Big Joe Williams's "Highway 49." Nice Winwood organ on "Who's Been Talking?"

LINK➤ *Alexis Korner — The Alexis Korner Collection Castle (U.K.) Import*

In the 1950s, Alexis Korner and his partner Cyril Davies had a London-based group called Blues Incorporated. So began the British blues movement, which begat Eric Clapton, the Rolling Stones, and so on. Do the work and track down the import.

The Chess Box **Chess 9332**

Released as a 3-CD set in 1991, this is probably the best Chess Box. Throughout his three decades of recording, Howlin' Wolf's home was almost exclusively on Chess. Most of the music was released as singles, and this presentation allows the listener a reasonably paced tour that begins with 1951's ramshackle electric near-gospel blues nightcrawler "Moanin' at Midnight," and ends in 1973 with Wolf's optimistic memory of the South "where the women treat me like a king." Wolf sings with a voice that radio personality Wolfman Jack adopted. It's gravelly and nasal, sincere and beastly; sometimes, as on 1953's "Mama Died and Left Me," he sings in a higher register and into a falsetto near-yodel (blues singer Tommy Johnson did the same). Ultimately, Howlin' Wolf's voice shapes his musical personality; he also played a mean harmonica, and a good example of his devastating style can be heard on 1954's "I'm the Wolf," one of his best songs. It's fun to hear Howlin' Wolf tell the story of Little Red Riding Hood, howling his way through the story on one of several talking tracks. The mood changes some on CD2's simmering first track, "Don't Mess with My Baby," recorded in 1955. Next up is "Smokestack Lightnin'," with its unmistakable groove, Howlin' Wolf's best harmonica (and best howling) on record. By now, he's been working with the same session musicians for several years: Otis Spann on piano, Willie Dixon on bass, Willie Johnson or Hubert Sumlin on guitar, and drummer Earl Phillips—the best in Chicago. Burnett wrote most of his own songs, but also competed with Muddy Waters for Willie Dixon's latest tune. Dixon's slow-and-easy "Spoonful" gets its finest rendition here, followed a half-year later in June 1961 by his "The Red Rooster." Both songs affected the Rolling Stones and other rockers in a big way. CD3 picks up in 1964, and mostly covers the next four years. Dixon's "Hidden Charms" leads off, soon followed by his famed "Built for Comfort" ("I ain't built for speed"—a song about a large man). "Louise" features his best use of a raving guitar accented by paired saxophones; it's a classic. Buddy Guy's scrambling guitar line, Howlin' Wolf's desperate vocals, and the scrawny instrument sounds make "Killing Floor" hardcore and essential. Wolf's 1970 tracks with British blues musicians complete one of the finest blues collections.

LINK➤ *Ike Turner — I Like Ike! The Best of Ike Turner* **Rhino 71819**
Ike Turner played guitar on many of Howlin' Wolf's sessions. He also played on one of the first rock 'n' roll records (Jackie Brentson's "Rocket 88") and with his own Kings of Rhythm. Setting aside his history with Tina, Ike's work in rock and blues stands on its own.

Ain't Gonna Be Your Dog: Chess Collectibles, Vol. 2

Chess 9349

This 2-CD set is a potpourri. The first 14 songs come from Memphis, and don't sound all that good. At track 15, Chess takes over, and everything sounds better. Serious collectors may care deeply about alternate takes ("Poor Boy," "My Baby Told Me," and several others), the studio version of "To the Big House," and many tracks previously unreleased in the U.S. (many were heard on 1970s bootlegs), including a solid "Poor Wind That Never Change" and the weary "Getting Late." There are many treasures here, notably 1968 acoustic solo versions of "Woke Up This Morning" and "Ain't Going Down That Dirt Road," both very carefully recorded with wonderfully clear guitar.

LINK➤ *J.T. "Funny Papa" Smith — The Howling Wolf: 1930–1931* **Yazoo 1031**
Two songs about wolves are included on this collection. One, called "The Howling Wolf," provided Smith with his Howling Wolf nickname. His acoustic Texas blues set an early standard, but faded from the spotlight after a prison sentence and some local touring.

Hunter was born in Memphis in 1895, ran away from home before she was a teenager, and was performing in Chicago's low-rent venues by age 12. Hunter started recording in 1921, first for Black Swan and then for Paramount. She wrote "Down-Hearted Blues," which became Bessie Smith's first hit record. The two singers gained popularity; by the mid-1920s, Hunter was performing regularly in NYC's nightclubs. She spent some of the 1930s and 1940s abroad, performing in Paris nightclubs and appearing with Paul Robeson in the London production of *Show Boat*. Hunter also entertained U.S. troops in Asia. She left music in 1956 to become a nurse; her career in that field lasted 23 years. In 1977, at age 82, Hunter staged a successful NYC nightclub comeback. She died in 1984.

Young Alberta Hunter: The '20s and '30s — Jass 6

This is the real thing: nearly two dozen songs from ten sessions. The collection leads off with 1935's "You Can't Tell The Difference After Dark," a swaggering bit of sensuality that tosses off inadequacies visible only in the daytime. The vaudevillian "Second Hand Man" finds an experienced showbiz hand at the top of her game. Hunter's 1939 version of "Downhearted Blues" is performed with top musicians, notably Charlie Shavers (trumpet), Buster Bailey (clarinet), and Lil Armstrong (piano). Hunter did another version in 1922 with Eubie Blake's Orchestra. With Fletcher Henderson's Dance Orchestra, she sings "Bring It With You When You Come." (Also released as Vintage Jazz 6, Stash 123, and Mojo 310.)

LINK➤ *Alberta Hunter — Complete Recorded Works, Vols. 1–4*
Document 5422-5425

The first two volumes (1921-23 , 1923-24) feature Hunter with top jazz players Fletcher Henderson, Eubie Blake, Don Redman, and Fats Waller. Vol. 3 (1924-27) includes Louis Armstrong, Sidney Bechet, Clarence Williams, and other New Orleans greats.

Amtrack Blues — Columbia 36430

Hunter recorded four Columbia albums in the late 1970s and early 1980s, but only one is available on CD. (1981's *Glory of Alberta Hunter* and 1982's *Looking for the Silver Lining* are worth searching for on LP or cassette.) On all of these albums, Hunter highlights older material, while adding some original work. Here, in 1978, the oldies include "The Darktown Strutter's Ball," "My Handy Man Ain't Handy No More," and "Nobody Knows You When You're Down & Out." Hunter's accompaniment on these albums is pure jazz, and she brings out the best in experienced hands like Doc Cheatham and Vic Dickenson. "Amtrack Blues" is, of course, a newer song.

LINK➤ *Ruth Brown — Miss Rhythm* ***Rhino 82061***

Definitive 2-CD anthology of an R&B diva, one associated with Atlantic Records' early years. Brown's arrangements are on the jazz side of R&B, and her material is modern. In short, she's the 1950s step beyond Billie Holiday that precedes rock music. Lots of passion and style.

Mississippi John Hurt

Avalon, MS, is a tiny rural settlement, but it's where John Hurt spent most of his life, deep in a forgotten South. Hurt was born in nearby Teoc in 1892. He developed his own guitar technique on an instrument his mother bought when he was 9 years old. He played locally and didn't get paid much, but he caught the attention of Tommy Rockwell in 1928. Rockwell recorded Hurt for Okeh in Memphis, TN; when the records proved successful, Hurt recorded some more in NYC later that year. The Great Depression ended Hurt's career, and he supported himself by picking cotton, working the railroads, and laboring on a cattle farm for the next 35 years. Eventually, two students from Washington, D.C.—Richard Spottswood and Tom Hoskins—tracked Hurt down and brought him to the big city. Suddenly, Hurt was featured in *Time* and *Newsweek*. He enjoyed three happy years of performances at festivals, coffeehouses, and college campuses before his death in 1966.

Avalon Blues: The Complete 1928 OKeh Recordings **Columbia 64986**

Although Yazoo has long kept these 13 songs alive as *1928 Sessions* (Yazoo 1065), Columbia's 1997 release eliminates the slight static and sounds better. Either way, Hurt's music is very easily enjoyed; his singing emphasizes gentle melody, and his guitar provides a pleasant rhythm that nicely complements his storytelling. The first two Memphis sides are "Frankie" (a variation on "Frankie & Johnny") and "Nobody's Dirty Business," a tune similiar to "Ain't Nobody's Business." All of the other songs were recorded in NYC. The best include "Louis Collins" (with its repeating guitar figure that becomes a hymn for a murdered man) and a darkly memorable "Spike Driver Blues," about John Henry.

LINK➤ *Various Artists — Blues Masters, Vol. 7: Blues Revival* ***Rhino 71128***

Covers mainly the 1960s for a documentary view of old players made young again (Mississippi John Hurt, Mississippi Fred McDowell), young players finding their way with older material (Paul Butterfield), and straightforward electric blues (Muddy Waters, Junior Wells).

Avalon Blues 1963 **Rounder 1081**

One of the most consistently pleasant blues albums ever made. "Avalon Blues" recaps the song that provided the clue to Hurt's hometown and led to this, his first session in 35 years. The pearl is "Richland Woman Blues," with its catchy chorus: "Hurry down, sweet daddy. Come blowin' your horn. If you come too late, your momma will be gone." Hurt's eloquent guitar and a relaxed voice adds lovely details to popular tunes like "Candy Man Blues," but it's the small pieces, the ones that last a minute or so, that capture the heart—the harmonica solo and unaccompanied voice on "Liza Jane," for example, are just beautiful.

LINK➤ *Chris Smither — Small Revelations* ***Hightone 8077***

Smither is not quite a blues singer and not quite a folk singer, but his music is pleasant enough. On this 1998 CD, he does a sweet rendition of "Sportin' Life" and a bunch of good originals. Try also his 1993 Happier Blue *album (Flying Fish/ Rounder 70622).*

Worried Blues 1963 — Rounder 1082

The companion piece to *Avalon Blues* 1963, this live recording is also even-tempered and relaxed. "Lazy Blues" states the entire album's case in a single song: a gentle man with a knack for interesting guitar figures, making gentle music. "Sliding Delta" is so informal it nearly falls apart, but "Nobody Cares for Me" regains focus with its simple melody and lonely, whispering vocal. The title song picks up a boogie rhythm and some fancier licks; Hurt is slightly off-mike, but sincere and picking away pretty hard. He closes with "I've Been Cryin' Since You've Been Gone," a solitary wish for a lost love to "come on home." Overall, a sincere, intimate session.

LINK➤ *Mississippi John Hurt — Legend* **Rounder 1100**

This 1997 release finds Hurt in an informal late-night recording session in either 1963 or 1964, very relaxed and confident in music that he'd been playing for decades: "Louis Collins," "Nobody's Dirty Business," "Frankie and Albert," and so on. Slightly harsh sound, slightly unpolished performance.

The Immortal Mississippi John Hurt — Vanguard 79248

Most John Hurt albums were recorded in the early 1960s, so he sounds much the same from one to the next. The repertoire doesn't change much, either. Of the three Vanguard albums, this is marginally preferred for several traditional tunes: "Since I've Laid My Burden Down," "Nearer My God to Three," and "Moaning the Blues." (Pat Sky, who produced, plays second guitar.) "Stocktime (Buck Dance)" is a sweet instrumental, and so is "Hop Dance." "Richland Woman Blues" is repeated here. *Today!* (Vanguard 79220) has "Candy Man," "Louis Collins," a nice "Corinna Corrina" and "Beulah Land." *Last Sessions* (79327) has more traditional songs, and some fluff; Hurt is also in slightly poorer voice.

LINK➤ *John Hammond — The Best of John Hammond* **Vanguard 79153**

"Stateboro Blues," "Key to the Highway," and "They Call It Stormy Monday," are among the many blues classics—electric and acoustic—Hammond successfully tackled in the 1960s. Superior guitar work, good voice, too. Hammond is the son of producer John Hammond.

Memorial Anthology — Genes 9906/7

There are two good reasons to buy this 2-CD set. First, Hurt beautifully performs just about all of his best songs (plus "Lovin' Spoonful," "CC Rider," and more standards) in two Washington, D.C., coffeehouses. Second, in a half-hour interview, the old blues man tells folksinger Pete Seeger about sneaking off after his mother fell asleep to practice guitar as a boy, straightening railroad tracks with 20 other men (Seeger sings part of a Leadbelly tune about the work), reactions of Avalon citizens to Hurt's sudden fame, making up songs, and so on. It's 1964, and Hurt is having the time of his life. The recording is lively, and the music is spellbinding.

LINK➤ *Various Artists — Before the Blues, Vol. 3* **Yazoo 2017**

This survey of early music includes many names associated with blues, such as Hurt, Cow Cow Davenport, Texas Alexander, and Blind Blake. The point here is to explore music that preceded the development of blues. Most of these songs, or styles, are from the 1800s.

Joseph Benjamin Hutto was born in Blackwell, SC, in 1926. He was raised on gospel music during a Georgia boyhood, which saw him singing with the Golden Crown Gospel Singers, and learning to play the drums, the piano, and the guitar. Hutto moved with his family to Chicago in 1949. He found work there with local bands, but decided against a career in music around 1955. After laying off for a decade, Hutto tried again in 1965; he made several well-regarded albums for Vanguard and Delmark. This led to a steady stream of work in Chicago clubs, especially at Turner's Blues Lounge, a small bar at 39th and Indiana on Chicago's south side. Hutto also performed at colleges, festivals, and other folk and blues venues. He died in 1983, but many of his innovative slide guitar techniques live on in the music of his student and nephew Ed Williams, who performs as leader of Lil' Ed and the Blues Imperials.

J.B. Hutto and the Hawks: Masters of Modern Blues — Testament 5020

A very credible version of "Dust My Broom" opens this 1966 album. It's the sort of song that inspired Hutto to re-enter the blues business. Next up is a Roosevelt Sykes tune, "Mistake in Life," handled with aplomb by Fred Below on drums and world-class harmonica harmonica player Big Walter Horton. Hutto is the real thing: a bluesman who confidently and expertly plays the guitar and moans his vocals. St. Louis Jimmy Oden's "Goin' Down Slow" features Hutto's slide guitar, as does "Sloppy Drunk," a tight little dance tune. Racier lyrics on "Wild Wild Woman" and "Pet Cream Man" are tough to understand because of Hutto's singing style and so-so engineering.

LINK➤ ***Various Artists — Chicago: The Blues Today! Vol. 1*** — ***Vanguard 79216***

J.B. Hutto and his Hawks are responsible for a third of Sam Charter's spotlight on Chicago artists who ought to be better known. (The Hawks are bassist Herman Hassell and drummer Frank Kirkland). Space on the disc is shared with Otis Span and Junior Wells (with Buddy Guy).

Hawk Squat! — Delmark 617

These sessions were recorded at two 1966 sessions (with one more song from 1968). Sunnyland Slim joins in, most often on the organ. This raucous bar music is the place to start with Hutto. For a really good sense of his work, try the slow-singing, bass-heavy, guitar-splashy "If You Change Your Mind," a lounge song with spirit. Another good example of Hutto's style is the stop-and-start "20 Percent Alcohol," sung to a neighborhood woman with a drinking problem. "Hawk Squat" is a rollicking guitar workout, but the sting of Hutto's guitar and Sunnyland's potent organ is most deeply felt on "The Feeling Is Gone." Once again, the recording quality could be better.

LINK➤ ***J.B. Hutto — Slidewinder*** — ***Delmark 636***

Improved 1972 fidelity, although the 1960s spunk had faded somewhat. Very impressive guitar work on the title song and elsewhere, but raw energy has given way to a slicker, more mature approach. Hutto's vocals are also easier to understand. Well worth the investment.

James came from the Mississippi Delta region, and like many bluesmen, he traveled to Chicago, made his fortune, and died young. He was born in 1918 in Richland, picked up guitar while working as a farm laborer, and met Robert Johnson and Sonny Boy Williamson II after his family moved to a plantation in Belzoni, MS. James was shy and reluctant to record, but often accompanied Williamson on his local radio show. He was essentially tricked into making his first record, "Dust My Broom." His growing popularity led to a recording career for the Meteor, Flair, and Modern labels. After moving to Chicago, James met nightclub owner Bobby Robinson, who owned several R&B and blues labels (Fire, Enjoy, and Fury). James worked for Robinson from 1959 until 1963. James died that year of a heart attack after years of drinking and tough living.

The Sky Is Crying: The History of Elmore James

Rhino 71190

This single-CD anthology covers the years 1951 to 1961, the first half of James's career. Appropriately, the 1951 recording of "Dust My Broom" begins the set, with an electrified riff that became James's signature. Some of this set's best material comes from the excellent *Whose Muddy Shoes (Chess/MCA 9114)*, but the aching lead guitar of "The Sky Is Crying," recorded for Fire in 1960, is stunning; 1957's "It Hurts Me, Too" is similar, but adds the contrast between J.T. Brown's deep-throated tenor sax and the edgy scatter of James's vocal. His top-notch Chicago blues band shines on the stop-time "Sunny Land," one of several excellent dates for Flair. In all, this is a fine introduction.

LINK➤ *Fleetwood Mac — Pious Bird of Good Omen* **SONY (Import) 8117**

U.K. compilation of Fleetwood Mac's early years (1967-68), when guitarist Peter Green was in charge, and when Elmore James was among the band's primary influences. Many of these tracks are new versions of blues classics; originals include the hit "Albatross."

King of the Slide Guitar: The Fire/Fury/Enjoy Recordings

Capricorn 42006

The contents of this 2-CD box, which covers 1959–63, are more electric, modern, tighter, and commercial. Not that the repertoire has changed much; there are new versions of "The Sky Is Crying," "Dust My Broom," "Done Somebody Wrong," "It Hurts Me, Too," and other James standards, but all are fresh and fleet. These remain his best songs, but producer Robinson made the best of all material, as on the jumping "Shake Your Moneymaker" and the "Broom" rehash, "Go Back Home Again." The unorthodox rhythm of "You Know You've Done Me Wrong," and the country/city blend of "Pickin' the Blues" show considerable originality. Tall box format; good liner notes.

LINK➤ *Elmore James — Let's Cut It* **Virgin/Flair 91800**

Hard-to-find single CD completes the James story with the 1954–56 years. Probably for completists only; many of the best songs are repeated on the other two anthologies.

Nehemiah Curtis James was born 1902 in Yazoo City, MS, and grew up on a plantation where his mother was the cook. His father was a minister and a bootlegger who abandoned his family. James learned guitar from a friend, then mastered piano. He left Mississippi to work in Weona, AR, and befriended a brothel pianist, whose fancy clothes and lifestyle he adopted. In time, James became a bootlegger, gambler, and lumber worker. He made some recordings for Paramount in 1931, but they didn't sell; the Great Depression led James back to his preaching father, for whom he led a gospel choir, first in Texas and then in Alabama. He was ordained as a minister and traveled the South. Back in Mississippi in the 1940s, James left music; he was rediscovered in 1964 by guitar player John Fahey and two friends. For several years, James appeared at folk festivals and recorded. He moved to Philadelphia, where cancer took his life in 1969.

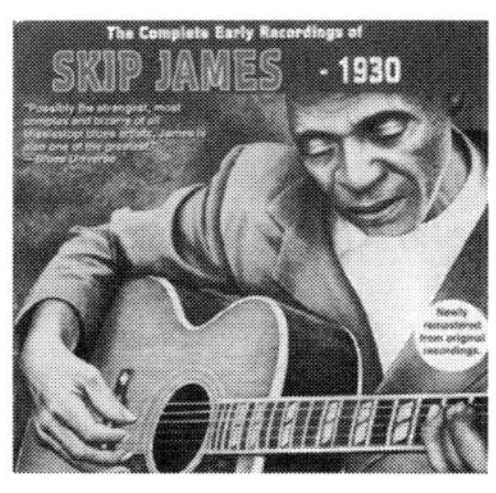

The Complete Early Recordings of Skip James

Yazoo 2009

The scratchy sound on these rare recordings is initially off-putting, but a few tries on "Devil Got My Woman" brings the lyrics and guitar work to life. Some say this tune was sung in response to a lost love (James's wife, 16, left him for a friend); this music, so dark and brooding, is probably James's second-best-known song. "I'm So Glad" is a peppy, spiteful song that sold more than a million records when it was recorded by Cream in 1968. Listen very carefully to hear James's rapid-fire guitar. In addition to deep blues, there are uplifting spirituals ("Be Ready When He Comes") and sprightly piano pieces ("If You Haven't Any Hay" and "How Long 'Buck'").

LINK➤ *Various Artists — Roots of Rock* **Yazoo 1063**

James was just one of many old blues singers whose songs were made famous by rock bands. Robert Wilkins's version of "Prodigal Son" led to a Rolling Stones song. Memphis Minnie recorded "When the Levee Breaks" decades before Led Zepelin. And so on.

Devil Got My Woman

Vanguard 79273

This 1964 album continues the story and presents several songs that could not be easily heard on the Yazoo CD. The best of these songs is the mellow and hopeful "Illinois Blues," performed on guitar, and "22-20 Blues" with its dramatic piano (sounding at times like Broadway). The latter is a song about a gun used to even the score with an unfaithful lover. The brooding "Devil Got My Woman" is back, and this time the lyrics are intelligible. The easy, optimistic gospel rhythm of "Look at the People" is masterfully controlled and quite unique. "Mistreating Child Blues" is a fine piano blues. Mesmerizing.

LINK➤ *Various Artists — Roots of the Blues* **New World 80252**

Beginning with field hollers and very early vocals (by Tangle Eye, who sings "Katie Left Memphis"), and on to prisoners singing "Berta Berta," this single CD helps set the stage for Skip James and his generation.

Skip's Piano Blues **Genes 9910**

A dozen piano blues that once again sound quite different from other work. James sings out (favoring middle ranges and using high notes only as accents) and plays his piano loudly. Close-miking makes the piano sound as though it's in a brothel. "All Night Long" is a barrelhouse rouser, and James has a rollicking good time with "Little Boy, How Old Are You?" The rhythmic complexity of "22-20 Blues" encourages comparison with Thelonious Monk and other iconoclastic jazzmen. James's version of "How Long Blues" is also very inventive, and the lyrics on "Black Gal" are very funny. James deserves far more credit for his blues piano; sadly, this album is not well known.

LINK➤ *Thelonious Monk — Monk's Music* ***OJC 84***

Monk was an iconoclastic jazz musician with an unusual sense of time and rhythm. He was also a great piano player with skills that far outdistanced most competitors. This is one of his best; try also Alone in San Francisco *(OJC 231), an unaccompanied solo album.*

She Lyin' **Genes 9901**

Eric Clapton was clearly influenced by Skip James, and this 1964 set vividly illustrates the connection. (Close your eyes and listen to both voice and guitar on James's opener, "All Night Long.") Overall, the mood here is mellow; a mid-toned vocal is sometimes punctuated by a gentle falsetto and by James's spotless acoustic guitar. The title song is a real find; it doesn't appear on any other album. There are especially articulate versions of James's most important songs—"Crow Jane," "Drunken Spree," "Devil Got My Woman," and more. "Hard Time Killing Floor Blues" gets its definitive version here; the Depression's misery comes through. Stereo recording quality is very good. Start here!

LINK➤ *Various Artists — Blues Masters, Vol. 6: Blues Originals* ***Rhino 71127***

Here's a wonderful starting point for any blues collection. There really isn't any particular connection between all of these songs, except that they're among the best in blues, from Elmore James's "Madison Blues" to Bo Diddley's "I'm a Man" and Howlin' Wolf's "Back Door Man."

Today! **Vanguard 79219**

James was 62 when he was coaxed out of retirement to make this album. He sounds nothing like the man on the 1930 recordings; here he is happy, and his voice is so high and lilting that it sometimes leaps into a falsetto. James is wistful and even a little apologetic when he tells the story of his stay during the "Washington D.C. Hospital Center Blues." The Depression song "Hard Time Killing Floor Blues" is a memory, not the impossible meditation on poverty from 44 years before. There's a light touch to all of James's guitar playing, as well as some delightful piano work on "How Long." And this time, "I'm So Glad" is practically a children's ditty.

LINK➤ *Various Artists — Three Shades of Blues* ***Biograph 107***

Three artists: Bukka White, Skip James, Blind Willie McTell. Each contributes a handful of songs. White's are from a 1974 date and include "Glory Bound Train." James's were cut in 1964 in Virginia, and McTell's songs come from 1949, with Curley Weaver on guitar.

Jamesetta Hawkins was raised on gospel music. She started singing on the radio as part of the Los Angeles Baptist Choir in 1943, when she was 5 years old. By 1950, James's family was living in San Francisco. There, she and two other girls formed a group called the Peaches (so called for James's nickname). In 1954, the girls were in L.A. working with Johnnie Otis and making hit records. "The Wallflower" was their first hit , reaching number 2 on the R&B charts; more followed. Otis also provided Hawkins with her stage name, Etta James. When the Peaches broke up, James recorded for the Chess label in 1960; she stayed there until 1971. Drug problems waylaid James's career through much of the 1970s, but she fought her way back. In 1978, she opened for the Rolling Stones, and in 1984, she sang at the opening ceremony of the Olympic Games. Today, James continues to record and tour.

R&B Dynamite — Flair 91695

These early recordings go back to 1956, when the Bihari brothers brought Etta James to a New Orleans studio. The session was important enough to gather together some of the city's best sidemen, including Lee Allen, Dave Bartholomew, and Earl Palmer (essentially, the Fats Domino and Little Richard studio band). James wails. She takes even a simple 1950s R&B tune like "Number One," calls the listener for intimate words, and screams out in loving ecstacy. Very musical. James does a fine job with her own "W-O-M-A-N" (not the later hit), digging down deep for soulful accents, and hitting the cutesy little-girl intonations just right. Really fine singing, pretty good material.

LINK➤ *Various Artists — Essential Women in Blues* **House of Blues 1257**

A spectacular 2-CD survey that places Etta James in context among Sippie Wallace, Dinah Washington, Ma Rainey, and Memphis Minnie while leaving room for younger singers like Big Time Sara, Michelle Willson, and Francine Reed. Excellent job!

Rocks the House — Chess 9184

Working on a tiny stage in a Nashville club specially selected for its superior acoustics and receptive audiences, this 1963 performance captures James at her very best. She starts—or more accurately, she and the singing, grooving audience start—with "Something Got a Hold on Me." The song resembles R&B, but as James testifies her way through it takes on a shape all its own. James finds her way slowly on "Baby, What You Want Me to Do?" stretching and straining her voice for emphasis; the crowd is practically cheering her along. There's much more here, too: "Money (That's What I Want)," "Sweet Little Angel," and B.B. King's "Woke Up This Morning" are among the better tracks. Buy this CD today!

LINK➤ *Michelle Willson — Evil Gal Blues* **Bullseye Blues 9550**

Willson is the latest blues diva to rock the house. She started young, worked her way through gospel and community theater to a band called Animal Train, then broke out with this jump blues/R&B hybrid. Big voice, nice expressive personality. Great band, too.

Tell Mama **Chess 9269**

A classic old Chess album, budget priced and probably worth owning even if you've already invested in the 2-CD set. James sings out with all her gospel heart, and she has all the brassy, funky accompaniment she needs. That's what makes "Tell Mama" a bonafide classic. Three saxopones, one trumpet, all perfect. Comprised of a dozen songs recorded mostly in 1967, this CD presents one terrific soul or R&B song after another. "I'd Rather Go Blind" is a slow, jealous burn. "Steal Away" is a late-night lover's plea to run away with another. Don Covay's "Watchdog" frames James's angry vocals (and the backup singers) alongside stinging horns; once again, the song is about jealousy.

LINK➤ *Various Artists — Drop Down Mama* **Chess (MCA) 93002**
Another classic old Chess album or, more accurately, early 1950s singles that have been together in this form since 1970. Johnny Shines sings out on "So Glad I Found You," and Robert Nighthawk feels the magic of love on "Sweet Black Angel." Plenty more, all as good.

The Essential Etta James **Chess 9341**

It all starts with a sad, slow dance ("She was standing there with my man") from 1960 sung by a girl who watches her love marry somebody else; "All I Could Do Is Cry" is one of the greatest songs Etta James has ever recorded. It was also a huge hit. It's the kind of torch song that she sings so well. Although her reputation soundly rests on sassy R&B and victim songs, James aces several pop music standards here with full orchestra. "One for My Baby (And One More For the Road)" is an example. The good stuff happens when James is standing in front of a few backup singers, who coo their commercialized gospel while the horn and rhythm section percolates. That's the setup for "Something's Got a Hold On Me"—another stunning milestone in 1960s popular music. "I Prefer You" trades the gospel style for 1960s girl group, adds a powerful horn section, and tops off with a gripping lead vocal. Spectacular numbers keep coming, each with raw integrity and the deepest possible emotion: "842-3809 (Call My Name)," "It Must Be Your Love," "I'd Rather Go Blind," Tell Mama," and on and on. When the 1960s ended, so did James's run. She recapped "W.O.M.A.N." in 1972 and decided to record several dark, raucous Randy Newman songs in the 1970s. Included here are three of his most cynical: "You Can Leave Your Hat On," "God's Song (That's Why I Love Mankind)," and "Let's Burn Down the Cornfield."

LINK➤ *Maxine Brown — Golden Classics* **Collectibles 5116**
Gerry Goffin and Carole King's song, "Oh No, Not My Baby," was among Brown's few really big hits, but this 1960s soul and R&B singer has long been respected as one of the very best in the business. This collection surveys her uptown style.

Blind Lemon Jefferson

Jefferson was born to a large family in the east Texas town of Couchman or in nearby Worthman, probably in the mid-1890s. He may have been blind at birth, and the nickname "Lemon" may have been slang for his complexion. Around age 20, Jefferson moved to the poor neighborhood of Deep Ellum in Dallas. He sang on the streets and at parties, then traveled extensively after living for a decade in Dallas. (Leadbelly claimed to have been one of his traveling companions.) A terrific singer with a two-octave range, and a gifted interpreter who enlivened any type of song, Jefferson was a natural recording artist. From 1926 until 1928, he was a star in the "race records" industry, the first successful male blues singer on record. Jefferson owned a $725 car and employed a chauffeur. Then, inexplicably, his talent faded. By late 1928, Jefferson was working as a porter in Chicago. He died in December of that year.

Blind Lemon Jefferson **Milestone 47022**

The cover art provides a close-up view of Jefferson's famed "painted-on tie." (He was apparently a good dresser; why the tie was painted remains a mystery.) About two-thirds of these 25 tracks were cut in 1926 and early 1927; five come from 1929. Songs like "Jack of Diamonds" and "Easy Rider Blues" were popular among many Texas singers, and it's instructive to hear how much Jefferson could add to a standard, making it his own. One of the best songs is "Rabbit Foot Blues," mostly because of Jefferson's refined and clever guitar work. Nice sad-eyed vocal on "Bad Luck Blues," too. Overall, there is less hiss on this album, but the sound is still seriously inferior.

LINK➤ *Various Artists — Before the Blues, Vol. 1* ***Yazoo 2015***

"Bamalong Blues," by Andrew and Jim Baxter, is a simple fiddle-and-guitar tune. Rube Lacy performs "Mississippi Jail House Groan," considered a dance, not a blues in the "early days" prior to 1920. Buell Kazee picks his way through "John Hardy," a "bad man" song.

King of the Country Blues **Yazoo 1069**

Start with "Matchbox Blues," a song that's been covered by many rock artists. Listen through the hiss and scratchiness and hear the crazy (and difficult to copy) guitar patterns that immediately set Jefferson apart from other musicians. The same approach distinguishes "Hot Dogs," which is just plain fun. "Corrina Blues" shows off a very big voice, one that could fill a room, then melt hearts with its tenderness and subtlety. "See That My Grave Is Kept Clean" was covered by Bob Dylan; through the surface noise, Jefferson articulates a somber, dark, hopeful mood. The variety of these melodies and Jefferson's wide range of creative approaches make this album absolutely essential.

LINK➤ *Bob Dylan — Bob Dylan* ***Columbia 8579***

Dylan's first album ends with a passionate rendition of Jefferson's "See That My Grave Is Kept Clean," but several others are based on blues. "You're No Good" came from Jesse Fuller, and "Fixin' to Die" is based on Bukka White's "My Time of Dyin'." More blues, too.

Blind Willie Johnson

Johnson was a gospel singer with stylistic similarities to blues, and a race recording artist who outsold label-mate Bessie Smith. He was probably born in 1902, either in Marlin or Tempe, TX, both about 100 miles from Dallas. When he was around age 5, his stepmother, retaliating against a husband who beat her, threw lye into his face, intentionally blinding him. Young Johnson took to religion early, became a Baptist preacher, and earned his living by singing with a tin cup around his neck. He met and married Willie B. Harris around 1926, and she became his recording partner after Johnson was discovered by Columbia in 1927. By 1930, his recording career was over, a victim of the Great Depression. Johnson later lost his house in a fire. He and his wife slept in their wet clothes on top of the ruins, using only newspapers for blankets. As a result, Johnson caught pneumonia and died in 1947.

The Complete Blind Willie Johnson

Columbia 52835

The music on this 2-CD set is also available on *Praise God I'm Satisfied* (Yazoo 1058) and *Sweeter As the Years Go By* (Yazoo 1078). These are all old recordings, and neither set sounds appreciably better than the other. Columbia gets the nod because blues historian Sam Charters wrote the liner notes from interviews with people in Johnson's life. Vocally, this is earnest, gravel-voiced material; a brilliant slide guitar player singing his heart out for the Lord. The raw emotion of Johnson's voice may be off-putting, but repeated listenings reveal considerable beauty and magnificent craftsmanship. Most often, the complement is Johnson grinding his way through the lower octaves, his presentation lifted by the delicate higher sounds of his guitar and the earnest, pedestrian vocals by wife Willie B. Harris. Most often, she simply sings unison behind him; sometimes as on "Keep Your Lamp Trimmed and Burning," the construction is a call-and-response with extended guitar breaks. Johnson's recordings were made over a series of five sessions in various Southern cities. The finest material was recorded at the first session, held in Dallas in 1927: "I Know His Blood Can Make Me Whole," "Jesus Make Up My Dying Bed," "Mother's Children Have a Hard Time," and one of his best-known songs, the passionate, enraged "If I Had My Way, I'd Tear This Building Down." The third session (New Orleans, 1929) is notable because Johnson departs from his usual boisterous rhythm patterns in favor of a quieter mood, at least for the first half of "Let Your Light Shine on Me." It's lovely.

LINK➤ *Peter, Paul & Mary — Peter, Paul & Mary* **_Warner Bros. 1440_**

"If I Had My Way" was one of PP&M's signature songs; as folk revivalists and protest singers, they transformed Johnson's song into social commentary—with all of the passion intact. Most of the other songs on this debut album are originals.

Unlike most of his contemporaries, Lonnie (Alonzo, originally) Johnson grew up with city jazz, not country blues. He was born in 1894 in New Orleans, and learned to play as part of his father's string band. By 1917, he toured Europe with a troupe; he then returned to St. Louis, where he worked on riverboats. By 1925, Johnson was recording for the Okeh label. He also worked with Louis Armstrong and Duke Ellington (he plays on "The Mooche"), and accompanied many other stars. Johnson also became a popular performer on the black vaudeville circuit, TOBA (an acronym for Theater Owners' Booking Association; performers often referred to it as "Tough on Black Artists"). He even had his own radio show, originating from NYC. Although the Great Depression ended a successful career, Johnson did enjoy several comebacks, notably in the 1960s. Johnson died in Toronto in 1969 after an automobile accident.

Steppin' on the Blues **Columbia 46221**

When Lonnie Johnson plays guitar, the notes are very carefully selected, the music is well-groomed, and the presentation is meticulous. Even in his first Okeh sessions in 1925, Johnson's voice is clear and expressive, essentially fronting a jazz band on "Mr. Johnson's Blues." Double-entendre blues abound on "Sweet Potato Blues" and on "Toothache Blues," a two-part duet with the popular singer Victoria Spivey. (The two singers mine the reliable drilling-filling rhyme in a vaudeville-style bit here.) Several duets with jazz guitarist Eddie Lang (known here as Blind Willie Dunn), accompaniment for singer Texas Alexander, and Johnson's fantastic solo piece "Playing with the Strings" are among many varied highlights from 1925–32. Essential!

LINK➤ *Louis Armstrong — Hot Fives, Vol. II* **Columbia 44422**

Johnson's 1927 guitar duets with Armstrong's horn are among jazz's treasures. Johnson guests on "I'm Not Rough," "Hotter Than That," and "Savoy Blues." This is one in a distinguished series; all are worth owning.

He's a Jelly Roll Baker **Bluebird 66064**

Johnson spent the Depression years working in Cleveland (in music and factory jobs—whatever was available). In 1937, he rejoined the scene in Chicago; he recorded 34 sides for Bluebird there from 1939 until 1944. Johnson's voice is strong and incisive. He also has the right piano accompanist in Lil Armstrong on "Crowing Rooster Blues" and the prehistoric R&B tune "That's Love." In addition to consistently superb guitar work, excellent songwriting, and the hit title song, there's real emotion on "The Victim of Love." It's the story of a woman standing in the rain waiting for her man to return from World War II—a tale Johnson tells in a very personal way. He addresses mistrust and payback in "Nothing But A Rat." Highly recommended.

LINK➤ *Arthur "Big Boy" Crudup — That's Allright Mama* **RCA 61043**

Crudup is known, mainly, as the man whose songs provided young Elvis Presley with raw material for rock 'n' roll. Elvis's first song for Sun Records was this CD's title track.

Blues & Ballads **OBC 531**

More ballads than blues, in fact. Johnson had been working at Philadelphia's Ben Franklin Hotel when guitar player Elmer Snowden connected him with writer Chris Albertson, who supervised this 1960 session that brought Johnson back into the limelight. Kid Ory's jazz classic, "Savoy Blues," is presented as a bluesy guitar duet by Johnson and Snowden. A nifty, up-tempo version of "St. Louis Blues" is stamped with decades of show-biz experience. Bessie Smith's "Back Water Blues" and Eubie Blake's "Memories of You" are elegant and slow and go down easy. "Jelly Roll Baker" is outstanding—a signature song for Johnson, and he revels in singing it. There's plenty of great guitar work on that song, too.

LINK➤ *Lonnie Johnson — Blues, Ballads and Jumpin' Jazz (Vol. 2)* *OBC 570*

More from the 1960 session, this time with "Birth of the Blues," "On the Sunny Side of the Street," and "Stormy Weather"—all songs more closely associated with jazz than blues. Six are instrumentals featuring Snowden.

Losing Game **OBC 543**

Johnson's voice is burnished with a fine tenor's glow; here, he simply accompanies himself on guitar. The material is not all strictly blues, but it never strays far. "Lines in My Face" and "Losing Game" are soulful R&B presented with blues guitar accompaniment—difficult to pigeonhole. "New Years Blues" and "New Orleans Blues" are essentially slicked-up urban acoustic versions of country blues. Johnson's renditions of "Summertime," and "What a Difference a Day Makes" are superb. But the blues instrumental "Slow and Easy" is the dazzler. The dreary "Four Walls and Me" puts to rest any lingering doubts about Johnson's pure blues—it's one of the saddest, most poignant urban blues on record.

LINK➤ *Eddie Lang — Jazz Guitar Virtuoso* *Yazoo 1059*

In 1928 and 1929, Lang recorded a series of duets with Lonnie Johnson (represented here by "Blue Room," "Blue Guitars," and "Midnight Call Blues"). Lang also accompanied Bessie Smith, Texas Alexander, and other black musicians—unusual for a white guitarist.

The Complete Folkways Recordings **Smithsonian Folkways 40067**

Lonnie Johnson was that rare blues performer who could work with a variety of material and still touch the heartstrings. In his world, ballads and blues were closely related. "Mr. Trouble" offers a taste of each style. Even a standby like "How Deep Is the Ocean?" retains its honesty, and with Johnson's slick guitar, never turns cheesy (though "Prisoner of Love" gets pretty melodramatic, even with the tasty guitar break). There's a healthy dose of beautiful traditional work here, expertly performed—"Pouring Down Rain," "Teardrops in My Eyes," and the desperate "Juice Headed Baby" (about his drunk, evil woman). Pop tunes include "Summertime" and "Careless Love" (which was sung by many blues singers).

LINK➤ *Sarah Vaughan — With Clifford Brown* *Mercury 814-641*

Nearly perfect jazzy renditions of popular songs, scatting and grooving to Jimmy Jones's piano, Joe Benjamin's bass, and Roy Haynes's drums. This is very sweet. Both vocalist Vaughan and trumpeter Brown are at the top of their form.

There is a persistent legend in the blues that Robert Johnson traded his soul to the devil in exchange for superior talent as a musician. Johnson, born in 1911 in Hazlehurst, MS, showed little musical ability as a child; he took up harmonica as a teenager and started on guitar in the late 1920s, but showed only modest promise despite considerable help from local musicians. After the death of two wives (one died in childbirth, the other from exhaustion), Johnson traveled extensively (to Chicago, Detroit, New York City, and throughout Texas and Arkansas). He took his music very seriously, and when he returned to Hazlehurst, local musicians, including Son House, had only one "explanation" for Johnson's astonishing musicianship—this grew into a tale of Johnson standing at a crossroads, handing his guitar to the devil (in the person of a large black man), and gaining remarkable talent in exchange for his soul. Johnson's early death—he was poisoned as punishment for messing with another man's wife—only lent credence to the story.

The Complete Recordings **Columbia 64916**

Although his repertoire included many popular songs, Johnson is known as the consummate blues player. Only about 30 of his songs were recorded, and these are mostly blues. All are included on this top-selling 2-CD set (along with many alternate takes). Some songs will be familiar because they've been covered by Eric Clapton, the Rolling Stones, and so many other musicians—songs like "Crossroads Blues," "Love in Vain Blues," "I Believe I'll Dust My Broom," and "Sweet Home Chicago." The quintessential Johnson song is arguably "Terraplane Blues" in which his guitar work is especially inventive, and his vocal is both confident and spirited (Johnson's periodic use of falsetto is especially effective). The terraplane was a popular car that could travel up to 80 mph. "Phonograph Blues," one of Johnson's best-sung songs, demonstrates his impressive depth, range, and superb vocal style. Complete lyrics with explanatory notes illuminate already glowing music by focusing attention on the singer's voice—one of the best in blues. (Happily, the sound quality is not bad at all.) There's big-time showmanship here, as on "They're Red Hot," but the magic is in the almost otherworldly desperation in Johnson's voice and scrambling guitar on "Crossroad Blues," whose second take is even more spare and chilling than the first. The harsh (nearly electric) guitar and the resignation of Johnson's vocal on "Me and the Devil Blues" doubtless contributed to the legendary origin of his talent. Johnson's work radiates more beauty and majesty with each listening session; in his tender and intelligent handling of lyrics, and in his phenomenal guitar playing, there is much to discover here. The 1990 2-CD reissue has sold over 500,000 copies.

Janis Joplin had a tough time fitting into the teenage world of conservative Port Arthur, TX, so she left. She tried Houston and Austin, but there really was only one place she could find the poetry, forward-thinking, free lifestyle, raw sexuality, and advanced music scene, and that was in San Francisco. After a false start, and a brief return to Austin, Joplin returned to San Francisco and connected with Big Brother and the Holding Company. Her timing was perfect. The rock scene blossomed during the summer of 1967, just after she appeared at the Monterrey Pop Festival with the band. She cut an album with Big Brother, then moved on to her own Kozmic Blues Band, and then to the Full Tilt Boogie Band. Very aggressive living, sex, alcohol, drugs, depression, and a quest for bigger thrills led to the inevitable: death by overdose in 1970. Joplin was 27 years old.

Big Brother & The Holding Company: Cheap Thrills — Columbia 9700

Caught up in the revolution with its R. Crumb cover art and Hell's Angels's seal of approval, this 1968 album was Joplin's first for Columbia. It's unclear whether this is rock, blues, or psychededlia, but it all works. The group's version of "Summertime"—with the stunning heat of electric guitars, the beauty of their sunshine, and Joplin's pained voice—represents a high-water mark for the rock era. The overplayed "Piece of My Heart" remains Joplin's sexiest vocal, with "I Need a Man to Love" second best. The live closer, "Ball and Chain," requires some patience with late 1960s indulgences, but the other Fillmore number, "Combination of the Two," is entertaining R&B.

LINK➤ *Various Artists — Blues Down Deep: Songs of Janis Joplin*
House of Blues 1251

Tracy Nelson sings "What Good Can Drinkin' Do," Lou Ann Barton performs "One Good Man," and Otis Clay does "Piece of My Heart." The real peach is Etta James on "Ball and Chain," but Koko Taylor's "Get It While You Can" is also high on the list.

I Got Dem Ol' Kozmic Blues Again Mama! — Columbia 9913

Three decades after its release, this recording emerges as the great lost modern blues album. It's also the best record Janis Joplin ever recorded. Her voice wails. The band is kickin'. The arrangements are primo, with horns in all the right places and excellent blues organ from Richard Kermode and Gabriel Mekler. The sound quality is very good, too. Groove to Joplin's scatlike manipulations of lyric lines and the endless power of her screamlike wails. Joplin's best on "Maybe," where the horns seem to mimic her emotional power. "To Love Somebody" is pure 1960s soul, and the slightly psychedelic "Kozmic Blues" glimmers. Listen once more, and you'll agree: this album is absolutely essential!

LINK➤ *Janis Joplin — Janis* ***Columbia 48845***

A 3-CD career retrospective includes the good and bad from 1971's Pearl, *plus some interesting collectibles: a demo (played on acoustic guitar) of "Me and Bobby McGee," a longer concert version of "Ball and Chain," and more rarities. Not essential, but interesting.*

The ebullient Jordan was the king of "jump blues," a fast-paced, stagey form that contributed to rock 'n' roll's development. Jordan grew up in show business, watching his father lead the band for the Rabbit Foot Minstrels. He attended a Baptist college, studied music, and by 1936, at 28, was playing saxophone for Chick Webb's big band. When Webb died in 1938, Jordan formed his own small group, the Tympany Five. They signed with Webb's former label, Decca, and for 15 years, recorded dozens of hits. Jordan and the Tympany Five also made short musical films, and became famous among black (and some white) audiences. By 1953, tastes had changed, and Jordan's act survived only in nightclubs, and later as 1940s nostalgia. Jordan died of a heart attack in Los Angeles in 1975.

The Best of Louis Jordan — MCA 4079

By combining a vaudevillian's smile with the stylish swing of big band music and a convincing voice that could deliver even the most ridiculous lyric with a flair ("there ain't nobody here but us chickens"), Louis Jordan developed a show business art form. Is his "jump blues" really blues? Well, maybe. "Caldonia" borrows a little from the blues, but Jordan's shrieking "what makes your big head so hard?" certainly stretches the heritage. Rousers like "Choo Choo Ch'Boogie," "Barnyard Boogie," and "Saturday Night Fish Fry" are stereotypically Jordan, and his slow material is equally fine. Jordan's 1954 rendition of "Nobody Knows You When You Are Down and Out" is the Broadway version of convincing.

LINK➤ *Original Cast Album — Five Guys Named Moe* **_Columbia 52999_**
This 1992 cast album is full of verve, nonsense, and a suprising number of slow songs that work as well as the fast ones. Great versions of "Caldonia" and "What's the Use of Getting Sober (When You Gonna Get Drunk Again)." Lots of fun and very nicely performed.

Five Guys Named Moe: Original Decca Recordings, Vol. 2 — MCA 10503

"Reet, Petite, and Gone" shows the sophisticated side of Jordan—it's not just a bouncy melody and a flashy presentation. He follows the formula, but plays some interesting games with rhythm and intonation. On "Five Guys Named Moe," Jordan twists talking blues, swing, and a cappella, and comes up with something wholly original (although Jordan wrote many of his hits, this one came from Larry Wynn and Jerry Bresler). Jordan and his cohorts have a very good time with "I Like 'Em Fat Like That," and "(You Dyed Your Hair) Chartreuse." Jordan did what worked—and crossed boundaries; try "Push Ka Pee Shee Pie," which he calls "the new calypso bebop."

LINK➤ *Bill Haley & the Comets — From the Original Master Tapes* **_MCA 5539_**
The direct line from jump blues to rock 'n' roll is immediately evident. All of the hits are here—including cover versions and variations of popular R&B tunes customized for white audiences. Twenty tracks, nicely remastered.

Albert King

Five years after he was born in the Delta town of Indianola, MS, in 1925, Mary Blevins's son took her new husband's name and became Albert Nelson. Living near Forrest City, AR, he taught himself to play guitar using homemade instruments and eventually purchased a used guitar that he played upside-down and backwards (he was left-handed). In the 1940s, Nelson drove a truck and played weekends at T-99 club on Highway 61 in Osceola, AR. By 1953, he had followed other musicians north to the Chicago area, but he soon relocated to St. Louis. There, King built a club career, cutting records when he could. In 1958, King adopted his Gibson Flying "V" guitar (he named it Lucy). A 1966 Stax recording contract made him a star. In the mid-1970s, when Stax folded, King jumped to RCA's Utopia label, and kept recording for another decade. He died of a heart attack in 1992.

Door to Door — MCA 9322

Although this album is credited to Albert King and Otis Rush, the two musicians don't play together. Instead, there are 8 songs by King (from 1953 and 1960–61) and 6 by Rush (from 1960). They have little in common. Rush's "All Your Love" grooves on a Latin rhythm, and his "You Know My Love" is soulful R&B. Crosscut with saxophones, the acid disdain of King's guitar lashes out against his bad woman on "Won't Be Hangin' Around." King updates the country blues with some street-smart piano on "Bad Luck," with his worn-out early morning voice; like "Murder" (with its slick guitar licks), it's from the 1953 Parrot sessions.

LINK➤ *Rory Gallagher — Edged in Blue* — ***Edsel (Import)***

A 2-CD career retrospective of an Irish guitarist who grew up on U.S. blues records. Gallagher became well known in the U.S. as a result of recordings with Albert King and Muddy Waters. He died at age 46 in 1995.

Let's Have a Natural Ball — Modern Blues 723

This CD collects sessions for King and Bobbin records made from 1959 until 1963. It's vintage Albert King—his guitar slicing through two saxes and a trumpet, the rhythm section pumping hard, and his voice singing along the top of the heap. When King's great, as he is on "I Get Evil," few blues players can compete with his musicality. Big-time credit also goes to the band, particularly Johnnie Johnson, who plays piano on most of these tracks. Two instrumentals, "This Morning" and "Dynaflow," link King's blues to the sturdier forms of jazz. The horns lead on "Let's Have a Natural Ball," a tight, very commercial R&B number.

LINK➤ *Little Jimmy King & the Memphis Soul Survivors* — ***Bullseye Blues 9509***

With his Memphis Soul Survivors, hard-core electric guitar player King runs through some acidic R&B and some funky workouts. The first CD from a promising young guitar player.

Born Under a Bad Sign **Mobile Fidelity 577**

"If it wasn't for bad luck, I wouldn't have no luck at all." Blues lyrics just don't get any better. In the ultimate self-pity song, "Born Under a Bad Sign" defined 1960s electric blues, or more specifically, the kind of blues so expertly composed. It's performed by Stax musicians Steve Cropper (guitar), Donald "Duck" Dunn (bass), Al Jackson (drums), and Booker T. Jones (piano), plus the Memphis Horns. "Personal Manager" is a simmering slow song that plays King's long, long guitar off those horns with a chilling effect. Two ballads are outstanding showcases for King's sweet voice: "The Very Thought of You" and "I Almost Lost My Mind." Amazing that it's the same man performing.

LINK➤ *The Best of Booker T. and the MG's* *Rhino 81281*

The heart of Memphis soul, this instrumental quartet played on a fabulous number of hits. They are: Booker T. Jones (piano), Steve Cropper (guitar), Al Jackson (drums), and Donald "Duck" Dunn (drummer). Definitive.

I'll Play the Blues for You **Stax 8513**

The title song is one of the great slow blues, punctuated by the sparks of Albert King's electric guitar, the periodic grinding of the rhythm section, and the occasional lonesome horn behind King's spoken ramblings. King makes it all seem so natural, so easy. The Bar-Kays come to life alongside the Memphis Horns on the rainy "Breaking Up Somebody's Home," which simultaneously manages both dreary and funky moods. And once again, King's vocals are quietly expressive in the midst of his flaming guitar solo. "Little Brother (Make a Way)" is very 1972, a relentlessly earnest positive plea for doing the right thing. Not King's best, but many highlights are here, nevertheless.

LINK➤ *Tinsley Ellis — Fanning of the Flames* *Alligator 4778*

Ellis lacks the on-target songwriting and precision of emotional impact, but he's a spirited electric guitar player and overwrought singer likely to appeal to fans of Albert King. This 1989 album is probably his best so far; Alligator has released four others as well.

Live Wire/Blues Power **Stax 4128**

A live recording made at San Francisco's Fillmore Auditorium in 1968, in which King essentially explains the blues to a rock audience. Amidst his jagged electricity, he shouts, "This is Blues Power!" and sets to talking, describing people who have the blues, then shooting out a mighty funky solo. In what amounted to a one-man show (the band just follows along), King controlled the energy in that room, teaching, preaching, knocking people out with with every slow, carefully chosen sound on "Blues at Sunrise"; the rapt attentiveness is nearly palpable 30 years later. This is stark, perfect, very slightly psychedelic guitar playing, among the best on record from the 1960s. Don't miss it.

LINK➤ *Various Artists — Fillmore: The Last Days* *Columbia/Legacy 31390*

The end of an era: Bill Graham closed the Fillmore East and West auditoriums in 1971. Artists celebrating and remembering include Taj Mahal, It's a Beautiful Day, Santana, Tower of Power, Quicksilver Messenger Service, and Elvin Bishop.

The Ultimate Collection **Rhino 71268**

With so much fine Albert King music available on just a handful of CDs, it almost doesn't make sense to buy a 2-CD boxed set. Conversely, this box will satisfy most people's needs for Albert King's music (all of the important songs are included), and those who enjoy his music will find four 1964 tunes from the Coun-Tree label, three 1976 tunes for Utopia, four more from his 1977 Tomato recordings, and one more from Fantasy. Of 39 songs on this set, 24 were released on Stax (his best material, in fact), mostly on singles, and most of these are available on current CDs. Still, this is a fine career retrospective of a fine blues musician. The best Coun-Tree single is "C.O.D," with a few piercing horns and the predictable lyric line, "Come to me babe, come to me C.O.D.," with the typical shipping and postal references. Of the later material, the excellent songwriter Mack Rice contributes "Cold Women with Warm Hearts," which gets the full treatment with three extra guitar players, three keyboards, and five backup singers—it's the kind of big blues experience that lights up a room. Rice's "Cadillac Assembly Line," also done up large but without the singers is a modern story song ("gonna get me a job on the Cadillac assembly line"). Allen Toussaint produced 1979's *New Orleans Heat* album, another major-league instrumental treatment, and "The Feeling" nicely blends Toussaint's distinctive Cajun style with King's slow, sizzling blues format.

LINK➤ *Albert King — King of the Blues Guitar* ***Atlantic 8213***

One of several compilations of Stax singles, this is the one with the most consistently excellent selection of songs: 17 in all, including "Born Under a Bad Sign," "Kansas City," "Laundromat Blues," and plenty of other hits.

The Best of Albert King **Stax 60-005**

Of the several Albert King collections, this one's interesting because it doesn't deal with much of the best-known material. Instead, there's the hard-core guitar leading Howlin' Wolf's "Killing Floor" and some of the most striking emotional guitar ever recorded as part of Elmore James's "Sky Is Crying" (many have attempted this, but few have succeeded as completely as King on this take). Both songs come from 1972's *Years Gone By* (Stax 8517). The horns and guitars still resonate, but "I Wanna Get Funky" suffers from 1974 lyrics. In addition to "I'll Play the Blues for You" and "Blues Power," there's a "Honky Tonk Woman" misadventure and a surprisingly good "Hound Dog."

LINK➤ *Deborah Coleman — I Can't Lose* ***Blind Pig 5038***

Newcomer Coleman has two major-league assets: a rich, deep voice that's ideal for electric blues and a natural talent for electric guitar. She instinctively knows how to sculpt and time her presentation. This 1997 album is terrific. She even rocks out Billie Holiday's "Fine and Mellow."

When Riley King's parents separated in 1929, he was just 4 years old; King left the tiny town of Itta Bena, MI. He lived with various relatives until 1940, when he was old enough to move to Memphis on his own. After a false start, King found himself a job on WDIA, a radio station for black listeners. He became well known, and when the Bihari brothers visited Memphis, Ike Turner turned them on to King. Records were recorded, and some became hits. In 1955, B.B. King left the radio station to tour with his own band. He never stopped. He stayed with the Bihari brothers' RPM label (subsequently renamed Kent) until 1961, then switched to ABC-Paramount. In 1966, he joined forces with former accountant Sid Seidenberg, who became his manager. Seidenberg's behind-the-scenes work brought B.B. King and the blues to white audiences. King has become a worldwide ambassador of the blues.

King of the Blues — MCA 10677

It doesn't get any better than this: a spectacular 4-CD box surveying 43 years, nearly his entire career. "Miss Martha King" was recorded at WDIA in 1949. It's a raw R&B tune tinged with old-time jazz from trombone player Sammie Jett. Just two years later King's signature sound is essentially in place: a large vocal with oversized notes held in place for dramatic effect, tenor saxes below to fill, electric guitar to punctuate vocal lines (but rarely beneath them), and a drummer to keep time in the background. That's the format for 1951's "Three O'Clock Blues," and for so many other King tunes. Another King classic, "Everyday I Have the Blues," first shows up as a 1955 RPM single with more of a rolling, aggressive horn line. And despite the tried-and-true formula, King's versatility is stunning: he does a superb vocal with Duke Ellington's band on "Don't Get Around Much Anymore," for example. By 1963, King's approach was fully evolved. "How Blue Can You Get?" is one of many songs expertly arranged by Maxwell Davis; a solo horn balances each of King's lyric lines; a tight horn section comes in at the end of each line, often in place of the guitar, which is reserved for funkier solo breaks. "Goin' Down Slow" is another of King's best: it's a spoken word story about a blues man who leaves the South for success in Chicago. (It's notable for the line "SET 'EM UP!!—cousin's payin' for it.") King's guitar gets a good workout on the hit "Sweet Sixteen" and on "Lucille" (King's name for his guitar). In 1969, new producer Bill Szymczyk did a superb job with two of King's all-time best: "Why I Sing the Blues" and "The Thrill Is Gone." This box contains so much good music, it's nearly impossible to cover even the highlights in a single review. There's a stunning rocked-out version of "Eyesight to the Blind" (which King wrote) on a 1971 live set from Japan and the last disc, which covers 1976–91, contains some unexpected fun, like a Ole Miss concert version of "Caldonia" and some jazz-blues combinations with the Crusaders. King's voice is thinner in the later years, but his talent never fades. A substantial investment that pays considerable dividends, this box should be part of every blues CD library.

LINK➤ *Ray Charles — Genius & Soul: The 50th Anniversary Collection* *Rhino 72859*

Few musical performers measure up to B.B. King in terms of sheer output and longevity. Charles is no less extraordinary. This 5-CD box is his legacy. Every important song is here, but Rhino's producers went much further than usual to include collectibles. Essential.

Spotlight on Lucille — Flair 91693

It's not always easy to find B.B. King's collections on Flair Records (distributed by Virgin), but they're often worth the search. *Singin' the Blues/The Blues* (86296) is filled with jazzy singles recorded for Crown in the 1950s. This superb collection of instrumentals comes from 1960. On "Slidin' and Glidin," King trades guitar licks with his longtime tenor saxman, Bobby Forte, in a swinging big band format; on "Blues with B.B.," King goes for a twangy tone and performs with just a small rhythm section until the horns jump in. "Calypso Jazz" was a concert favorite, and "Shoutin' the Blues" is simple and satisfying. An excellent guitar record, highly recommended.

LINK➤ *Charlie Christian — The Genius of the Electric Guitar* *Columbia 460612*

It all starts here. Christian was a stunning young guitar player who gained renown as part of Benny Goodman's band. This is jazz, but it's essential listening.

Live at the Regal — Mobile Fidelity 548

Good 1964 performance at Chicago's Regal Theater finds King with rollicking horns and a driving rhythm section. He opens with "Everyday I Have the Blues," real tight and yet he allows himself a very practiced form of loosening up on his vocals. The crowd knows his music, and gets crazy on the first few notes of "Sweet Little Angel." The cheering, in fact, almost seems ingeniuous (King, after all, is not a teen heartthrob) as it leads into the serious "It's My Own Fault." Still, King does his thing, responds to the crowd's shouts with honest rapport, and moves on through "How Blue Can You Get?" and the danceable "Please Love Me."

LINK➤ *Various Artists — Blue Flames: A Sun Blues Collection* *Rhino 7096*

The history of the Sun studios doesn't begin and end with Elvis Presley. Jackie Brentson recorded what might be rock 'n' roll's first disc, "Rocket 88," in 1951, and Rufus Thomas was one of many soul and blues musicians who worked there. B.B. King did, too. A good sampling of Memphis style.

Completely Well **MCA 31039**

This 1969 album was King's first to break through to general (white) audiences. The principal reason is the hit "The Thrill Is Gone," but several other songs are nearly as good. One is "So Excited," with its appealing combination of electric guitar effects, no-nonsense Memphis horn rhythms, and a very attentive bass and drum combination. This album definitely rocks more than other King efforts, and it fits nicely into rock's history from this era; "Confessin' the Blues" is a little cumbersome and thick, but it does shake the room. The subtlety that King brings to "Cryin' Won't Help You Now" is welcome; its understatement is one of the album's treats.

LINK➤ *Jimmy Johnson — Barroom Preacher* ***Alligator 4744***

Johnson's guitar cuts like a knife, but Johnson chooses his movements with taste and care. He also sings with a soulful tone and style that works for R&B as well as blues. Recorded in 1993. Pure, unadulterated blues. Available only on cassette.

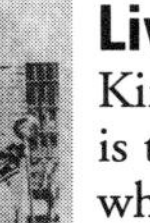

Live in Cook County Jail **MCA 31080**

King recorded several live albums, but this one, from 1971, is the best of the lot. Recorded with an audience of inmates who clearly hold the man and his music in high regard, King really delivers the goods. WIth two saxophones, a trumpet, bass, and drums, it's a small band with a big sound. After a lengthy spoken introduction, King gets into "Everyday I Have the Blues," "Three O'Clock Blues," "The Thrill Is Gone," and other near standards. As on the other live albums, King loosens up a bit, but never strays far from the energetic, sizzling tried-and-true. A further inducement: none of this music is included in the boxed set.

LINK➤ *Chris Cain Band — Cuttin' Loose* ***Blind Pig 74090***

Cain's got B.B. King's clear, resonating voice down pat. And, he plays like him, working with similar charts. "Pick Up the Tab" is a B.B. King sound-alike: horns, guitar break. and all. But Cain's no copycat—his work is wholly original. From 1990.

Blues Summit **MCA 10710**

This 1992 album may not be B.B. King's best, but it's a whole lot of fun to hear him duet with so many fine blues stars. The roster includes Irma Thomas, Ruth Brown, Buddy Guy, Joe Louis Walker, Robert Cray, Lowell Fulson, John Lee Hooker, Koko Taylor, Albert Collins, and Etta James. King's voice is a little hoarser than it was two decades earlier, but the top-notch fidelity and really excellent musicians compensate. Plenty of sizzling moments, particulary from Cray, Walker, and Webster. Really distinctive "I'm Gonna Move Out of This Neighborhood" by King and his own group. Very solid "Stormy Monday," too. Overall, it should have been even better.

LINK➤ *Various Artists — The Simpsons Sing the Blues* ***Geffen 24308***

Look at this as "Blues 101" for the next generation. It's funny, but it's also a showcase of blues by musicians who love their music. And for every "Moanin' Lisa Blues" and "Do the Bartman," there's a version of "God Bless the Child" or "Born Under a Bad Sign." Lighten up—this is fun!

Freddie King

Freddie Christian was born near Gilmer, TX, in 1934. His mother and uncle taught him the acoustic guitar. In the late 1940s, King's interest shifted to electric guitar. Fortunately, his family moved to Chicago in 1950, a move that provided the teenager with ample opportunity to see Jimmy Rogers, Eddie Taylor, and Robert Jr. Lockwood in clubs and street concerts. Eager to become a part of the scene himself, King became a skilled sideman. He first recorded under his own name in 1956. In 1960, King signed with Federal Records (part of the Cincinnati-based King Records; no relation). Within a productive eight-year period, King recorded many hits, including several that sold to white audiences. Most notable of these was "Hide Away," which reached number 29 on Billboard's pop charts. King became one of the most famous blues guitarists, a fact that inspired Eric Clapton and other British blues-rockers to cover his songs. King died in 1976 of heart failure.

Just Pickin' — Modern Blues 721

Two dozen tracks, and not a word uttered. This is all instrumental guitar music, performed by one of the 1960s best in the genre. The tracks were recorded from 1960 to 1964, and they're consistently interesting. In the 1960 and 1961 sessions, King is mostly accompanied by a second guitar, piano, bass, and drums. Several well-known King bounce their happy way along, unencumbered by the structure demanded by a vocal. This is true of "Hide Away," "Sen-Sa-Shun," and the lighthearted "Just Pickin'." The second half of the album is generally accompanied by the same group, with a few saxophones are added. Skillful craftsmanship makes for a pleasant listening session.

LINK➤ *Shuggie Otis — Shuggie's Boogie* — ***Epic/Legacy 57903***

In the short list of truly extraordinary blues guitar players, Freddie King and Shuggie Otis would be ranked high. This mostly instrumental collection from the early 1970s is an absolute pleasure; Otis's imagination and his knack for innovation is stunning.

Hide Away: The Best of Freddie King — Rhino 71510

This spectacular 1-CD anthology begins with a 1956 R&B duet with singer Margaret Whitfield. "Have You Ever Loved a Woman," from 1960, has tastes of a style now associated with B.B. King—plenty of open space for guitar solos and piquant vocals in carefully chosen spots. King jumps to falsetto for emphasis. The 1961 hit "Hide Away" showcases a fairly melodic electric guitar and some neat effects. King always nails the basics, but he knows how to put on a show, whether it's his rippling effects on 1961's "Sen-sa-shun," or showing progressive rock bands how it's supposed to be done on 1971's "Palace of the King." Stunning versatility!

LINK➤ *Led Zeppelin — Led Zeppelin* — ***Swan Song 19126***

A defining moment in the evolution of blues to rock to something bigger: a sonic assault resulting in heavy metal. Amidst the showboating and layering, there is blues down below.

Lester Kinsey, a.k.a. Big Daddy Kinsey, was an old-style country blues player from Mississippi. He moved north in 1944, settled in Gary, IN, and after WW II found a job in a steel mill. Kinsey played blues on weekends, and as his sons grew up they joined him. In the late 1960s, the group became known as Big Daddy Kinsey and His Fabulous Sons. The group faded away in the 1970s, but brothers Donald, Ralph, and Kenneth became professional musicians. Donald (lead guitar) played with Bob Marley, and frequently with Peter Tosh. He later formed the Chosen Ones, a reggae band, with his brother Ralph (drums). Ron Prince, a friend, joined to play rhythm guitar. In time, the group took shape as the Kinsey Report, with Big Daddy Kinsey singing lead and Kenneth on bass. The group's 1980s renown has faded somewhat, but its members still perform and record. Donald now sings lead vocals.

Bad Situation — Rooster Blues 2620

Before Donald and his brothers busted out with their own Kinsey Report band, they shared billing with Big Daddy Kinsey, a terrific blues vocalist. He's totally in the game here with a roughhouse Delta voice and endless street credibility in a rocked-out 1984 session. On "Slow Down," the elder Kinsey trades vocal licks with a gospel-sounding girl group, and on the autobiographical "Gary, Indiana," he's got Pinetop Perkins on piano. The big story on this song and throughout the album, is the searing electric guitar played by son Donald, and the groove laid down by the whole band. "Sharp Axe" cuts hard in the direction of Howlin' Wolf and Lightnin' Hopkins. Highly recommended!

LINK➤ *Roosevelt "Booba" Barnes — The Heartbroken Man Rooster Blues 2623*

Barnes grew up with the juke joints, tried the north, then returned to Mississippi. With his Playboys band, Barnes maintains a level of raw authenticity, but he's thoroughly modern, too. If you like the Kinseys, you'll probably go for Barnes. From 1995.

Edge of the City — Alligator 4758

With riveted steel percussion, rock-hard rhythm, and the sculpted electricity of two guitars, the Kinsey Report could have been just another midwestern bar band. What sets the group apart? Smart arrangements, for one thing. On a tune like "I Can't Let You Go," the rhythm section carries the flow, the guitars add spice, and Donald Kinsey's decidedly nontough voice adds the necessary credibility. Donald is an amazing guitar player, but he knows when and how to wield that axe for maximum impact. On that particular song, St. James Bryant adds a moody organ. A very consistent Alligator debut (from 1987) contains plenty of compelling material, notably "Come to Me" and "Poor Man's Relief."

LINK➤ *Kinsey Report — Midnight Drive Alligator 4775*

This 1989 sophomore outing continues in a similar direction, but doesn't make a whole lot of progress. Sacked by so-so songwriting, Donald's guitar continues to sizzle, but the smooth sense of balance is sometimes buried by overproduction. Still, this was one hot band.

Huddie (*HUGH-dee*) Ledbetter was born in 1885 and grew up near Mooringsport, LA. He was strong, smart, talented, and often busy playing at social events. Leadbelly left home as a teenager and probably hung around with Blind Lemon Jefferson in Texas. In 1917, Leadbelly killed Will Stafford in a fight. He was jailed in the dreadful Huntsville penitentiary, but convinced the governor to pardon him by singing a song. A big man with a quick temper, Leadbelly was jailed again in 1930, this time in Angola. He tried another song for a different governor, but folklorist John Lomax showed up, recorded him for the Library of Congress, and arranged a second pardon. In 1934, Leadbelly became Lomax's driver. He moved to Manhattan, lived on welfare, and spent time recording, playing small parties, and performing with folk music friends like Woody Guthrie. Leadbelly died of amyotrophic lateral sclerosis in 1949.

King of the 12-String Guitar — Columbia 46776

These 18 sides were recorded by Leadbelly for ARC in the first few months of 1935. "Becky Deem, She Was a Gamblin' Girl" is one of his stronger songs, a powerful demonstation of the force of his voice. (Sadly, many lyrics are very hard to understand.) "Death Letter Blues" comes in two parts, both impressive for their guitar work. The song is about the loss of a love ("taking my baby to the burying ground"). Many of these songs are melodically spare, more like stories told to music than singable tunes. "Daddy I'm Coming Back to You" is more in the "Goodnight Irene" vein, with verses and choruses, and a memorable melody. Not essential.

LINK➤ *Various Artists — Prison Worksongs* — ***Arhoolie 448***

Recorded by Dr. Harry Oster at the dreadful Angola State Penitentiary in Louisiana, this is the kind of world where Leadbelly was discovered by Alan Lomax. The music has its own appeal—as do the stories behind the music.

Midnight Special (The Library of Congress Recordings, Vol. 1) — Rounder 1044

The Lomaxes recorded Leadbelly at the Louisiana State Penitentiary and in many other locations from 1933 until 1942. Elektra released some of these recordings on LP in 1966. In 1991 and 1994, Rounder released all the recordings on 6 CDs. This disc begins with two versions of "Irene" (also known as "Goodnight Irene"), a song about a girl who was too young (hence: "I'll see you in my dreams"). "Midnight Special," perhaps Leadbelly's best song, is about a train whose light shone on prisoners wanting to be freed; the melody and rhythm are perfect. The song is a musical kin to "Take a Whiff on Me," a cocaine song. Good "Roberta," "Matchbox Blues," too.

LINK➤ *Koerner, Ray & Glover — Blues, Rags & Hollers* — ***Red House 76***

A 1963 classic by three young white musicians who skillfully captured the essence of the hot Mississippi sun, the misery of the cotton fields, the abuse, relentless sadness, and the relief that only music could bring. The musicianship is extraordinary.

Gwine Dig a Hole to Put the Devil In (The Library of Congress Recordings, Vol. 2) **Rounder 1045**

After a version of "C.C. Rider," comes the song Leadbelly sang to shave more than 22 years off his prison sentence, "Governor Pat Neff (Sweet Mary)." It's not his best song, but it was certainly his most successful. There's a good version of "Becky Dean (She Was a Gambling Gal)" followed by two of Leadbelly's most popular songs, "Medicine Man" and "Alberta." Once again, the sound is rather hazy (but remarkably clear, considering the technology and recording conditions). "Mama, Did You Bring Any Silver (Gallis Pole)" is notable for a relentlessly fast guitar bed, and "Green Corn" is a fast-footed, high-spirited country dance. "Turn Your Radio On" is a novelty pop tune.

LINK➤ *Various Artists — Prison Songs, Vol. 1: Murderous Home* *Rounder 1714*
This CD is part of the Alan Lomax collection, a massive undertaking involving dozens of titles. These pieces were recorded at Parchman Farm, Mississippi's State Penitentiary. Percussion is supplied by work gangs splitting firewoord; songs are chained choruses.

Let It Shine on Me (The Library of Congress Recordings, Vol. 3) **Rounder 1046**

Roughly half of this 1940 set is religious songs. The first track is a 12-minute discussion about religion that contains several songs that are under a minute long. These include an unaccompanied "You Must Have That True Religion, Halleloo" and "Backslider, Fare the Well." Each is offered a second time on tracks following the interview. Leadbelly is joyous and uplifting on "Let It Shine on Me," with a rhythm that doubles its speed to exhilarating effect. All are 19th-century songs that Leadbelly learned as a child. Topical songs here include "Mr. Roosevelt," "Mr. Hitler," "Scottsboro Boys," and "Howard Hughes."

LINK➤ *Various Artists — Folkways: A Vision Shared* *Columbia 44034*
A wonderful celebration of Leadbelly and Woody Guthrie. Little Richard and Fishbone share in "Rock Island Line," Willie Nelson sings "Philadelphia Lawyer," Bruce Springstein does "Vigilante Man," and Sweet Honey in the Rock sings "Sylvie." Spectacular!

The Titanic (The Library of Congress Recordings, Vol. 4) **Rounder 1097**

"Mister Tom Hughes Town" is about the dangers of Shreveport, LA—a place where a mama would never want her young boy to go. "Shreveport Jail" naturally follows, but the most important songs here are also the toughest to discern in the dim sound. "The Titanic" was the first song Leadbelly learned to play on the 12-string guitar; it's essentially a folk ballad that glosses over story details (no lyrics included; pretty sparse liner notes, too). "Hestitation Blues," a popular Leadbelly song, contains the chorus "How long will I have to wait?" On "Boll Weevil," Leadbelly again performs something that isn't quite blues, but defies any other category.

LINK➤ *Leadbelly — Nobody Knows the Trouble I've Seen (The Library of Congress Recordings, Vol. 5)* *Rounder 1098*
More of the same, highlighted by a two-part telling of "The Hindenberg Disaster," plus a very brief "Rock Island Line." Also includes "Bring Me a Little Water, Silvy" and "Nobody Knows the Trouble I've Seen." Probably the weakest in the series.

Go Down Old Hannah (The Library of Congress Recordings, Vol. 6)

Rounder 1099

The CD starts with a monologue leading into Victoria Spivey's song about a woman dying of tuberculosis: "T.B. Blues." Leadbelly then talks his way into a handsome rendition of the Leroy Carr song "How Long? A 12-minute monologue about square dances (called "sookey jumps") follows, complete with some terrifically fast snippets of "Tight Like That," "Gwine Dig a Hole," and others. (By now, Leadbelly has done this talk-then-sing routine so many times, he sounds rehearsed.) After a discussion about Christmas, a set of religious songs fills the CD's second half. Highlights include "Old Time Religion," "Amazing Grace," and "Swing Low, Sweet Chariot." The best in this series.

LINK➤ *The Weavers — Wasn't That a Time* **Vanguard 147/50**

The Weavers—Pete Seeger, Lee Hays, Fred Hellerman, and Ronnie Gilbert—were a folk group that often performed with Leadbelly. They were good friends, too. The Weavers' style, from 1949 through the 1950s, was folk music sung in harmony with lots of political involvement, too. A 4-CD box.

Where Did You Sleep Last Night?

Smithsonian Folkways 40044

Recorded in the early 1950s, the Folkways CDs are clear, well recorded, and easy to enjoy. After a pleasant "Irene," there's "Pick a Bale of Cotton" with the harmonizing Oleander Quartet earnestly singing along. "Cotton Fields" (lyrics: "When I was a little baby, my mother would rock me in the cradle") is very appealing and autobiographical. "Bring a Little Water, Sylvie" is a work song with a catchy melody. In an extraordinary, essential collection, "Rock Island Line" stands out; Leadbelly didn't write this song, but he helped to make it famous. It's fascinating to hear an authentic "(There is a House in) New Orleans," too. An amazing 34 songs on one CD!

LINK➤ *Larry Johnson — Midnight Hour Blues* **Biograph 138**

Folk-blues singer Johnson delivers a winning performance with the help of John Hammond, who contributes National Steel guitar and harmonica. Recorded in 1971, about 40 years after Johnson was born a sharecropper's son in Georgia.

Bourgeois Blues (Lead Belly Legacy, Vol. 2)

Smithsonian Folkways 40045

"Fannin Street" is another name for "Mr. Tom Hughes Town," about the lure of Shreveport's most colorful (and dangerous) district. When Leadbelly was traveling, he came across the word "bourgeois," liked it, and built a slashing protest song around its meaning. Friends Woody Guthrie and Cisco Houston provide the backup vocals for a 1946 performance of "Alabama Bound." "Don't You Love Your Daddy No More?" is cross between a pop song and a blues. "John Henry" is performed "right"—as a dance tune with the repeating "it is going to be the death of me." Sonny Terry plays the harmonica on that one. Hearty music, well played and nicely varied.

LINK➤ *Cisco Houston — The Folkways Years* **Smithsonian Folkways 40059**

Whitney Houston's mother was a close friend of Woody Guthrie and was deeply involved in the politics, music, and fun of building a new world. She sings beautifully, and this is a fine sampling of her work.

Shout On (Lead Belly Legacy, Vol. 3) — Smithsonian Folkways 40105

This 1998 release of 32 more Leadbelly songs completes the series. There's a jubliant version of his "Governor Pat Neff" (lyrics: "I knew my wife would jump up and shout. When the train rolls up, I come stepping out. 'Mary, Sweet Ma-a-ary'"). Freedom has never sounded so sweet. The sun was called "Old Hannah," the relentlessly hot circle that made life so miserable in prison. Leadbelly wrote a song about it, a love song about getting out of prison someday called "Go Down, Old Hannah." He performs "John Henry" with Sonny Terry and Brownie McGhee and sings a version of "Down in the Valley" called "Birmingham Jail." Excellent work throughout.

LINK➤ *Various Artists — Before the Blues, Vol. 2* **Yazoo 2016**

Music from the era around 1920, this thoughtful look back at the past is complete with intelligent liner notes that explain the origins of songs and styles. Along with the Tennessee Chocolate Drops and Eck Robertson are more familiar players like Blind Lemon Jefferson. Very easy listening.

Leadbelly's Last Sessions — Smithsonian Folkways 40068/71

On three nights in the fall of 1948, Frederic Ramsey recorded Leadbelly in his NYC apartment. Taking advantage of the new magnetic tape format, he recorded Leadbelly with previously unavailable clarity. Then Leadbelly's family stubbornly refused to authorize the tapes unless a record company was willing to release the material in complete form. The sessions began informally—Leadbelly had no guitar with him, but felt like singing—with the first 34 tracks unaccompanied. They're terrific! "Miss Liza Jane" is "an old, old song," pure and from the heart. A captivating version of "Blue Tail Fly" is performed so simply—nothing more than an honest voice with a pleasant sense of humor. With the same friendly informality, the second session combined some chat and plenty of music. It's hard not to smile the first time Leadbelly's guitar is heard so clearly on "Dancing with Tears in My Eyes"—especially after suffering through piles of older, foggier recordings. There's some Pig Latin, and a "Hawaiian Song"—remember, Leadbelly was a collector of songs, not strictly a bluesman. "The Grey Goose" features assembled friends gently singing "Lord, Lord, Lord" in the background. With almost 100 songs on this 4-CD set, there's a great deal of variety: "Tight Like That," "Hesitation Blues," "Springtime in the Rockies," and "Nobody Knows You When You're Down and Out," which Leadbelly performs with less desperation than Bessie Smith. All told, listening to this set is like having Leadbelly visit your living room.

LINK➤ *Woody Guthrie — Library of Congress Recordings* **Rounder 1041**

Guthrie recorded this 3-CD set in 1940, and although the quality isn't as good as on other CDs, it's the single best collection of his honest, effective, poignant folk music. The liner notes are excellent. Very highly recommended.

Born in Monticello, MS, in 1929, Lenoir was always known as "J.B." and not by any first name. His father taught him to play guitar, and his mother also played and practiced with him. After perfecting his skills at local parties and picnics, Lenoir moved to New Orleans for a few years. He worked behind Sonny Boy Williamson and Elmore James, but it wasn't until 1949's relocation to Chicago that his own career took shape. With the friendship and guidance of Big Bill Broonzy, Lenoir got jobs at blues clubs; by 1951 he had signed with Chess. Lenoir left the label to record for J.O.B. and then Parrot, but returned to Chess's Checker subsidiary in 1955. He remained a fixture on the Chicago scene through the 1960s and traveled to Europe twice as part of a concert tour package. Sadly, a 1967 automobile accident caused a heart attack that took his life.

1951–1954: His JOB Recordings — Paula 4

Keep your eyes open for a CD release of *Natural Man* (a collection of Lenoir's Chess sides that includes the topical "Eisenhower Blues") and *The Parrot Sessions* (from 1954–55, on the Relic label; his best work). The JOB recordings are not as lavishly produced as Lenoir's work for the other two labels; basically, it's Lenoir singing and playing his guitar with Sunnyland Slim on piano, and Alfred Wallace on drums. The songs are mostly midtempo and the writing could be more distinguished, but the fundamentals are in place. There's a pleasant "Let's Roll," followed by a slow story song, "People Are Meddling (in Our Affairs)," about the end of a love affair.

LINK➤ *Various Artists — Blues Is Killing Me* — ***Paula 19***

Baby Face Leroy Foster was a topnotch gin drinker, according to Sunnyland Slim, who smiled when he heard the name. Floyd Jones was quieter, with a gift for social commentary. They're among a handful of Chicago's lesser-known bluesmen on this early 1950s collection.

Vietnam Blues: The Complete L+R Recordings — Evidence 26068

More than most blues singers, Lenoir sung about specific contemporary events. He starts out with "Alabama Blues," listing the reasons why he's not going back to Alabama. (The killing of sisters and brothers is high on the list.) He questions God's intentions on "God's Word." In "Shot on James Meredith," Lenoir tells what happened on June 6, 1966, when Meredith was "shot right down just like a dog." And "Vietnam Blues" is a wish to stop the war and a prayer to the president to "clean up your house before you leave." Pointed commentary and less angry songs are mostly accompanied by Lenoir's own guitar. Expertly recorded in 1965 and 1966.

LINK➤ *Various Artists — Blues Masters, Vol. 10: Blues Roots* — ***Rhino 71135***

Beginning with two African griot performances (Jali Nyama Suso's song "Kedo" and the Mandingo Griots on "Tutu Jara"), the action moves to a Southern prison for Robert Pete Williams, then to "One String" and a Texas prison camp work gang. Interesting roots.

Lewis was born in Greenwood, MS, in 1893, but his family moved to Memphis, TN, when he was a child. Lewis taught himself to play guitar; as a young man, he traveled through the South and lost a leg in a train mishap. After returning to Memphis, Lewis played on street corners, and found a job as a street cleaner with the city's sanitation department. Rediscovered by Sam Charters in 1959, Lewis left his job to concentrate on music in the early 1960s; he became popular in clubs and at festivals. Lewis also appeared on *The Tonight Show*, where he played the old bluesman to the hilt: "Why should I marry when the man next door to me's got a wife?" He became known as a showman and raconteur, playing himself in 1974's *W.W. and the Dixie Dance Kings* (starring Burt Reynolds) and appearing in various documentaries. Lewis continued to record until his death in Memphis in 1981.

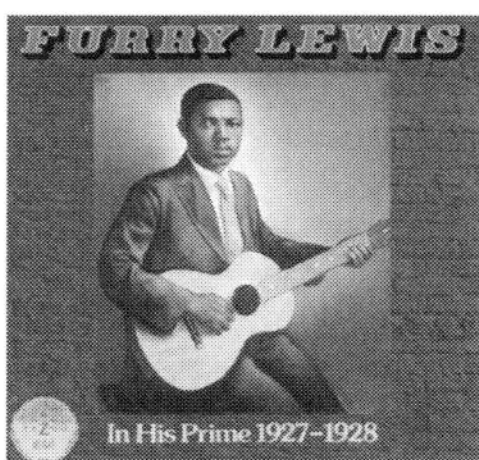

In His Prime 1927–1928 **Yazoo 1050**

These recordings were not especially popular, and by most accounts, Lewis was not a well-known Memphis musician when these records were released. There is no single song that stands out, but Lewis's voice is pleasant and expressive. He knows how to present a song, and his guitar riffs are often captivating. It all comes together on 1927's "Good Looking Girl Blues," which casts its spell through a tidy repeating riff, and a solid vocal treatment. Repeated listenings focus one's attention not so much on Lewis's singing voice, which is fine, but on his guitar—the central force on "Furry's Blues," "Falling Down Blues," and many others.

LINK➤ ***Cannon's Jug Stompers — The Complete Works 1927–1930 Yazoo 1082/3***
Early jug band music—street music by banjo, jug, guitar, and harmonica, or kazoo. "Walk Right In" (lyric: "Daddy let your mind roll on . . . ") will be familiar, especially the kazoo. Entertaining years later, this album was very influential on 1960s folkies.

Shake 'Em on Down **Fantasy 24703**

It's easy enough to understand what all of the excitement was about. Here's a bluesman who presents the whole package—impressive guitar work, songs that beautifully represent the blues form, and a voice that carries through the decades. This CD brings together two 1961 albums. The highlight is a lengthy meditation on the folk blues, "John Henry," with verse after verse building the power of an American hero, and stunning guitar bridges between those verses. "White Lightning" is an especially dark blues brought on by strong liquor; it contains a handsome trainlike pattern on guitar and the familiar "train I ride is sixteen coaches long" lyric.

LINK➤ ***Var. Artists—Beale St. Get-Down: Bluesville Years, Vol. 3 Prestige 9907***
Furry Lewis starts the collection with his rangey voice and tight, smart guitar on "John Henry," "Casey Jones," and "Shake 'Em On Down." Memphis Slim contributes "Mean Mistreatin' Mama" and "Letter Home." Six more by the lesser-known blues singer Memphis Willie B.

Lipscomb was born in 1895 and spent most of his life as a poor farmer, living in a small sharecropper's shack near the Brazos River near Navasota, TX. Strictly speaking, Lipscomb wasn't a blues singer, but a songster—a Texas musician who performed ballads, breakdowns, popular songs, and anchored a small town's social life. Songsters generally preceded professional musicians who traveled from town to town in the South. Lipscomb worked the farm on weekdays; on Saturdays, he performed long into the night for black audiences. Sundays were spent performing for white neighbors at afternoon picnics. In 1960, Lipscomb was discovered by Chris Strachwitz and his partner, Mack McCormick. As a result, Lipscomb recorded during that decade for Arhoolie. By 1970, he had signed with Reprise. Lipscomb retired in 1974; he died at home in 1976. Fortunately, the story of his life is detailed in an oral autobiography, *I Say Me for a Parable*.

Texas Songster — Arhoolie 306

Lipscomb seems to know every song in the country blues canon. His articulation is clear, and his fresh delivery makes even the most familiar song a special experience. The first 11 tracks—half the album—were recorded in Texas in 1960. Many songs will be familiar because they were sung, with some variations, by many blues musicians: "Sugar Babe," "Jack O' Diamonds," "'Bout a Spoonful," for example. Lipscomb is especially effective on "Ella Speed," a song about a loose woman's demise and funeral, sung by her murderer. Eleven more songs and some brief monologues were recorded in Berkeley in 1964, including "Willie Poor Boy" and "Motherless Children." Satisfying and essential.

LINK➤ *Various Artists — Don't Leave Me Here: The Blues of Texas, Arkansas, and Louisiana 1927–1932* — *Yazoo 1004*

Two reasonably well-known names here are Henry Thomas, who often represents the earliest version of blues on collections like this one, and Blind Lemon Jefferson. Texas Alexander's here too, with "98 Degree Blues." Fine work from those whose names are unfamiliar, as well.

You Got to Reap What You Sow — Arhoolie 398

This 1964 session was recorded in Chris Strachwitz's Berkeley living room. Lipscomb's encyclopedic knowledge is based, at least in part, on a remarkable memory. He used to hear his uncle singing "Charlie James" in the fields; he recalled "Come Back Baby," a 1930s hit; and he remembered hearing "Spanish Fang Dang" from a Mexican field hand one night years ago. The melody for "Cocaine Done Killed My Baby" has been reworked many times with other lyrics by blues and folk writers. Lipscomb sings "Titanic" as though it was a fresh memory (Blind Willie Johnson's version was called "God Moves on the Water"). "You Rascal You" is also a highlight.

LINK➤ *Various Artists — Country Negro Jam Session* **_Arhoolie 372_**

Pure, unadorned country blues, the sort of informal harmonies and easy good times that would have accompanied a summertime picnic. No famous names, but the music's captivating. Various fiddles, washboards, and earnest voices. Wonderful.

Captain, Captain! **Arhoolie 465**

The third volume of Lipscomb's wonderful music was released on CD in 1998 (hopefully, more are on the way). Once again, the quality of the recording is exquisite, particularly the first dozen tracks, recorded in 1966. These include the title song (a work song learned from a convict when Lipscomb was a boy), several impressive guitar solos (very entertaining; they go down easy), and the cloying guitar temptation, "Night Time Is the Right Time." Lipscomb's creative instincts are extraordinary. The standouts among the dozen tracks from 1960 (all previously unissued) include "Angel Child," "Going Back to Georgia," and "Mance's Talking Blues." Just a guitar and a voice—but what results!

LINK➤ *Roy Book Binder — Polk City Ramble* **_Rounder 3153_**

A modern-day songster who collects tunes and makes them his own, the iconoclastic Book Binder recreates his mentor Reverend Gary Davis's "Baby Lay It On You," Blind Blake's "Police Dog Blues," other classics, and a pleasing range of original songs. Very good guitar playing.

BOOK: I Say Me for a Parable **da capo 030680610X**

While hoping Arhoolie will release more of Mance Lipscomb's music on CD, and in the absence of anything else with even adequate sound, the only way to delve further into Lipscomb's music is either to track down obscure LPs or to read this wonderful book. It's an oral history compiled by Austin musician Glen Alyn. Not many books so completely capture a man, his times, and his world. This is mostly a collection of reminiscences, but Alyn has skillfully knitted them together into a coherent, compelling life story. There are so many memorable scenes: the day Lipscomb was sent to the cotton fields to pick an adult-sized 50-pound quota, and the exteme pain he suffered as a result; his pride in working up to 150 pounds as an adult. There are Lipscomb's memories of his mother, Mama Janie, a Chocktaw Indian healer. Also recounted is his boyhood friendship with a local sheriff, who was the man who killed Bonnie and Clyde. Attention is also paid to the "discovery" of Lipscomb and his performances for large numbers of white listeners at concerts in Berkeley and elsewhere. It's a story that's remarkable and truly American. Told with impressive insight into the realities of Lipscomb's "back life" early years, the book also explores the reasons why his music and repertoire developed as they did. Indeed, Lipscomb knows his music, knows himself, and was smart enough to say "yes" when Alyn asked to record the tapes that formed the basis of this autobiography. Very highly recommended reading.

Milton Campbell was born in Inverness, MS, in 1934. Although he never achieved big-time fame, he has been one of the most reliable blues performers for decades. Campbell picked up guitar by listening in local clubs and by copying what he heard on the radio. He found work at picnics and other gatherings, and became as interested in country music as he was in blues. In the early 1950s, Campbell worked in several bands, playing for Ike Turner and Willie Love, among others. By 1953, he was cutting his own records for producer Sam Phillips; over the next 16 years, Little Milton's string of hits for the Bobbin and Checker labels made him a popular performer. In the 1970s, he recorded for Stax and some smaller labels; he moved on in the 1980s to Malaco, where his popularity grew. Campbell has not stopped recording or performing live for nearly a half-century.

The Sun Masters — Rounder 35

Sun released 6 of the 13 tracks on this reissue CD. They're straightforward, not beautifully recorded, but effective just the same. "Beggin' My Baby" is typical. A slightly hoarse but supremely stylish Little Milton performs a simple R&B love song, while a drummer flails away in the background. A pair of saxophones jumps in to vary the mix. "Lookin' for My Baby" follows the same formula, with some unappealing overmodulation. The best tune, "Alone and Blue," is a distinguished sad-eyed vocal with minimalist accompaniment from a quiet piano, the saxes, and a drummer. There's a nice staccato break in the middle of the song, too. "Re-Beat" updates the jump blues formula.

LINK➤ *Little Milton — Greatest Hits* — ***Malaco 7477***

Bookending the other side of Little Milton's career is this collection of overly slick, highly arranged soul songs from his 1970s and 1980s work with the Malaco label. Little Milton's voice remains gripping, and the guitar is in the mix, but the real magic is found in the earlier work.

Welcome to the Club: The Essential Chess Recordings — Chess 9350

In 1961, Little Milton recorded "My Song." His voice is smooth and commanding; the background instruments include a high-tuned xylophone, and the vocalists are a doo-wop group. Months later, Milton cut "Someone to Love" with his stinging guitar, a rocking rhythm, a shouting vocal, and breakout horns. Those are the two sides of Little Milton: the energetic and fast-moving, and the slickly romantic. This collection covers roughly a decade, from 1961 through 1969, and includes an impressive array of hit songs. One of his biggest hits, 1965's "We're Gonna Make It," is based on a favorite theme—overcoming money troubles. It's a classic 1960s blues: a resilient male lead vocal, an insistent beat, horns that accent and then blow a full chorus, and backup singers that take over for the horns. A number one R&B hit, "Feel So Bad" is slower and tougher on the soul. Milton's vocal is dark and depressed, but the funky groove set up by his electric guitar, Louis Satterfield's bass, and Maurice White's drums lift the spirits for a world-class R&B tune. Little Milton's style is so identifiable and satisfying that even a pair of Coca-Cola jingles fits right in ("Things Go Better with

Coke"). Blood, Sweat & Tears did a version of "More and More" and it's interesting to hear how much the were influenced by Little Milton's 1967 version. With spectacular R&B horn arrangements, consistently excellent vocals that influenced a generation of rockers, and stunning production, this album is pure joy. Digital remastering really improves the sonics. Essential.

LINK➤ *Junior Parker — Junior's Blues* ***MCA 10669***

"Wanna Ramble" will be immediately familiar because of its shoutlike chorus. Parker's smooth voice and tight harmonica breaks spelled commercial success—and built on a rougher effort for Sun Records (available as Mystery Train [Rounder 38]). An unabashedly commercial approach to the blues.

If Walls Could Talk **Chess 9289**

Compare this album with *Welcome to the Club* to hear how much a record's sound can be improved with skillful remastering. It's back to slightly mushy but good-spirited 1969 sonics for Little Milton's best album. The title track was a solid hit, and it's among his best work: a thrilling vocal holds center stage while the relentless horns keep everything moving. Most of this album is not blues, but soul with pop horn arrangements, gimmicky instrumentation, and earnest interpretations. "Blues Get Off My Shoulder" and "Your Precious Love" could only come from 1969. The saving grace is Little Milton himself, whose vocals are slick, professional, and expert. Cool horns, too.

LINK➤ *Fontella Bass — Rescued: The Best of Fontella Bass* ***Chess (MCA) 9355***

Great gospel and soul singer known for the hit song "Rescue Me," this single CD retrospective also includes "You'll Never Know," "Don't Mess Up a Good Thing," and "Soul of a Man." The Dells are the background vocalists.

Tin Pan Alley **Stax 8582**

From 1971 until 1975, Little Milton recorded for Stax; these are his best singles. He started strong with August 1971's "If That Ain't a Reason (For Your Woman to Leave You)." Here, Milton sings the choruses with some backup singers, but nearly talks some of the verses. Additional heat comes from horns and a distant second male chorus. "That's What Love Will Make You Do," his other big Stax hit, was released in December 1971. It's more funky (a characteristic of several tracks here), with distinctively tiny guitar sounds, a danceable beat, and those horns. Little Milton knows how to deliver a soulful song; his "I'm Gonna Cry a River" is a classic.

LINK➤ *Little Milton — Grits Ain't Groceries* ***Stax 8529***

Little Willie John's "All Around the World" became Little Milton's signature tune, "Grits Ain't Groceries," and he lays down a hot version in this 1972 L.A. club date. Sweaty, sincere, and soulful, this CD helps explain why the man has been successful on the "chitlin' circuit" for decades.

One of the all-time greatest blues harmonica players, Walter Marion Jacobs grew up in New Orleans. By age 12 he was already on his own, learning what he could from Sonny Boy Williamson in Helena, AR, while making his way to Chicago. In short order, he caught the attention of Big Bill Broonzy and Tampa Red. It was 1946, the Maxwell Street scene was happening, and Little Walter was 16 years old. Muddy Waters hired him to play harmonica in 1948. By 1952, he was fronting his own band, which became known as little Walter and the Nightcats. Periodically he recorded and performed with Muddy Waters. By the 1960s, gigs were no longer plentiful, and Jacobs began drinking heavily. He toured Britain with the Rolling Stones in 1964, but a 1967 Chess comeback session showed how seriously alcoholism had damaged his technique and creativity. Jacobs died in 1968 after an angry street brawl.

The Essential Little Walter — Chess 9342

One of the finest blues collections ever released, and a must-have for every blues lover. Jacobs's skillful presentation of the blues harmonica as a lead instrument in a rocking blues band has never been equaled. This 2-CD set covers just over a decade, from "Juke," recorded in May 1952, through February 1963's "Dead Presidents." The unsung hero on these recordings, and on many Chess recordings, is drummer Fred Below. Often it's the interaction between Jacobs's organlike harmonica and Below's fancy drumming that makes a song work. This is certainly true of "Fast Boogie," a personal favorite because the color and texture of the harmonica sound—more gripping than any horn or stringed instrument—manages to resemble several over the course of a few minutes. There is so much heart and soul in this music, and it is magnificently performed (the word "virtuoso" is accurately applied to Jacobs here). "Lights Out" is stellar work, and many of the hits rise well above standard fare: "Blues with a Feeling" and "Tell Me Mama" are among many examples. Willie Dixon pushed hard to convince both Jacobs and Chess to record "My Babe," and it became a huge hit—the result of a perfect match between song and singer. With its dip into baritone, Jacobs's voice generates a handsome blend of soul and blues; on the right song, he's a pleasure. For better or worse, every strong vocal performance here is followed by a knockout harmonica demonstration, and it's easy to forget the vocals when faced with the energy and feel-good tone of the instrumental "Roller Coaster" (with Below again contibuting in a big way). Robert Lockwood, Bo Diddley, and Luther Tucker play guitar on that number, and Dixon plays bass. The 1958 number "Key to the Highway," a Jacobs song subsequently made famous by several rock bands, is slow and sophisticated; it's one of several tracks indicating change in direction and personal growth. The latter half of the 1950s brought more exploration ("As Long as I Have You") and occasional returns to firmer ground from past years. By 1963, Jacobs was blending jazz with R&B; it's a kick to hear his harmonica holding its own in a duet with a baritone saxophone played by Jarrett Gibson and an organ played by Billy Emerson.

LINK➤ *Walter Horton — Fine Cuts* **Blind Pig 70678**

Big Walter "Shakey" Horton was a central figure during the golden age of Chicago blues (he arrived around 1953 and became a top session man). This was his first album as a a leader; it was cut in 1977 with an enthusiastic, capable group of young sidemen.

Blues with a Feeling: Chess Collectibles, Vol. 3 — Chess 9357

This 2-CD set contains 40 tracks that are mostly marked "previously unreleased in the U.S." In some cases, Chess serves up an alternate take of a hit song, like a rocking "Juke" from 1952, or "Blues with a Feeling" from 1953. Generally, these cuts lack some of the precision of the released material, but the high quality of the music makes these versions worthy of investment. "Thunderbird" is one of several songs that were released as singles (this one in 1955); its style recalls train songs, although the pace is somewhat slower. "Flying Saucer" is one of the rougher songs; the effect of rock 'n' roll on Little Walter's music is evident in this 1956 single. The same group (Lockwood, Tucker, Dixon, and Below) smoothed out the approach just three months later with the instrumental "Teenage Beat." The rhythm straddles rock and blues. The alternate version of Jacobs's own "Temperature" is one of the best songs on this set; it's a slow, steamy Chicago blues with a sexy Little Walter vocal. Most of Jacobs's material is original, but his choice of classic blues often suits his voice and presentation. Jacobs does a fine job with Big Maceo's "Worried Life Blues" and with Arthur Crudup's "Mean Old Frisco," for example. The first 2-CD set is clearly the place to start with Little Walter, for all the right reasons: choice of material, accumulated hits, fine performances, and superior sound.

LINK➤ *William Clarke — Serious Intentions* **Alligator 4806**

L.A.-based Clarke is a powerful harmonica player whose songwriting updates the music heard in the 1950s in Chicago without sacrificing its essence. For better or worse, Clarke also sings and tends to be generous toward guitar players, leaving less time for his harp. His best, from 1992.

Robert Jr. Lockwood

When Lockwood was a teenager in Helena, AR, his mother married Robert Johnson. It was the mid-1930s; Lockwood was about 15 years old and a promising organist. His stepfather wasn't much older, and the two became friends. Johnson taught Lockwood the guitar, and they also did some road work together. When Johnson was murdered in 1938, Lockwood found his own way. He traveled to Memphis, St. Louis, and Chicago and became known as one of the first bluesmen competent on the electric guitar. In 1941 Lockwood cut some sides for Bluebird. Then it was back to Helena, where he worked with Sonny Boy Williamson at KFFA radio's *King Biscuit Time* program. By 1950 Lockwood finally settled in Chicago and enjoyed a reliable career as a session man. He moved to Cleveland a decade later, but maintained his Chicago presence on record and in clubs. He's also been a regular on the festival circuit.

Steady Rollin' Man **Delmark 630**

A very pleasant 1970 recording of Lockwood's standard repertoire benefits from a whistle-clean recording and several handsome instrumentals. Lockwood's long experience with this sort of material results in a refined growl and some reasonably hot guitar licks. He's best on "Western Horizon," a variation on Elmore James's "Dust My Broom." "Steady Groove" and "Lockwood's Boogie" showcase his guitar. The instrumentals are also the best place to enjoy the Aces, a top-notch backup trio as integral to the Chicago blues as Muddy Waters. (Comprising the threesome are guitarists Louis and Dave Myers and drummer Fred Below.) Most of this music is on the subdued side; it's well done, rarely boisterous. All told, there's very solid work here.

LINK➤ *Homesick James — Juanita* ***Evidence 26085***

A 1993 album by a steady rolling cousin of Elmore James. Homesick James is an especially good lyricist, a man who's skilled at telling stories through music. His lead guitar is smart and impactful; his voice reflects years of experience. Recorded when he was 83.

Plays Robert & Robert **Evidence 26020**

When Robert Johnson took up with Robert Lockwood's mother, he also inherited her son's admiration. Johnson, about four years older than Lockwood, taught him some songs. The two traveled together for a while before Lockwood pursued his own direction. This 1982 solo acoustic album shows him returning to his roots. About half of these songs are associated with Johnson, including Lockwood's favorite theme, "Steady Rolling Man." Others include "Sweet Home Chicago," "Walking Blues," and "Rambling on My Mind." Lockwood's 12-string guitar work is intriguing and very nicely recorded. A rough, sincere singing style maintains a balance between contemporary crowd pleasing and King Biscuit Flour authenticity. Recorded in Paris.

LINK➤ *Various Artists — Modern Chicago Blues* ***Testament 5008***

Although Lockwood isn't on this collection, you'll find many of his contemporaries here, including Johnny Young, Big Walter Horton, and Maxwell Street Jimmy. From 1962–66.

Born in NYC in 1946 to a musical family; MacLeod's grandfather recorded Gaelic music for RCA, and his mother played classical music. As a child, MacLeod stuttered; he took up music to overcome the problem. By junior high, MacLeod was working in local bands. A family move to St. Louis introduced him to the blues. MacLeod enlisted in the Navy, and stationed in Norfolk, VA, he gigged at coffeehouses in the mid-Atlantic states. He also backed up Emmylou Harris and Juice Newton, among others. Along the way, MacLeod learned about Charley Patton and Son House; after some conflict about his own background, he started writing blues based on his own experiences. Personal changes led to Boston's Berklee School of Music, L.A. studio work, touring with Mary MacGregor ("Torn Between Two Lovers"), and a return to blues in 1978. MacLeod began his recording career in the 1980s.

Come to Find — JVC XRCD 23

By merging acoustic blues traditions with a contemporary approach, MacLeod has done some reinventing of the blues. He's an expert at coaxing wonderful tones and statements from his guitar. The snap and crackle of MacLeod's guitar on "Since I Left St. Louis" satisfies the soul, and his "hey buddy" ways of personal storytelling makes an immediate connection with the listeners. MacLeod's early-morning voice comes close to rural Southern style on "Mystery Woman." The best song is arguably Willie Dixon's "Bring It On Home," one of two that features Charlie Musselwhite. Originally engineered to the highest possible standards (AudioQuest 1027), the music sounds even better on JVC's XRCD pressing. Very fine work.

LINK➤ *Gary Primich — Company Man* — ***Black Top 1136***

Another white guy who's taking the blues in new directions, Primich writes smart lyrics (a cynical view of being a "Company Man" for the title song, etc.). The frantic energy throughout this 1998 album is due, in part, to his electric harmonica. Country flavor, too.

You Can't Take My Blues — AudioQuest 1041

Loose and confident, this 1996 set starts out with a gently rocking "One Good Woman." Carey Bell's harmonica pierces through the song, driving the rhythm section to progressively higher, funkier levels. "Papa John" was supposed to be recorded on *Come to Find* as "Charlie James." Violinist Papa John Creach had agreed to join MacLeod on the number. When Creach died, the song became a tribute, with Heather Handy in his place. "Papa John" is paced by a unique skipping beat that MacLeod often favors. This happy party keeps rolling along with distinctively MacLeod tunes like "Bus with No Destination," and "You Can't Take My Blues." Stunning audio fidelity.

LINK➤ *Doug MacLeod — Unmarked Road* — ***AudioQuest 1046***

With a detailed approach to guitar recording, this fine-sounding 1997 effort sometimes recalls Leo Kottke. MacLeod boogies with "Necessary Clothes," and Jeff Turmes's bass on "Home Cooking" just plain feels good. Excellent MacLeod guitar on "Old Country Road."

Sam Maghett was born in Grenada, MS, in 1937. His family didn't have much money; young Maghett made his own guitar and taught himself to play by observing other musicians at local events. Boyhood friend Morris Holt, who became well known as Magic Slim, learned with him. Seeking better opportunities, Sam's family moved north to Chicago in 1950; there he started hanging out with blues musicians and eventually found work with Homesick James and others. Magic Sam put together his own band in the mid-1950s and recorded for Cobra; he was drafted in 1959. Sam deserted in 1961, did some jail time as a result, and then picked up again in Chicago's blues clubs. His reputation grew during the 1960s; late in the decade, he was entertaining San Francisco rock fans at the Fillmore. Sam also played at the 1969 Ann Arbor Blues Festival, where he was a sensation. He died later that year from heart problems.

1957–1966 — Paula 2

These seven Chicago sessions feature Magic Sam alongside other top musicians. The sound quality varies from adequate to good, but the music is fine. Sam does "All Your Love" with Little Brother Montgomery, and his guitar retains a bell-like tone on every stroke of his hand. Five tracks were recorded with a girl group in the background in the 1960s; because the mix is rather cluttered, 1960's "You Don't Have to Work" requires some imagination. The cleanest sound and the best rocking blues can be found on 1966's "Out of Bad Luck" and "She Belongs to Me," both performed with Otis Spann on piano and Mighty Joe Young on guitar.

LINK➤ *Magic Slim — Zoo Bar Collection, Vols. 1–6* **Wolf 120.301-306.**

Magic Slim and the Teardrops recorded some extraordinary blues in Nebraska's Zoo Bar, and this material is one of Wolf's best-selling discs. They're a Chicago blues band with a friendly, accessible feeling. Second guitar player John Primer deserves special mention.

The Late Great Magic Sam — Evidence 26070

It's hard to believe that this music was recorded in 1963 and 1964. The rhythm section, especially Johnny "Big Moose" Walker's organ, gives it away. Listening only to the guitar, to the way that Magic Sam leaves a tune's basic melody line and shoots off improvisational fireworks, this could be 1970 or later. In this era, the songs were shorter in length, but even two-and-a-half minutes of "All Your Love" suggest a pioneer seeking new frontiers. Sam's also quite good on "Baby, You Torture My Soul," an organ-based soul song. Here and on "Sometimes," Magic Sam presages his "want to boogie" shouts within a more formal, conservative structure. Very good work.

LINK➤ *Various Artists — A Tribute to Magic Sam* **Evidence 26086**

Magic Slim was a childhood friend who played with Magic Sam, and followed his buddy north to Chicago. Eddie Shaw was also close to Sam, and they recorded together. Bassist J.W. Williams has no direct connection. All wholeheartedly contribute here.

West Side Soul **Delmark 615**

Recorded in 1967, this is an essential look at maturing Chicago blues. Maghett starts "That's All I Need" with a soulful vocal and an admirable tone and delicacy on his electric guitar. The pace slows for the low-down guitar and dejected vocal of "I Need You So Bad," then a big dose of energy kicks in for "I Feel So Good (I Want to Boogie)." The essence of this music—and the reason why it still attracts attention three decades after it was recorded—becomes clear as Magic Sam sings out the word "boogie," stops and starts his talking blues, and opens full up for his guitar breaks.

LINK➤ *Eddie C. Campbell — King of the Jungle* ***Rooster Blues 2602***

Ignore the stupid cover photo (Campbell as a blues-playing caveman). Campbell digs way down for darkly expressive electric Chicago blues. Smart selection of Chicago blues, topnotch accompaniment from Carey, Lurie Bell, Clifton James, and others. From 1977. Superb.

Black Magic **Delmark 620**

Recorded about a year later, in 1968, this album adds some R&B feeling to an already viable Chicago sound. Eddie Shaw's tenor sax makes all the difference, as his solo on the first track, "I Just Want a Little Bit," proves after only an instant's listening. The mix is a bit thicker on "What Have I Done Wrong?" and the emphasis is shifting from Magic Sam as a solo guitarist with a band to a full-scale ensemble approach. His singing is key, especially on "Easy, Baby," one of his best songs. Taking a page from Freddie King's book, Sam serves up a peppy guitar solo on "San-Ho-Zay."

LINK➤ *Li'l Ed & the Blues Imperials — Roughhousin'* ***Alligator 4749***

With Ed Williams's slide guitar at the center, this Chicago crew was a coarse-sounding organization that could rock the house. This 1986 release was recorded in a single night; it includes a grinding version of "Mean Old Frisco."

Magic Sam Live **Delmark 845**

Some of the first nine tracks were recorded live at Chicago's Alex Club in 1963 with a band that included Eddie Shaw on tenor sax and Tyrone Carter on electric piano. Others from this group are from 1964, with Shaw and A.C. Reed on tenor sax. Eight more songs were recorded at the Ann Arbor Blues Festival in August 1969 with just Bruce Barlow on bass and Sam Lay on drums. The Alex material won't win any audiophile awards, but Magic Sam's long, inventive guitar solos are about five years ahead of their time. It's thrilling to hear his added sophistication on 1969's "Strange Things Happening" and the overwhelming encore to "Looking Good." Recommended.

LINK➤ *Various Artists — Sweet Home Chicago* ***Delmark 618***

Magic Sam's band featured Eddie Shaw for this 1966 session; Luther Allison cut his tracks in 1967, and so did harmonica wizard Louis Myers. Magic Slim played guitar, and Lucky Lopez finished the set. A fine sampling of Chicago in the mid-1960s.

Henry St. Claire Fredericks was born in NYC in 1942, but was raised in Springfield, MA. His mother sang gospel and his father arranged jazz. In the early 1960s, when Fredericks attended UMass, he became fascinated with a wide range of African-American music, and began singing country blues and other roots music in Boston folk clubs. He moved to L.A. in 1965 and found a kindred spirit in Ry Cooder, with whom he formed the short-lived Rising Sons band. By recreating Southern acoustic blues for educated white audiences, Taj Mahal developed a fan base. (The stage name came to him in a dream.) An educated, curious, creative man, Taj Mahal has become known as a music historian and a very eclectic musician. His film work includes *Sounder*; he also wrote the music for the Broadway show *Mule Bone*, which was based on a play by Langston Hughes and Zora Neale Hurston. Taj Mahal lives in Hawaii.

Giant Step/De Ole Folks at Home **Columbia CGK 18**

Two albums that were popular on underground radio stations in 1969 and the early 1970s retain some of that Fillmore-hip flavor. The songs on Giant Step are performed by an electric band, but Mahal keeps things authentic and straightforward on "Good Morning, Little School Girl." Occasionally, Mahal and company sound like faux Burrito Brothers ("Six Days on the Road"). They settle into a light Chicago blues groove, complete with Taj Mahal's harmonica on "Bacon Fat," and a bluesy style is applied to "Keep Your Hands Off Her." On the one hand, this is an honest tribute—on the other, it's a bunch of musicians not doing the job as well as their influences. *De Ole Folks at Home* is entirely different. It starts with Taj Mahal singing unaccompanied, clearly relishing the chance to play the part of a Southern laborer on "Linin' Track." He's credibly rough and nasal on "Candy Man," a blues standard, and on "Stagger Lee." Mahal's got the right instrument—a National Steel–bodied Acoustic Guitar—but the mix is too loud, and it draws undue attention to a musician whose work hangs a notch lower than Reverend Gary Davis and other heroes. Despite the obvious weaknesses, this is honest music by a man who clearly adores the likes of "Fishin' Blues" and "Cluck Old Hen"; Mahal performs the songs with an earnest desire to turn his audience on to this music. Besides, it's a pleasure to hear someone who so totally enjoys his work.

LINK➤ *Alvin Youngblood Hart — Big Mama's Door* ***OKeh/550 Music 67593***

With some background help from Taj Mahal, Hart recreates the magic and majesty of 1920s and 1930s blues. His repertoire includes Charlie Patton ("Pony Blues"), and Blind Willie McTell ("Hillbilly Willie Blues"), but most of the work is original. Highly recommended.

World Music — Columbia 52755

One of the best things about Taj Mahal is his willingness to explore areas beyond the strict boundary of blues. Here he explores a world of differences, working with both original material and compositions by other musicians. Mahal begins with "When I Feel the Sea Beneath My Soul," which nicely sets the wide-ranging mood. He next sings of "My Ancestors" and then settles into the reality of Bob Marley's "Slave Driver." African memories return during a brief "Kalimba" interlude. In time, Mahal finds himself with "Cajun Waltz" and "Brown Eyed Handsome Man" before eventually returning to a reprise of "When I Feel the Sea Beneath My Soul." An intelligently conceived, well-executed album from 1993.

LINK➤ *Var. Artists — Preachin' the Gospel: Holy Blues* — ***Legacy 46779***

Although they're quite distinct from each other in today's carefully categorized music industry, gospel and blues grew up together as brother and sister. This is why you'll find Blind Willie Johnson and Joshua White alongside Washington Phillips, Arizona Dranes, and Reverend John Blakey on this wonderful collection.

Taj's Blues — Columbia 52465

This appealing collection of blues songs starts out with three tracks with Ry Cooder from the Rising Sons days in 1967. There's a decent version of "Stateboro Blues," and the band's at its energetic best on Sleepy John Estes's "Everybody's Got to Change Sometimes" (Cooder is astonishing on this piece). Taj Mahal's work on brass dobro on Mississippi John Hurt's "Frankie & Albert" is delightful, as are his vocal and the subdued choruses from the Pointer Sisters. There's a friendly, comfortable, familiar air to 1972's medley from the film *Sounder*. Trying to copy Elmore James's work on "Dust My Broom" was a tactical error, though. Still, Mahal's admiration comes through.

LINK➤ *Taj Mahal — In Progress & In Motion* — ***Columbia/Legacy 64919***

Long-awaited 3-CD set covers Taj Mahal's entire career. Highlights include "Take a Giant Step" and "Corinne, Corrina," from his Rising Sons era (with Ry Cooder); several 1968 cuts with the Rolling Stones; five early 1970s tracks with the Pointer Sisters; plus a very healthy sampling of his work for Columbia (and some tracks from other labels.)

Señor Blues — Private Music 82151

This beautifully recorded 1997 CD was nominated for several Grammy Awards. Taj masterfully synthesizes so many musical styles. "Queen Bee" is somewhere between gentle reggae and electric blues. "Think" is probably R&B—it's got the requisite sax solo, the background singers, and the unorthodox dance beat—but Mahal's doing something more complex here, too. "Sophisticated Mama" is an old Washboard Sam tune, performed in an old-time way with a taste of boogie-woogie gone electric. "Mr. Pitiful" is straight out of Memphis's Stax school. And "Señor Blues" is a Horace Silver jazz tune with two horns harmonizing and Taj's brief jazz vocal interlude.

LINK➤ *Radio Kings — Money Road* — ***Bullseye Blues 9601***

Imagining themselves in a time and place long gone, these guys love all kinds of blues. They are: Brian Templeton (harmonica, vocals), Michael Dinallo (guitars), and Bob Christina (percussion). All original, with very profound influences.

Mayall's father collected U.S. jazz and blues records. In 1955, young Mayall formed a blues band in his native Manchester, England; he was about 21 years old. He moved to London in the early 1960s and formed the Bluesbreakers in 1963. (The original band included bassist John McVie.) The group made a live album for Decca in 1964 that went nowhere. Mayall heard Eric Clapton on a Yardbirds single and invited him to join the band. Clapton's impact was immediate and profound. He stayed for a year and was ultimately replaced by Peter Green (who subsequently left with McVie and drummer Mick Fleetwood to start a new blues band, Fleetwood Mac). Mayall kept moving, often changing personnel. He toured the U.S., became well known via FM progressive radio in the early 1970s, and moved to the U.S. a short time later. Although his stardom vanished, Mayall periodically toured and recorded during the 1980s and 1990s.

Blues Breakers — **Mobile Fidelity 616**

This is the quintessential British blues album. The unbeatable band features Mayall on lead vocals, keyboards, and harmonica. Eric Clapton plays guitar and sings lead on "Ramblin' on My Mind." John McVie is the bass player, and Hughie Flint plays drums on most of the tracks. John Almond and Alan Skidmore also contribute saxophone on some tracks. The band starts with some Chicago blues: "All Your Love," but it's Clapton's guitar solo throughout Freddy King's "Hideaway" that transformed him into a guitar deity. Mayall's own "Little Girl" is one of his best, and his opening harp solo on "Another Man" is impressive. The up-tempo "Parchman Farm," with Mayall's sharp jabs of inflamed harmonica, was a concert favorite. Lots more great stuff.

LINK➤ *Various Artists — Harmonica Blues* — ***Yazoo 1053***

Quintessential harmonica blues from the 1920s and 1930s. An R. Crumb cover, plus performances by Jazz Gillum ("I Want You by My Side," with Big Bill Broonzy on guitar), Freeman Stowers ("Railroad Blues"), and other unsung heroes.

The Turning Point — **Polydor 823-305**

A pleasant, moody album culled from a 1969 Fillmore East performance, its soft-edged sound is promoted by the lack of drums, and the presence of Jon Mark (who plays acoustic finger-style guitar) and Johnny Almond (tenor and alto saxophones, flutes). The difference between this music and the Blues Breakers style (just five years before) is stunning; here, Mayall was opening the door to 1970s progressive music. There's a melancholy air throughout, articulated most successfully in the slightly jazzy "Thoughts About Roxanne." In contrast, "Room to Move" is a harmonica shuffle whose sure, quick pace made it one of Mayall's more memorable efforts from this period; Almond's vocal percussion solo is also wonderful.

LINK➤ *Mark-Almond Band — The Best of Mark-Almond* — ***Rhino 70571***

Two tracks may shake loose from memories of early 1970s progressive radio: the quiet-voiced urban portrait called "The City," and the lazy, not-quite-jazz, not-quite-blues "One Way Sunday." Warm and comfortable, the band's music was quite special in its time.

London Blues: 1964–1969 **Deram 844302**

This 2-CD set tells much of the story of British blues. It begins with a handful of bar blues, including Mayall's well-crafted harmonica solo on "Blues City Shakedown" from February 1965. The world changes with Clapton's psychedelic solos (nicely matched by Mayall's organ) on "I'm Your Witchdoctor" and "Telephone Blues"; both were defining moments in 1960s blues-rock, and produced with a big, complex sound by Jimmy Page. Next come four tracks from the essential *Bluesbreakers* album. Peter Green's work on "Looking Back" is terrific and gains authority as the band moves from 1966's catchy melodies to the very dark and serious music of one of Mayall's finest albums, *A Hard Road* (Deram 820-474). Throughout 1966, the horn section anchored by John Almond is a treat. But the real magic of this work is in the stinging, wounded, searching, room-shaking guitar of Mayall's superb creative partner, Green. The two are at their pure bluesy best on a 1967 single version of Otis Rush's "Double Trouble." By 1967's album *The Blues Alone* (Mobile Fidelity 662), Mayall's solos on vocals, harmonica, and keyboards showed how completely he had absorbed the U.S. idiom and made it his own. "Sonny Boy Blow" is a great blues number from this album. Although *Crusade* (London 820-537, also from 1967) employs a full band, Mayall is now the central figure. He proves himself to be a world-class blues singer on "The Death of J.B. Lenoir." By now, Mick Taylor (later of the Rolling Stones) is playing lead guitar, but Chris Mercer's tenor sax is bigger news. This group evolves into an even stronger unit for spring 1968's *Bare Wires* (Deram 820-538) and now includes the formidable saxman Dick Heckstall-Smith beside Mercer. These horns wail on "She's Too Young," centered by one of Mayall's best all-time drummers, Jon Hiseman. The personnel changes again for autumn 1968's *Blues From Laurel Canyon* (Deram 820-539). The album is a kind of travelogue from Mayall's first U.S. trip; it has plenty of style and no shortage of pretense (think: reverb, room with lots of candles, draped cloths, and black light). All told, this is one amazing trip because of the music itself—it's documentary proof of Mayall's underrated talents, and the fertile starting point for Cream, Led Zeppelin, and hundreds of lesser-known bands who were smart enough to simply copy what they heard here.

LINK➤ *Peter Green — Green & Guitar: 1977–1981* ***Music Club 50001***

Along with bassist John McVie and drummer Mick Fleetwood, Green founded Fleetwood Mac (the three had met in Mayall's band). Green left in 1970 after battling drug problems, and Fleetwood Mac's sound moved toward pop. Green remained true to the blues, however, as his solo work here demonstrates.

Room to Move: 1969–1974 **Polydor 517291**

The story continues with a July 1969 Fillmore East performance released as *The Turning Point* (Deram 823-305). It's a wonderful live show, a celebration that emphasizes musicality and instrumental virtuosity. Mayall's harmonica and Johnny Almond's flutes are standouts (their mouth percussion on "Room to Move" is also fun). By 1970's *Empty Rooms* (PolyGram 527-457), even the simplest songs, such as "Don't Waste My Time," were a delight; style, however, was overtaking substance. A new band featuring violinist Sugarcane Harris brought new energy to summer 1970's *USA Union*, but even autumn 1970's reunion (with Clapton, Taylor, and others) and many tries at contemporary lyrics couldn't correct the course. Still, the story does not end here. In 1972, Mayall was one of the best-known names on the blues scene, and he easily migrated to *Jazz-Blues Fusion* (a style, and also the title of an autumn 1971 album, PolyGram 527-460). With a superb team that included the excellent Freddy Robinson on guitar, respected jazz player Blue Mitchell on trumpet, and Clifford Solomon on saxophones, Mayall very effectively explored the space where the two related genres meet. By 1972's *Moving On*, the band was bigger, and the message was again pure blues; the music here is similar to Mayall's work around 1967, but bigger and more majestic ("Worried Mind" and "Red Sky" are fine examples). Most of the thrill is gone by 1973's *Ten Years Are Gone*; the funk and lack of clear direction on 1974's *Brand New Band* is somewhat embarrassing.

LINK➤ *Jack Bruce — Willpower: A Twenty-Year Retrospective* ***Atco 837-806***

Bassist and keyboard player Jack Bruce started his career in 1962 with Alexis Korner, and he's maintained a forward-thinking balance of jazz and blues for decades (stopping along the way to reinvent blues-rock with Cream in the late 1960s). A superb musician, Bruce is still quite underrated.

Mighty Sam McClain

McClain's had enough adventures in his 55 years for several lifetimes. He was born in 1943 in Monroe, LA. McClain was raised by a violent stepfather and left home after eighth grade. He hooked up with Little Melvin Underwood, who ran a fraudulent revue featuring a phony Chubby Checker. When the law caught up with Underwood, McLain found work with the Dothan (Alabama) Quartet. He next fronted a Pensacola bar band, where he drank most of his salary. A hit recording of Patsy Cline's "Sweet Dreams" led to an Apollo Theater appearance; two years later, McClain was making his money by selling marijuana. McLain narrowly escaped a major bust; he ended up destitute in Nashville. There, he worked at a pancake restaurant and sold his blood to raise money. McClain ended up on the streets, but then his life changed for the better. He recorded several albums for AudioQuest and toured Japan.

Give It Up to Love — JVC XRCD 12

In the style of Brook Benton and Otis Redding, McClain gathers up his soul and his humanity for the proud soul ballad, "Give It Up to Love," a song he wrote himself. Carlene Carter's "Too Proud" comes next, with Bruce Katz's organ and Kevin Barry's guitar digging deeper into the same vein, this time with a blues song grown from country roots. The delicate "Here I Go Falling in Love Again" works because McClain sings from his heart, thinking of his ex-wife Laura. "Lonesome Road" reflects on time spent in Nashville; while guitarist Barry lays down an acoustic solo, McClain's intensity finds relaxed hope. From 1993. From the heart.

LINK➤ *Mem Shannon — A Cab Driver's Blues* — ***Hannibal (Rykodisc) 1387***

Shannon's day job as a New Orleans cabbie provided the title. His biographical "Play the Guitar Son" tells the story of his father's gift of a guitar and hope for a better life for his son. Shannon's a fine guitarist and a storyteller with wry view of contemporary life.

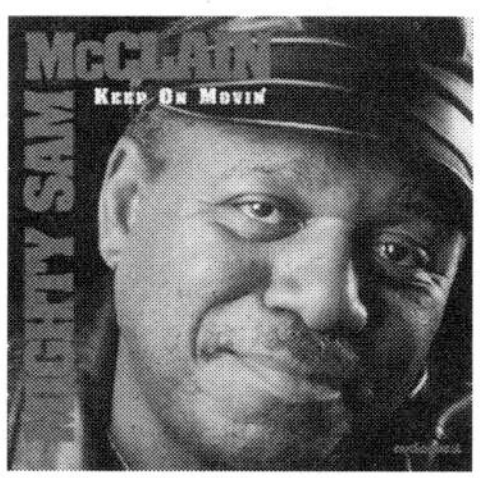

Keep on Movin' — AudioQuest 1031

Once again, McClain opens the album with an instant classic. "Can You Stand the Test of Love" is a McClain original, hardcore soul with four Memphis-style horns, and a sincere vocal performance evoking Sam Cooke. Al Green is looming in the background, too; McClain acknowledges the influence by singing his "Lord Will Find a Way." Kevin Barry's creativity complements McClain's soul, and once again, the singer wears his life's scars for all to see: that's "A Soul That's Been Abused." "I'm So Lonely," by McClain and Barry, is another great sad song. Incidentally, AudioQuest is an audiophile record company; the engineering is great.

LINK➤ *Terry Evans — Puttin' It Down* — ***AudioQuest 1038***

Evans is a McClain label mate with an intense approach to R&B. He's also an acoustic guitar player, but the range of talented sidemen makes his own instrument hard to find. Ry Cooder's here, so is bassist Jorge Calderon, and drummer Jim Keltner. Also available as JVC XRCD 14.

Mississippi Fred McDowell

For most of his life, Fred McDowell played his acoustic country blues for tips at picnics, barbecues, juke joints, parties, and on the streets of tiny Como, MS, where he lived from the 1930s until his death in 1972. McDowell was born in 1904 in Roswell, TN, and became a traveling musician (in other words, a hobo who played music); he worked odd jobs in Memphis, then married and settled in Como. When folklorist Alan Lomax found him in 1959, McDowell made his first recording, but not much changed for him until the mid-1960s, when Arhoolie Records released two LPs. This led to appearances at the Newport Folk Festival and dates at colleges and coffee houses. By the late 1960s, McDowell appeared with the Rolling Stones, who bought him a silver lamé suit and recorded one of his songs. But by 1971, stomach cancer was advancing. McDowell died a year later and was buried in his silver suit.

You Gotta Move — Arhoolie 304

Arhoolie producer Chris Strachwitz recorded most of these songs in February 1964 at McDowell's home near Como, MS. This is pure country blues, sung as it was 50 years before, largely unaffected by the fickle recording industry. McDowell's best on the driving "Shake 'Em on Down," with its jangling guitar effects, but slower numbers like "Louise" and "That's Alright" are no less memorable. Repeated listenings reveal a melodic gift—"Kokomo Blues" is one of several good examples. Decades of experience resonate in the depths of "Fred's Worried Life Blues." The Rolling Stones covered McDowell's "Gotta Move" on *Sticky Fingers*; the version here was recorded by McDowell in Berkeley, CA, in 1965. Quintessential country blues.

LINK➤ *Lonnie Pitchford — All Around Man* — ***Rooster Blues 2629***

Pitchford was born in 1955, but his youthful poverty, his one-string first instrument, and his rich country blues all mimic a life of 30 years earlier. He's a wonderful songwriter and performer, he's also an extraordinary guitar player. Songs by Bo Carter, Donny Hathaway, Elmore James, and Bobby Hebb.

Good Morning Little School Girl — Arhoolie 424

More from the February 1964 session with more emphasis on McDowell's remarkable slide guitar and wonderful vocals. "Fred's Rambling Blues" is a standout; McDowell reaches out with passion and supports himself magnificently, providing rhythm and dazzle on the slide guitar. Half of this album is filled with "church songs" (some from 1965)—McDowell regularly accompanied his wife, Annie Mae, on songs like "Amazing Grace," and "Get Right Church." Their duets are complex—three voices (Annie Mae, Fred, and Fred's guitar) intertwined without much harmony, but with considerable rough appeal in their rhythm and integrity. The version of "You Gotta Move" is terrific. Stellar slide work on "I'm So Glad, Got Good Religion."

LINK➤ *Fred & Annie Mae McDowell—My Home Is in the Delta Testament 5019*
Some of these songs are repeated on the above Arhoolie album, but many are not. "Waiting for My Baby" is vintage McDowell—a striking guitar hook upright against a rambling storyteller's vocal. Wife Annie Mae McDowell sings along on the spirituals.

Long Way from Home **OBC 535**

On the plus side, this 1966 UCLA session shows off McDowell's slide guitar in full-scale stereo and captures nuances unavailable on the Arhoolie sessions. On the minus side, McDowell's repertoire now includes warhorses like "John Henry," "Milk Cow Blues," and "The Train I Ride." Then again, the version of "John Henry" is dominated by some of McDowell's flashiest guitar pyrotechnics; it's a real crowd pleaser. McDowell is best on original work like "Gavel Road Blues"—it's here that the combination of voice and guitar becomes mesmerizing—but even "Big Fat Mama" maintains the session's somewhat mechanical feel. And while the mechanics are flawless, the humanity of the Arhoolie sessions wins out.

LINK➤ *Var. Artists — Blues Masters, Vol. 15: Slide Guitar Classics Rhino 71126*
McDowell doesn't make the cut, but there's plenty here to amuse: Johnny Shines on "Dynaflow Blues," Homesick James on "Homesick's Shuffle," even the Allmans' "Statesboro Blues," and a Ry Cooder cut, "All Shook Up."

I Do Not Play No Rock 'n Roll **Capitol 33919**

For the first two minutes of this delightful 2-CD set, McDowell explains how he came to play the bottleneck (slide) guitar. He then launches into a fast, tight, and flashy version of "Baby Please Don't Go," making the most of his three-piece band (which includes bassist Jerry Puckett and drummer Dulin Lancaster). McDowell follows with a rollicking "Good Morning, Little School Girl" and delivers some of his tastiest bottleneck work—and that's just a glimpse of things to come. At age 65, McDowell gives rock guitarists plenty to think about, and copy, on "That's Alright Baby," often sounding as if he's riffing on electric guitar. "Red Cross Store" makes use of a similar stop-and-start rhythm. These same techniques were used by blues-rock bands in the early 1970s; the Rolling Stones were among the many bands that were profoundly turned-on by McDowell's work. McDowell comes back to talk awhile, explaining the similarity between the blues and the "reel." His lesson on how the blues work leads into an improvisation called "Everybody's Down on Me." Next is "61 Highway," standard McDowell material, perfectly played. Spirituals, such as "Glory Hallelujah," whose framework is used to create an original work, follow. Eli Green was a frequent partner (he sings two songs on the first Arhoolie CD); Green taught McDowell one of this album's most exciting songs, "Write Me a Few of Your Lines." Fast-changing tempos make it a thriller. There's a whole lot more from these 1969 Capitol and Just Sunshine sessions, including special packaging and excellent liner notes. It's terrific—but listen to the Arhoolie CDs first.

LINK➤ *Elvis Presley — The Sun Sessions RCA 6414*
Elvis built a solid base with blues, then used it as a platform to reach stardom. Here's proof that Elvis really is connected to the blues in a substantial way: his (quite impressive) versions of "Milkcow Boogie Blues," "That's All Right (Mama)," "Mystery Train," and others.

Walter McGhee came from Knoxville, TN. As a boy, he became a good guitar player, and after about a decade's schooling, he hit the road in the later 1920s. McGhee earned money by playing in traveling shows and by singing gospel music. By the 1930s, McGhee had made a name for himself in Durham, NC; it was one of many area cities in which he made money from the streets. In the shadow of local favorite Blind Boy Fuller, McGhee did some recording; when Fuller died, McGhee took his place (and, according to some accounts, his name as well). Then McGhee moved to NYC and teamed up with harmonica player Sonny Terry, whom he knew from Durham. The two became deeply involved in the folk music community, frequently appearing at festivals and fund-raisers, as well as performing on the college circuit and on the theatical stage. McGhee retired in the 1980s, following the death of his partner.

The Complete Brownie McGhee — Columbia 52933

Calling this 2-CD set "complete" is misleading; these are McGhee's complete Okeh and Columbia recordings from 1940 and 1941. So this is McGhee as a solo performer in the days before his name was permanently attached to Sonny Terry. In 1940, McGhee cut some of his first sides in Chicago with two friends from North Carolina. Oh Red (a.k.a. George Washington) was a talented washboard player; he provides tasteful accompaniment on "Me and My Dog Blues." Jordan Webb joins in on harmonica on several songs, including the peppy "Step It and Go." Even on these early recordings, McGhee possesses a friendly, pleasant style; it's easy to understand why he became so popular with general audiences. McGhee's guitar work shines on "Death of Blind Boy Fuller," which is followed by more than a dozen recordings McGhee cut under the name Blind Boy Fuller #2. In May 1941, McGhee seemed to have a grand old time singing "Ain't No Tellin'" with a kitschy washboard man, Washboard Slim (Robert Young, a one-man sound effects department who becomes ridiculously noisy on "Key to the Highway 70"). In May 1941, McGhee cut a handful of gospel tunes with Webb and Washboard Slim under the name Brother George and His Sanctified Singers. The small group sound is the same, but McGhee's clearly singing gospel, not blues. By October, Sonny Terry's in place for "Workingman's Blues" and other songs. Disregarding a few clunkers, this is a very fine compilation.

LINK➤ *CeDell Davis — Feel Like Doin' Something Wrong* — ***Fat Possum 1004***

Blues journalist and aficionado Robert Palmer produced this album for Davis (born 1927 in Helena, AR), who plays his own version of country blues with a butter knife on his slide guitar. A gifted improviser, Davis plays music that's complicated, iconoclastic, and may require some patience.

The Folkways Years, 1945–1959

Smithsonian Folkways 40034

With this compilation of 6 Folkways albums, McGhee takes his rightful place as one of the finest vocalists in blues history. Fortunately, the sound quality of these recordings is generally very good, so McGhee can be heard in his glory. A reworking of "Red River Blues," known as "Rising Sun," is one of the best songs on this record; it's one of the few here performed with Sonny Terry. "Careless Love" was a pop song that made its way into many blues repertoires, and McGhee's vocal is particularly sweet and credible. McGhee was a keen collector of songs, and as a result, his repertoire was quite varied. "Pawnshop Blues" is a sparse reworking of a 1940 Blind Boy Fuller song; "Cholly's Blues" is an old song from the Blind Lemon Jefferson era. McGhee sings both call and response on "Long Gone," a chase tune about a convict escaping from prison and racing into freedom. The repeating rhythm pattern and McGhee's conspiratory tone focuses audience attention on the action; this style of performance is also quite old (and relatively rare on record). "Fore Day Creep" is about sneaking some sex before the break of day, then leaving before getting caught; once again, the tone is secretive. The religious material also plays well: McGhee's a spirited believer spreading the word on "I'm Gonna Tell God How You Treat Me." Not only is all of this solid work, it's also an interesting wide-angle view of McGhee's musical training and inclinations.

LINK➤ *"Philadelphia" Jerry Ricks — Deep in the Well* **_Rooster Blues 2636_**
Ricks excels on acoustic guitar, demonstrating skills earned while working with Brownie McGhee, Miles Davis, John Coltrane, Mississippi John Hurt, and others. A Philadelphia family man, he didn't tour, and he didn't get famous. Superb vocals, mostly original tunes.

Blues historians aren't certain of the year McTell was born (around 1900), but they're fairly certain that his family name was either McTear or McTier (both names are common around Thomson, GA, a cotton-growing area about 30 miles west of Augusta). McTell was nearly blind from birth; by age 20, he was traveling with carnivals and medicine shows. McTell's mother taught him to play guitar, and he picked up a wonderful sense of showmanship in his travels. McTell frequently performed with friends Curley Russell and Buddy Moss, mostly in the Atlanta area. By the late 1920s, McTell was recording regularly for several labels under assumed names, but the Great Depression ended this phase of his recording career. Mostly he played for tips on Atlanta's Decatur Street. Alan Lomax recorded McTell's work in 1940 for the Library of Congress. After World War II, McTell recorded for a then-new Atlantic Records, but with little success. He continued performing on Atlanta's streets and died in 1959.

The Definitive Blind Willie McTell Columbia 53234

The first thing you notice is the guitar—McTell is so facile that the 12-string often sounds like a pair of instruments. The next is a slightly nasal voice with easy musicality, a storyteller whose every word is interesting. On "Travelin' Blues," which McTell recorded for Columbia in 1929 as Blind Sammie, McTell talks some, punctuates with his guitar, maybe slides a few notes, calls-and-responds with voice and guitar, then reenters with a fragment of melody. Many of the riffs will sound familiar—they've been copied for decades (McTell perfected but probably didn't originate them). "Come On Around to My House Mama" will seem instantly familiar, even if its lyrics are not. McTell recorded these sides for Columbia and Okeh (a label Columbia acquired when McTell was recording under different names for both). McTell's repertoire included many rags, but none as well known as "Georgia Rag," delivered here with panache. On some songs McTell's guitar accompanies the more substantial (but less facile) voice of Curley Weaver. On others he duets with a somewhat shrill Ruth Mary Willis (who sang as Mary Willis or Ruth Day). By far the most satisfying combination is McTell accompanying himself on guitar on songs like "My Baby's Gone"; his voice takes on a hapless, sad quality that barely hides the tears. Weaver provides a second guitar on the bleak "Death Room Blues," and on the hopeful "Lord, Send Me an Angel." These sides were among about two dozen released on Vocalion. This 2-CD collection duplicates much of the Yazoo set, but lacks McTell's now-famous "Statesboro Blues."

LINK➤ *Blind Willie McTell — 1927–1933: The Early Years* *Yazoo 1005*

This single CD duplicates the best work on the Columbia set, but adds "Statesboro Blues," later an Allman Brothers anthem ("Wake up mama, turn your light down low . . . "). McTell grew up in Statesboro, GA. "Writing Paper Blues," a slow and dreamy blues from 1927, offers a textbook lesson in blues guitar accompaniment.

Atlanta Twelve-String — Atlantic 82366

Recorded in Atlanta for Atlantic Records in 1949, this record was quickly forgotten, and didn't perform much better in an early 1970s re-release. It's hard to understand why. "Kill It Kid" shows off some of McTell's flashiest guitar work; "Razor Ball" is another of his classics, as is the version of "Broke Down Engine Blues." The sound quality is fine, McTell's voice is confident, and the guitar work is spectacular. McTell is clearly enjoying himself, and the experience resonates through "Pinetop's Boogie Woogie," with very clever guitar work. "Last Time Blues" is better still. "Motherless Children Have a Hard Time" is one of several religious songs that complete a delightful album.

LINK➤ *Various Artists — Atlantic Blues: Guitar* — ***Atlantic 81695***

A nearly random collection of blues heroes whose records were released at one time or another by Atlantic Records. Because Atlantic's staff possessed extraordinary taste, this collection is quite wonderful. Performers include Tina Turner, John Lee Hooker, Big Joe Turner, Amos Milburn, T-Bone Walker, and McTell.

Pig 'n Whistle Red — Biograph 126

This 1950 session is energetic and fun—McTell and frequent partner Curley Weaver (also on guitar and vocals) run through popular and religious favorites. McTell is in excellent voice, and the duo's country harmonies are engaging. The formula works best on "You Can't Get Stuff No More," a good example of "hokum"—slightly cornball, often fast-paced songs akin to vaudeville songs. "Honey, It Must Be Love" and "Pal of Mine" are among several pop songs. They're not at all bluesy, but the fancy guitar work often earned a few coins tossed into a hat. The original Pig 'n Whistle Red, by the way, was a barbeque stand where McTell and Russell played for tips.

LINK➤ *Curley Weaver — Georgia Guitar Wizard (1928–1935)* — ***Story of Blues 3530***

Don't let the nondescript album art dissuade you. This is a world-class blues album by arguably the finest six-string guitar player in blues history. Weaver was a frequent partner for McTell, Barbecue Bob, and Buddy Moss—not as famous, but likely the superior talent.

Last Session — OBC 517

McTell missed the 1960s blues revival by several years, but this 1956 recording seems a part of that story. When he's singing "Baby, It Must Be Love," his experience shows. McTell's (spoken word) story behind "The Dyin' Crapshooter's Blues," long a part of his songbook, makes sense of a song beautifully performed. The version of "Kill It Kid" (about finishing a bottle of liquor) is a powerful rouser; it too, is preceded by a story. The vocals are consistently clear, and full of personality and showbiz spin. Some say McTell's voice is a little slurred here, perhaps the result of alcohol or ill health, but the criticism is mostly unfounded.

LINK➤ *Blind Willie McTell — Complete Library of Congress Recordings (1940)* — ***Document 6001***

McTell was at the center of the Atlanta blues community, and here he talks about his experiences as a recording artist, as well as about old songs and blues history. McTell also performs a wide range of music, from "Amazing Grace" to "Murderer's Home Blues."

Memphis Minnie was a longtime fixture on the Chicago blues scene, a key figure in the transition from country to city blues. Minnie was born Lizzie Douglas in the southern Louisiana town of Algiers in 1897, and raised in Wall, MS. Lizzie's family called her "Kid," and she started performing as Kid Douglas, both in nearby Memphis and with touring shows and circuses (including Ringling Brothers, throughout the South). She and husband Joe McCoy (Kansas Joe) settled in Memphis, where they were discovered by a Columbia talent scout in 1929. The couple recorded over 50 sides before the Depression effectively shut down the record business. The two moved to Chicago and became part of the local blues scene in 1930. Minnie continued working in Chicago until the mid-1950s, when poor health forced her to retire. Minnie spent her later years in a Memphis nursing home and died of a stroke in 1973.

Hoodoo Lady (1933–1937) — Columbia 46775

Program your CD player to run these tracks in chronological order to hear the development of a blues master. Start with "Ain't No Use Tryin' to Tell on Me (I Know Something on You)," a 1933 solo piece peppered with spite. Next, move on to one of the 1936 songs, "If You See My Rooster," produced with a complement of string bass, piano, and simple percussion (as well as Minnie's controlled rooster impressions). "Hoodoo Lady" is among Minnie's best-known songs; the 1936 version here captures some voodoo magic, a country blues theme. Overall, Memphis Minnie's vocals, guitar playing, style, and presence make this album essential for every blues library.

LINK➤ *Frank Stokes — The Memphis Blues* — ***Yazoo 1008***

One of the more essential Yazoo CDs, this is actually a collection of songs by various Memphis musicians from the 1920s and early 1930s that includes a Memphis Minnie performance, plus songs from Stokes, Furry Lewis, Will Weldon, and others.

Early Rhythm & Blues — Biograph 124

Only 5 of the 16 songs on this CD were made by Memphis Minnie, and these feature her on electric guitar with Sunnyland Slim on piano and unidentified musicians playing bass and drums. The other tracks—by Jimmy Rogers, St. Louis Jimmy, Little Brother Montgomery, Pee Wee Hughes, and Sunnyland Slim—are all very good and provide a meaningful context for Minnie's seminal work (her influence on the young Muddy Waters is quite evident here). Two takes of Big Bill Broonzy's "Night Watchman Blues" are the key tracks; they feature a very muscular electric guitar, a power-packed rhythm section, and a raw sexual vocal from Minnie. Little Brother Montgomery's piano solo "A&B Blues" rocks!

LINK➤ *Lucille Bogan — 1923–1933* — ***Story of Blues 3535***

An 18-track survey of a confident female singer whose work frankly addressed sexuality, physical abuse, drinking, and other taboos. After listening to this collection, you might explore three other Document volumes.

John Chatman was born in Memphis, TN, in 1915. When he was old enough, he'd spend time listening to the musicians on Beale Street, and picked up piano. Although he occasionally worked in clubs, he started his professional career as an itinerant blues traveler, spending time in Helena, AR, before settling in Chicago in 1939. He began recording that year, first as Peter Chatman (his father's name), then as Memphis Slim. Within a year or so, he'd recorded a popular tune, "Beer Drinking Woman," for Bluebird and played piano with Big Bill Broonzy. The two musicians stayed together for about four years before Slim left to form his own House Rockers band. Slim continued to record through the 1940s and 1950s. He toured Europe in 1960 and moved to Paris two years later. After several comfortable decades of performing and recording, Slim died in Paris in 1988.

The Bluebird Recordings, 1940–1941 **RCA 66720**

These tracks are more than a half-century old, but they sound wonderful. Memphis Slim sings beautifully—his voice is radiant, and his piano playing is incandescent. On "Beer Drinkin' Woman," served here in two helpings, Slim tells the story of a scam queen. He breezes through "You Didn't Mean No Good" with the utmost sincerity; even when times are bad, as on "Empty Room Blues," Slim's voice retains a touch of sunshine. Memphis Slim was someone who clearly enjoyed making music. His enthusiasm is infectious, and his music can't help but make you feel better. Slim's piano style is quite varied: "Old Taylor" features a boogie-woogie rhythm, while "This Life I'm Livin'" is a sad old piano blues. Superb!

LINK➤ *Mose Allison — Allison Wonderland* ***Rhino 71689***

Allison's music exists somewhere between quiet cocktail lounge jazz and a sophisticated city update on the simple beauty of country blues—preceisely why it makes sense to hear "Parchman Farm" and "Seventh Son" beside "The Tennesse Waltz" and "Hey Good Lookin'."

The Real Folk Blues **Chess 9270**

These early 1950s sides were not recorded for Chess; they were made for Premium and later acquired by Chess. The title is utterly irrelevant, a leftover from a 1960s marketing campaign. The sound here is mellow, electric, and a bit soft around the edges. Mostly, Memphis Slim is part of a band with two saxophones, a guitar, bass, and drums. The musicians often find a groove, as on the prerocking "Tiajuana" and "Trouble, Trouble"; the latter becomes a series of tasty duets between Slim's piano, the tenor sax, and guitar. The best work is the down-tempo lost-love blues, tunes like "Slim's Blues" and the well-known "I Guess I'm a Fool."

LINK➤ *Washboard Sam — Rockin' My Blues Away* ***Bluebird (RCA) 61042***

The washboard was a viable percussion instrument (and an inexpensive one). Here, its finest practitioner performs with the perfect accompaniment of Big Big Broonzy (guitar), Memphis Slim (piano), and other Chicago legends. Great songs, superb performances.

Rockin' the Blues **Charly 210**

Memphis Slim's recordings for the Vee-Jay label are among his finest, but at present, they're hard to find. You might have some luck tracking down this album or Vee-Jay's original *At the Gate of Horn* (which contains 12 tracks, compared to the 16 included here). Besides Memphis Slim's extraordinarily capable piano magic and steady voice, Matt "Guitar" Murphy's electrifying guitar makes this album quite special. Add two saxes and songs like "Messin' Around with the Blues," "Rockin' the House," "Slim's Blues," "Wish Me Well," and "Mother Earth." The result is a blues album that should find a place in every library. Recorded in 1958 and 1959.

LINK➤ *Mercy Dee Walton — Pity and a Shame* ***OBC 552***

Walton's best known for his lonely "thousand miles from nowhere" song, "One Room Country Shack," but much of this 1961 album is as effective. A talented storyteller, his portrait of "The Drunkard," with slightly off-kilter piano playing and Sidney Maiden's fine harmonica, is excellent.

Memphis Slim: USA **Candid 79024**

Memphis Slim's discography is frightening because dozens and dozens of his LPs contain tracks duplicated on others. This collection is a safe harbor: it features a dozen or so tracks released in 1961. (There's also an excellent album by the same name recorded in 1954 for Chicago's United Records that features Matt "Guitar" Murphy in Memphis Slim's House Rockers band.) Most of the songs here are originals, performed with harmonica player Jazz Gillum and guitar player Arbee Stidham. Tunes include "Born with the Blues," "Harlem Blues," "Key to the Highway," and "Bad Luck and Troubles." There's even a version of the traditional folk song "John Henry," too.

LINK➤ *Various Artists — Blues Masters, Vol. 12: Memphis Blues* ***Rhino 71129***

A brief, somewhat scattered salute to Memphis, many of these tracks were recorded in Chicago or NYC by artists no longer associated with Memphis. Whatever. It's all good blues, beginning with the Memphis Jug Band, by way of B.B. King and Willie Nix, and on to Rufus Thomas.

Raining the Blues **Fantasy 24705**

A pair of 1960 albums (originally *Just Blues and No Strain*) finds Memphis Slim comfortable, capable, and easy to enjoy. He starts "Beer Drinking Woman" as an unaccompanied solo. "Blue and Disgusted" is another fine song in the same vein. "Harpie" Brown plays on four tracks, including a sweet and tender "Motherless Child." Bassist Wendell Marshall fills out the sound on "Teasing the Blues," a gentle instrumental. Lafayette Thomas's guitar is also heard in the background; these two sideman participate in most of the tracks. Thomas does a nice job simulating raindrops on "Raining the Blues," while Slim quietly pumps gloom through his piano. His artistry is understated and endlessly impressive.

LINK➤ *Various Artists — The Paramount Piano Blues, Vol. 1* ***Black Swan 12011***

With extensive liner notes that explain not only the music, but the Paramount Records business and race records in general, this CD is a very special history lesson. Artists from 1928–32 include Little Brother Montgomery, Wesley Wallace, Charlie Spand, and others.

One of the most refreshing voices in contemporary blues, Kevin Moore gained national notice with his first major-label release in 1994. Hardly an overnight sensation, Moore grew up in Los Angeles; he was influenced by gospel, R&B, and 1960s rock. Moore played in a cover band, then spent three years working behind Papa John Creach. Moore then worked on the publishing side of the business, as an arranger for Almo-Irving Music, a large firm. He released a forgotten album in 1980 for a Casablanca subsidiary, and in 1983 joined veteran saxman Monk Higgins in the house band at Marla's Memory Lane, an L.A. club. Country blues became a serious interest in 1990 while Moore was preparing for Rabbit Foot, an L.A. theater production. A short time later, he started performing blues regularly in clubs (where he became known as Keb' Mo'). In 1994 he was the second artist signed to the revived OKeh label.

Keb' Mo' — OKeh 57863

Easily the best debut album of the 1990s, Keb' Mo's 1994 release draws on country blues, but brings the genre up to date. Moore performs on various guitars, as well as harmonica and banjo. He's got a knack for arrangement. His guitar works as hard as his vocals to set mood and communicate emotion. The snappy dance "Angelina" is typical; it features a smart, articulate vocal with just a hint of breathlessness and just enough hoarse grit for authenticity, as well as a picking guitar style with tastes of harmonica. "City Boy" is a ballad, a memory song to be played when leaving the city. The drama of Tommy Eyre's keyboards and Keb' Mo's guitar is wonderful.

LINK➤ *Various Artists — Blind Pig Records: 20th Anniversary Collection* — *Blind Pig 2001*

Blind Pig Records has been one of the best things to happen to contemporary blues. This collection, which shows just how varied the label's roster has been, includes Jimmy Thackery, Carey Bell, Debbie Davies, E.C. Scott, and Deborah Coleman. A terrific collection.

Just Like You — OKeh 67316

Happily, Keb' Mo's second album is even better than his first. Songwriting is the reason why. The album also benefits from a wider range of colors and textures. "Perpetual Blues Machine" is an acoustic country blues, but with some city attitude. "More Than One Way Home" is an electric number with a unique rhythm (every Keb' Mo' song possesses a special sonic signature). It's a biographical song about Moore's old neighborhood, and perhaps the best demonstration of his vocal talent. Enhanced by background vocalists Jackson Browne and Bonnie Raitt, the title track offers a warm and personal view of friendship. With one remarkable song after another, this is a fabulous album that belongs in every blues collection.

LINK➤ *Keb' Mo' — Slow Down* — *OKeh 69376*

Released in 1998, Keb' Mo's third album is every bit as strong as his first two. Once again, the material is mostly original (although he does a version of Robert Johnson's "Love in Vain"). Highlights include "Henry," "Soon as I Get Paid," and "A Letter to Tracy."

Little Brother Montgomery

Eurreal Montgomery originally came from Kentwood, LA. His father ran a barrelhouse for local lumber workers, and it was here that "Little Brother" taught himself to play piano. By age 11, in 1907, Montgomery was on the road, picking up work at logging camps, picnics, and anywhere else he could. The trail led first to New Orleans, then to Chicago, but during the 1930s, Montgomery lived and worked around Jackson, MS. By 1942, he was back in Chicago, and stayed there for the rest of his life. Montgomery earned a living as a well-respected studio musician for Chess, Cobra, and other labels. He also played clubs and at festivals, and toured behind Otis Rush, Magic Sam, and other Chicago stars. Montgomery played both blues and Dixieland jazz with Kid Ory and others. With his second wife, Janet Floberg, he also operated a small record label as a cottage industry. Montgomery died in 1985.

Tasty Blues **OBC 554**

The after-hours tenderness of "Tasty Blues" sets an enticing mood for Montgomery's 1960 session. Besides the twinkle of Montgomery's easy, bluesy piano, Lafayette Thomas's guitar and Julian Euell's bass sympathetically fill out the instrumental. "Santa Fe" begins with an equally delicate introduction, but Montgomery jumps in with a railroad blues; its rhythm is suggestive of scenery briskly passing by. Montgomery's been singing "Vicksburg Blues" since 1929, stridently vibrating his falsetto vocal as if it were a guitar string. To a far lesser degree, Montgomery uses the same technique on the equally old "No Special Rider." Several solos remind the listener of the respect Montgomery has earned as a pianist. Fine and mellow.

LINK➤ *Various Artists — Atlantic Blues: Piano* ***Atlantic 81694***

Montgomery is represented by just one track on this CD colletion (which includes less music than you'll find on the comparable disc in the Atlantic Blues boxed set). Others, mostly on the boogie side, included Meade Lux Lewis, Jack Dupree, and Jimmy Yancey.

Chicago: The Living Legends **OBC 525**

Producer Chris Albertson begins the set with a stirring, effective blues composed by (of all people) Irving Berlin. Later on, there's an old-timey rendition of vaudeville's "Oh, Daddy," sung by Elaine McFarland and accompanied by Mike McKendrick on banjo. In fact, the old-time feeling prevails: "Up the Country Blues" is 1920s-style jazz, composed and sung in period style by Montgomery. "Prescriptions for the Blues" and "Sweet Daddy (Your Mama's Gone Mad)" are the real thing. It's Bessie Smith's era, played out in the Birdhouse in Chicago in 1961. But listen to that piano boogie: "Riverside Boogie." And "44 Vicksburg" is a 100 percent authentic piano blues. Nice work; handsome recording, too.

LINK➤ *Little Brother Montgomery — Goodbye Mister Blues* ***Delmark 663***

Obviously, Montgomery felt a passion for early jazz. That noble obsession is played out beautifully in three mid-1970s sessions; happily, his State Street Swingers reach beyond the obvious material. Most songs are fresh, unfamiliar, and tasty. But they're not blues.

Although he was born in East Orange, NJ, Mooney is associated with the blues scene in Rochester, NY. He learned from Son House, who lived for a while in Rochester; during the 1970s, Mooney became House's accompanist. Mooney moved to New Orleans in 1976 and released his first album through Blind Pig a year later. He formed Bluesiana in 1983 and toured with this eclectic outfit, often as an opening act for notables like Clarence "Gatemouth" Brown and Albert King. By the late 1980s, Mooney was again on his own, making his way with a very original take on rural blues, touring, and cutting albums for several small record companies. Despite a great many favorable notices from mainstream publications, such as Esquire, Mooney remains something of a blues insider's musician. At 43 years old, he's ready for a breakthrough. He certainly possesses the requisite talent.

Comin' Your Way **Blind Pig 70779**

Mooney's first album resonates with the humor and intensity of country blues, but adds ragtime, an old-time feel, and even a taste of vaudeville. At times, Mooney sounds like a novelty, but he's done his homework. As a result, when he performs on his National Steel Standard guitar or bottleneck, he's darned close to the real thing. Mooney's sense of timing and his vocal choices on "Brand New Woman" suggest authenticity. And "Take a Walk Round the Corner," a Leroy Carr tune, demonstrates his skill in renovating old blues, maintaining their integrity, and turning out something new. Son House's "Pony Blues" receives a similar treatment. Mooney's also an original, as "Hot Tub Mambo" suggests.

LINK➤ *Jesse Fuller — San Francisco Bay Blues* ***Original Blues Classics 537***

The title song is infectious, a bouncy tune ideal for Fuller's one-man band (the kazoo break is fabulous). In fact, just about every bit of music on this 1963 album will make you smile. Fuller is a beautiful entertainer, a person who makes other people feel great.

Testimony **Domino 1**

This album is not going to be easy to find, but it's probably worth the time and trouble. Working with a hot New Orleans band that includes Dr. John, Ivan Neville, George Porter, Jr. (the Meters' bassist), and drummer Johnny Vidacovich, this is Mooney at his most intense—the way concert audiences know him. The album is equally divided: Mooney wrote seven songs himself and covers seven others. Among his originals, "I Plead Guilty," "Maybe Baby," and "One Thing" are the best. The covers include Son House's "Levee Camp Moan" and the traditional "I Wish I Was in Heaven Sitting Down." The collection was released in 1992.

LINK➤ *Jimmy Thackery & John Mooney : Sideways in Paradise* ***Blind Pig 5006***

A somewhat unexpected collaboration between two bluesmen with vastly different styles. Here Thackery is all acoustic, performing on 6- and 12-string guitars, National Steel guitar, mandolin, and mandocello. The vocals are fun in an old-time, stylized way.

McKinley Morganfield was nicknamed "Muddy Waters" when he was a child; one story has him playing near a mucky creek bed. Born to a sharecropper family on the abusive Stovall plantation (outside Clarksdale, MS) in 1915, he sang field hollers, and learned harmonica as a boy and guitar as a teenager. Mostly, he lived in a small log cabin, worked hard as a field hand, and played parties with his small band. The 1940s signaled promise when Alan Lomax recorded Waters for a Library of Congress project. In 1943, Waters broke away from farm life and moved to Chicago, where he got a truck-driving job and played music at night. Work with Sonny Boy Williamson, help from Big Bill Broonzy, and performances with his own band led to a 1947 hit and the beginning of a 25-year relationship with Chess. World-famous, Waters recorded in the 1970s for Columbia; he died in his sleep in 1983.

The Complete Plantation Recordings **MCA 9344**

A year or two before Muddy Waters moved to Chicago, he worked as a tractor and truck driver on Howard Stovall's plantation in Clarksdale, MS. When Library of Congress historian Alan Lomax met the musician for their first recording session in 1941, Waters owned no shoes. Nor did he own a guitar. He borrowed Lomax's Martin to record these country blues, singing in a confident voice with a knack for melody and clear expression. The recordings, made in 1941 and 1942, are good, if sometimes fizzy. Most songs are originals, though some are based on the work of others. "Country Blues" is one highlight among many others. With the occasional accompaniment of other local musicians.

LINK➤ *Various Artists — Roots 'n' Blues, The Retrospective: 1925–1950* Columbia/ Legacy 47911

A wide-ranging survey of race music and folk music, these one hundred-plus tracks feature mostly obscure performers (Blues Birdhead, Freeny's Barn Dance Band) or respected artists whose star has faded (Lucille Bogan, Elizabeth Johnson), plus a good many famous names.

The Chess Box **Chess 80002**

This 3-CD set is an essential item. It spans 25 years, from 1947 until 1972, when Muddy Waters and Chess Records represented the pinnacle of blues on record. A closer look reveals a 15-year period at the red-hot center (ending in the mid-1960s) and a well-intentioned boxed set, circa 1989, whose 40 pages of liner notes seem thin by today's standards. These are minor nits, however. "Gypsy Woman," from 1947, showed some promise, but producer Leonard Chess brought Waters and bassist Big Crawford back into the studio for another try. The result was 1948's "I Can't Be Satisfied," which opened with a stinging guitar line and so effectively combined city and country blues that the first pressing sold out in a single day. "I Feel Like Going Home" is similar, but Waters's electric guitar effects and his edgier vocal make for a stronger song. Later that year, Waters found a more intricate groove with "Mean Red Spider," but this is still mostly country blues with a slight urban edge. This style—

Waters's guitar, perhaps a sideman, and Crawford's bass—continued through 1950's "Rollin' and Tumblin', Part 1" and Robert Johnson's "Walkin' Blues." Little Walter's harmonica really wails on "Long Distance Call" (one of this box's best tunes), but it isn't until 1954 when Waters's best band finally takes shape (on CD2): Little Walter (harmonica), Otis Spann (piano), Jimmy Rogers (guitar), and Willie Dixon (bass). Various drummers completed the package. This is the group that makes "I Just Want to Make Love to You," "I'm Ready," "Mannish Boy," "Trouble No More" and so many rocking blues standards. Band members were in and out for the rest of the 1950s, and James Cotton's influence was often felt in place of Little Walter's. CD3 covers the 1960s through 1972 and includes a spectacular version of "Twenty Four Hours" (with extraordinary harmonica work from Cotton). Waters's control is superb on "I Feel So Good," and his sentiment is magnificently expressed on "My Home Is in the Delta"—this is sharply dressed, elegantly played, often minimalist blues. Waters's economical use of notes and his moderate amplification produce a room-thumping impact; few blues players generate half of Waters's impact.

LINK➤ *Muddy Waters — His Best, 1947 to 1955* **_Chess 9370_**

Muddy Waters's music has been re-released many times, on many collections. The most recent is a pair of 2-CD sets. The second in this series is Muddy Waters: His Best 1956 to 1964 *(MCA Chess 9380). Both are part of the Chess 50th Anniversary Series.*

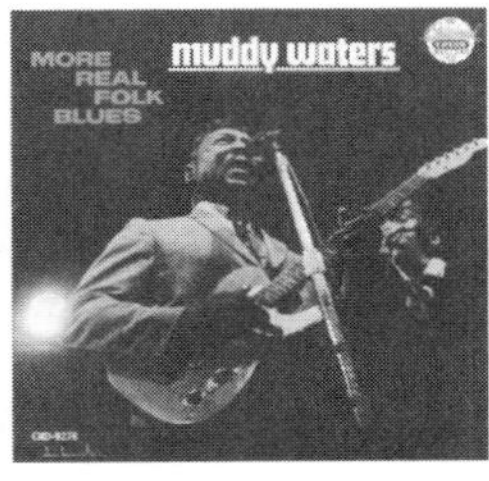

More Real Folk Blues — MCA 9278

A low-priced collection covering 1948–52, with only a few songs repeated in the Chess Box. Waters does two additional Robert Johnson songs especially well: "Kind Hearted Woman," and "Down South Blues," with its outstanding sad guitar. Most of these songs were recorded before Waters had a regular band; accompaniment is typically Big Crawford's bass and sometimes Little Walter's harmonica. As 1950's "Hello Little Girl" attests, the electricity of Waters's guitar with only touches of accompaniment define urban blues—this is astonishing work. "Early Morning Blues," from the same session, is also sublime. Jimmy Rogers (guitar) joins Little Walter for the proto-Chicago blues of 1952's "Landlady."

LINK➤ *Rolling Stones — Hot Rocks (1963–1971)* **_London 844-475_**

Although the hits songs are nearly all originals, the Rolling Stones acquired more than their name from Muddy Waters and his ilk. Where the Beatles were a pop group, the Stones took their power from the blues, particularly in the beginning. Contains all of their early hits.

One More Mile: Chess Collectibles, Vol. 1

Chess 9348

The combination of Chess's haphazard release schedule for Muddy Waters's recordings, and the consistently excellent work that he did through the 1950s and 1960s should encourage every listener—not just collectors—to consider this 2-CD set. The liner notes helpfully explain how each of these rare or alternate takes fits into Waters's remarkable story. There's a jump blues ("Muddy Jumps One") from 1948. Waters's stinging slide guitar emboldens "Burying Ground" and "You're Gonna Need My Help," both from 1949. The rocking "She's So Pretty" is one of a perfect handful from the Walter-Spann-Rogers-Dixon band of the mid-1950s; these are the set's inevitable highlights. The original version of 1960's "Tiger in Your Tank" (recorded with an entirely whole new band) is hotter than the live one on the Newport album. "Five Long Years" is an intense, incandescent blues from 1963 with top-notch piano from Otis Spann. "Thirteen Highway" is one of three more songs from this superior session. *Muddy, Brass & Blues* was very badly received in 1966, but here the brass is removed, the songs are remixed, and the effect on "Trouble in Mind" and "Trouble Trouble" is more satisfying—although Muddy Waters as a crooner is an odd creative choice. The tone is subdued (almost acoustic in feeling, although Waters plays electric) for 11 wonderful songs recorded in 1972 for Swiss radio. "Streamline Woman," "Baby Please Don't Go," and "Feel Like Goin' Home" combine country blues with urban sophistication in a way that is rarely captured on record.

LINK➤ *Muddy Waters — Rare and Unissued* **_Chess 9180_**

A 1984 release that resulted from a first detailed examination of the Chess vaults. None of this material duplicates the One More Mile *collection, and all of this 1947–52 work is excellent. (Much of this material was previously available only on bootleg recordings.)*

At Newport 1960

MCA 31269

Seeing Muddy Waters's band live must have been a major treat. This was the real thing—a concert at 1960's Newport Jazz Festival—featuring James Cotton (harmonica), Otis Spann (piano), and Pat Hare (guitar). The sound is fresher and livelier than studio work, and the crowd is into the music (even if it was probably unfamiliar to most). And if these aren't the very finest versions of "Baby Please Don't Go," "I've Got My Mojo Working," and "I'm Your Hoochie Coochie Man," the energy and image of a live date compensates. Probably not the first purchase, but worth owning for the many special moments.

LINK➤ *Siegel Schwall Band — Best of Siegel Schwall* **_Vanguard 79366_**

Although Paul Butterfield's Chicago band is the one most people remember, Schwall's group was also a popular white blues band from the same era. The songs here are mostly originals, interspersed with an occasional Willie Dixon or Howlin' Wolf tune.

Muddy Waters Sings Big Bill Broonzy / Folk Singer **MCA 5907**

This single CD includes two albums. One, from 1959, is a collection of songs written by or associated with Big Bill Broonzy.The second album, from 1963, is a reworking of Waters's 1950s hits with a stunning young Buddy Guy on guitar. Both albums are prime. Waters does an admirable job with all of the Broonzy songs, but "Lonesome Road Blues" and "Southbound Train" get under one's skin (once again, James Cotton's harmonica is a big reason why). Although the songs are familiar, the treatment is entirely new: *Folk Singer*'s style is deep and languishing, often slow and glimmering, perfect late night listening. Naturally, *Folk Singer* has nothing to do with white America's 1963 definition of folk music.

LINK➤ *Big Bill Broonzy — Big Bill's Blues* ***Topaz 1038***

A quick primer on Broonzy's work, contained on a single disc. His hit songs are here, but this is best viewed as a starting point. (Broonzy's best work is described in his own entry.)

Blues Sky **Epic 46172**

This single CD compilation of Muddy Waters's 1976–80 Columbia sessions isn't essential, but there's lots to enjoy in Johnny Winter's productions of his hero's music. "Jealous Hearted Man" successfully mixes Chicago blues with Winter's searing 1976 blues, and "I Can't Be Satisfied" is updated with the help of James Cotton, pianist Pinetop Perkins, and Winter on guitar. "Screamin' and Cryin'," with Perkins and Walter Horton (harmonica), is tasty, and downhearted. Some songs are slightly unfocused, but 1980's "Forever Lonely" finds the right groove with Winter, Bob Margolin, and Walter "Guitar Jr." Johnson on guitar, and Jerry Portnoy on harp. A mixed bag.

LINK➤ *Jerry Portnoy — Blues Harmonica Master Class*

If you want to learn to play the blues harmonica, buy this 3-CD set. Hundreds of musical illustrations are included on the CDs, and the set also comes with a 50-page book that explains techniques from tongue blocking to note bending. Contact International Blues Management, Box 523, Waltham, MA 02254, or visit www.harpmaster.com.

Muddy "Mississippi" Waters—Live **Blue Sky 35712**

A fascinating juxtaposition that really works. This 1978 live album, recorded with a top-notch band, finds Muddy Waters amidst all the excitement (and some of the excesses) associated with that era's concerts. The band is terrific: Pinetop Perkins (piano); Jerry Portnoy (harmonica); Johnny Winter, Bob Margolin, and Luther "Guitar Jr." Johnson (guitars); Willie "Big Eyes" Smith (drums); and Calvin Jones or Charles Calmese (taking alternate turns on bass). Listen to these guys wail on "Mannish Boy" and feel the heat of Waters's slide guitar on "Howling Wolf." Also a delight is the rocking rhythm of "Baby Please Don't Go" and the ever-present crowd going wild for "Deep Down in Florida." This CD really is a treat—it's a pity it's so often overlooked.

LINK➤ *Luther "Guitar, Jr." Johnson — Slammin' on the West Side* ***Telarc 83389***

Just one of the electric guitar player's albums worth hearing, this one was made in Louisana and covers everything from jump blues to quiet, contemplative acoustic work. Johnson is extremely skillful and quite talented. Try also 1990's I Want to Groove with You *(Bullseye Blues 9506).*

Charlie Musselwhite

There wasn't much work or much of a future in Kosciusko, MS, so Charlie Musselwhite's family moved north to Memphis, TN. He went to high school there and hung around with local blues musicians. At age 18, Musselwhite left Memphis, hoping to find work in Chicago. Mostly he found work for tips on the city's nightlife strip, Maxwell Street. In time, Musselwhite was frequenting Chicago's blues clubs, sitting in with Mike Bloomfield, J.B. Hutto, and others. This led to a 1966 Vanguard recording contract, which in turn led to airplay on underground radio stations in San Francisco. Now a renowned harmonica player, Musselwhite left Chicago for the Bay Area, where he became a regular at the Fillmore and in local clubs. He finally got past a chronic alcohol problem in the late 1980s, and his national fame has grown as a result of increased exposure and wise career decisions.

Memphis Charlie — **Arhoolie 303**

"Finger Lickin' Good" is the kind of song that Charlie Musselwhite performed better than anyone else. With several San Francisco notables providing background rhythm, Musselwhite cups the harmonica around the microphone and sets himself to inventing. He starts simply with a melody, but intentionally strains the tone for soulful emphasis. Then he cycles through a single chord over and over again, improvising. Musselwhite next hits hard on the beat, screaming through those tiny holes; he then turns mellow. All this happens within about a minute. These 14 songs, mostly Musselwhites, with some from Little Walter and a few public domain pieces, filled two albums; the first was released 1971 and the other in 1974.

LINK➤ *Robben Ford — Handful of Blues* — ***Blue Thumb 7004***

Refined jazz-blues guitarist (and son of San Francisco legend Charles Ford), Robben Ford's music was shaped by time with Charles Musselwhite (he performs on Memphis Charlie), Miles Davis, and the Yellowjackets (which he cofounded). Lots of skills here, and a pleasant musicality.

In My Time — **Alligator 4818**

While 1990's *Ace of Harps* (Alligator 4781) and 1991's *Signature* (4801) are recommended for their updated Chicago blues, and remarkable harp solos, the spirit of this 1993 release runs deeper. Musselwhite begins with two old-fashioned acoustic blues: his own "Stingaree" and Sleepy John Estes's "Brownsville Blues." The third tune and the final one are darker, reverent, beautiful gospel blues. On both tracks, the Blind Boys of Alabama provide understated support. "Bedside of a Neighbor," which ends the album, is a dignified elegy easily imagined in a sharecropper's sad shack. The maturity in Musselwhite's voice suits his material well.

LINK➤ *Blind Boys of Alabama — Holdin' On* — ***House of Blues***

The Blind Boys concentrate on gospel, but also sing traditional music and even some pop. This CD includes "You'll Never Walk Alone," and "He." Outstanding music.

Kenny Neal

The son of Baton Rouge blues musician Raful Neal, Kenny Neal started playing harmonica at age 3; by 13, he was performing in his father's band. Neal continued to grow under the tutelage of Rudolph Richard, who played guitar for his father's friend Slim Harpo. By the late 1970s, he was working for Buddy Guy. Neal and several brothers (six are professional musicians) formed the Neal Brothers Blues Band, which was based in Toronto, Canada. He then returned home to start a solo career. Neal's first record was released in 1986 by the local King Snake label, then re-released by Alligator a year later. Along with an ongoing relationship with Alligator, Neal has pursued other opportunities. In 1991, he was featured in Broadway's *Mule Bone*, a musical version of a 1930 play by Langston Hughes and Zora Neale Hurston, with contemporary songs by Taj Mahal. Neal won a Theater World award for his performance.

Big News from Baton Rouge!! — **Alligator 4764**

An enthusiastic 1986 debut performance, originally cut for King Snake. Neal enjoys himself as he rolls through funky, swampy rocking blues. He shifts from guitar to harmonica and demands some interesting rhythms from his band. "Evalina," with the catchphrase "Georgia women don't wear no shoes," gets way down into the Louisiana mud. More experienced than his years suggest, Neal's sparse guitar and his conspiratorial tone in the gravel-voiced "Caught Your Back Door Man" confidently stream through the King Snake Horns. The cleverly titled "Bio on the Bayou" is just that—a partly-spoken biography recalling his dad, Slim Harpo, Lazy Lester, Buddy Guy, and others.

LINK➤ *Raful Neal — Louisiana Legend* — ***Alligator 4783***

Raful Neal has been performing on harmonica since the 1950s; this 1990 album was produced by son Kenny Neal (one of his ten children, many of whom work in the music business). It's heartfelt, rocking, swampy, spicy, and a whole lot of fun.

Walking on Fire — **Alligator 4795**

All of Neal's Alligator albums are consistent and well worth owning; when you get the chance, pick up 1989's *Devil Child* (4774), 1992's *Bayou Blood* (4809), and 1994's *Hoodoo Moon* (4825). This disc comes from 1991; it seems to hit the bulls-eye more often because of song choices. "Look, But Don't Touch" is a splintering guitar workout sung with an appealing warning tone by Neal's sweetly gruff voice. Once again, the horn integration with the electric guitar is terrific. An old-time R&B feeling underlines the horns on "The Truth Hurts," and the horns shuffle with the rhythm on the seething title track. Solidly energetic and fun.

LINK➤ *Lazy Lester — Harp & Soul* — ***Alligator 4768***

Longtime Lousiana harmonica wiz Leslie Johnson hits hard on this 1988 album for King Snake. Kenny Neal plays guitar throughout, adding a contemporary flair to "Patrol Wagon Blues" that balances the likes of the R&B slow 1950s-style dance, "Take Me in Your Arms."

Robert Nighthawk

Robert Lee McCullum was born in Helena, AR, in 1909. As a boy, he taught himself the harmonica; his cousin Houston Stackhouse taught him guitar in 1931. The two often performed together. McCullum got into some trouble and headed for St. Louis in 1935. He became a popular blues musician there, and in 1937 recorded for Bluebird as Robert McCoy. He took his next stage name from a song he recorded for Bluebird called "Prowling Night-hawk." Nighthawk tended toward traveling; he shuttled between St. Louis, Chicago, and Helena during the 1940s and for much of the next 20 years. During this time, Nighthawk became a popular radio performer on Helena's KFFA and also on Memphis's WDIA. The late 1940s and early 1950s brought more recording sessions for Chess's Aristocrat label and for United. Nighthawk spent most of the 1950s and early 1960s performing in the South. He died in 1964.

Robert Nighthawk - Houston Stackhouse — Testament 5010

Nighthawk sings lead and plays guitar on eight of these 1964 tracks; he plays guitar behind Houston Stackhouse on most of the others, from 1967. Nighthawk's "Black Angel Blues" is classic in structure and superbly performed with a whistle-clean slide guitar solo and harmonica accompaniment from John Wrencher. Similarly, Nighthawk's version of "Maggie Campbell," which he learned from Tommy Johnson, is energetic and magical. Nighthawk was one of the great slide guitar players; a magnificent demonstration of his talent can be heard on "I'm Getting Tired" and "Crying Won't Help You." The engineering is very good; unfortunately, this is not true for the Stackhouse tracks. Stackhouse's earnest voice and Nighthawk's guitar make the set worth hearing.

LINK➤ *Houston Stackhouse — Cryin' Won't Help You* — ***Genes 9904***

Stackhouse worked not only with Nighthawk, but with Robert Johnson, Tommy Johnson, Sonny Boy Williamson, and others. He didn't record much. Try also Houston Stackhouse 1910-1980 *(Wolf 120.779).*

Live on Maxwell Street, 1964 — Rounder 2022

Recorded live on a Chicago street corner in 1964 with crowds and street noise in the background, this album has become a classic. It doesn't take much to imagine yourself leaning against the bricks of a crumbly apartment building, listening to Nighthawk's smooth lead and slide guitars and his dark, nasal voice. The best track is probably "Maxwell Street Medley," featuring two of Nighthawk's best-known songs, "Anna Lee" and "Sweet Black Angel Blues." Carey Bell's on hand for a few harmonica crowd pleasers, notably "Burning Heat." Drummer Robert Whitehead and rhythm guitarist Johnny Young also deserve plenty of credit.

LINK➤ *Robert Lee McCoy — Complete Recorded Works (1937–1940)* — ***Wolf 2***

Nighthawk recorded under the name Robert Lee McCoy during this period; this CD presents his best work, although the sound quality varies widely from one track to the next. Still, this music is among the finest blues guitar on record, and it's worth owning.

An extraordinarily prolific contemporary blues band with nearly two dozen albums to its credit, Washington, D.C.'s Nighthawks have been around since 1972. Guitar player Jimmy Thackery put the original group together with singer Mark Wenner, who also played harmonica. Drummer Pete Ragusa and bassist Jan Zukowski joined a short time later. At first, they covered Chicago blues tunes in D.C.'s bars and clubs, but soon expanded their repertoire and range of venues to include college campuses and rock and blues clubs throughout the East Coast. By the mid-1980s, as a result of endless touring and several major label recordings, the Nighthawks were nationally known. Thackery left in 1985 to form a new band, the Assassins. This made room for Wet Willie singer and sax player Jimmy Hall and former Sea Level guitar player Jimmy Nalls. Both stayed for about five years and were replaced by Danny Morris (guitar) and Mike Cowan (keyboards).

Open All Nite — Genes 4105

For a few brief shining years in the mid-1970s, the Nighthawks were just about the best young blues band in the U.S. Fortunately, Genes (JEN-us) has released the group's prime material. The tastiest ingredients on this straight-ahead rocking blues are Jimmy Thackery's thick, spicy electric guitar and Mark Wenner's harp. Both sound as if they've been to Chicago and come back with more modern ideas. There's authenticity, originality, and really tight craftsmanship behind "Nine Below Zero" and the teardrop guitar work of "Long Distance Call." The latter is a heart-wrenching slow blues; like many songs here, the instrumental work far outshines the vocals. From 1976.

LINK➤ *Chris Duarte — Tailspin Headwhack* — ***Silvertone 41611***

One of the most promising 1990s guitarists, Duarte's barroom guitar shows glimmers of Miles Davis, John Coltrane, Jimi Hendrix,and Stevie Ray Vaughan, who was his greatest influence. Duarte is a modernist; listen for studio hijinks, hip-hop, and some sampling.

Jacks & Kings, Vols. I and II — Genes 4120/4125

Here is some fun with rock 'n' roll and electric blues. Pinetop Perkins and several other musicians are along for the ride. This pair of late 1970s albums on a single CD features 20 tracks in all. There's a very credible version of "Born in Chicago" and a renovated version of Curtis Mayfield's "Love Me or Leave Me." It's a collection where blues classics like "Dust My Broom" and "The Sky Is Crying" cohabitate with such rocking oldies as "Sea Cruise" and "Little Queenie." Thackery's guitar binds it all together, and two horns pump up the action on the second album. Not a perfect set, but certainly entertaining.

LINK➤ *The Nighthawks — Best of the Nighthawks* — ***Genes 4140/45***

Neatly organized with nine blues tracks and ten rock tracks, the delineation doesn't make much sense once the CD starts to play. There's a rocking feeling to the band's blues and a blues feeling to its rock. Particularly good is "Shake and Finger Pop." Excellent starter kit.

It all starts here. Patton was the first widely known Delta blues man, one who set the style and the standard. No one's certain when Patton was born, but 1891 is a fair guess. His family moved from a rural Mississippi hamlet to the Dockery plantation, where Patton learned guitar. By 1910, he was locally famous, appearing regularly at picnics, juke joints, and parties—with the womanizing, drinking, and occasional night in jail that was common to the rambling lifestyle. Patton didn't record until 1929, the result of a successful audition with Jackson, MS, record store owner Henry Speir, who arranged a session with Paramount Records. A year later Patton became a country blues star. More sides followed in 1930, and for a short time, Patton was the label's top performer. In 1934, Patton's session for the American Recording Company was the work of a sick man. Patton died of a heart condition later the same year.

Founder of the Delta Blues — Yazoo 1020

This may be genius, and it may be seminal, but it's also very difficult listening. The recordings are scratchy and lacking in highs and lows. "High Water Everywhere" shows Patton in his most boisterous style—shouting the lyrics (about a 1927 flood) while playing the guitar so hard it nearly becomes a percussion instrument. "Pony Blues" suffers from especially poor sound, but careful listening reveals an unusual technique as Patton sustains his vocals for dramatic effect; it's another of his most popular songs. "Down the Dirt Road Blues" also employs sustained vocals, but the guitar figures are more easily heard (and very snappy). Despite the poor sound quality, this album is essential for any comprehensive blues CD collection.

LINK➤ *Masters of the Delta Blues: The Friends of Charley Patton* — *Yazoo 2002*

Another essential Yazoo CD, these two dozen tracks are heavy on Tommy Johnson and Son House. In addition, there are prime cuts by Kid Bailey, Bukka White, Ishmon Bracey, and Bertha Lee (her acidic voice is well suited for "Yellow Bee").

King of the Delta Blues — Yazoo 2001

A very appealing (and very scratchy) collection of oddities, virtuoso turns, and religious songs, this CD includes "Hang It on the Wall," one of Patton's most satisfying tunes. It's a fast, funny, freewheeling shuffle (actually a "breakdown"). "Pea-Vine Blues" is one of Patton's most-copied songs; it's a conversation on a train that ends a love affair (the P-Vine was a train that stopped daily at Dockery's Plantation). Patton sings slowly, but his guitar keeps up with the train's energy. Frequent recording partner Henry Sims is at his best on "Elder Green Blues." About half of this album is straight gospel; Patton is often spectacular, especially on "I Shall Not Be Moved."

LINK➤ *Var. Artists—Blues Masters, Vol. 8: Mississippi Delta Blues* — *Rhino 71130*

A reasonable progression from Tommy Johnson to Elmore James, with some interesting stops along the way. Patton's cohort, Willie Brown, sings "Future Blues," and Robert Petway does his "Catfish Blues" (which became Muddy Waters's "Rollin' Stone"). Much more.

Joe Willie Perkins came from Belzoni, MS. Although he's generally regarded as one of the finest blues pianists, Perkins started out playing guitar. He got a job with pianist Willie Love in the late 1930s, then moved to St. Louis, where he often worked with Big Joe Williams. In 1943, at age 30, Perkins linked up with Robert Nighthawk; the two rambled to Helena, AR, where they worked for KFFA radio. Perkins continued for several years in the King Biscuit studio band. By 1949, the band was in Chicago. In 1950, Perkins recorded Clarence "Pinetop" Smith's classic "Pinetop's Boogie" in Memphis. In time, Perkins settled down in Chicago, where he worked with various musicians. In 1969, he replaced Otis Spann in Muddy Waters's band. Perkins formed the Legendary Blues Band in 1980 with three former Waters cohorts. He continued to record during that decade. By the 1990s, Perkins had retired and was performing only occasionally.

Boogie Woogie King **Evidence 26011**

Recorded for France's Black and Blue in 1976, this should have been released as Perkins's first solo effort, but it wasn't. Evidence made the album available in the U.S. in 1992. The backup band is top-notch: Luther Johnson, Jr., on guitar, Calvin Jones on bass, and Willie Smith on drums. The material is also fine. "Pinetop Is Just Top" is a bluesy syncopation; a good version of "Pinetop's Boogie Woogie" follows. Perkins performs a chillingly slow version of "Sweet Black Angel," a song associated with Robert Nighthawk. His rendition of Robert Jr. Lockwood's "Take a Little Walk with Me" also goes down with natural ease. Good sound, too.

LINK➤ *The Legendary Blues Band — Red Hot 'n' Blue* ***Rounder 2035***

Perkins and former Muddy Waters's band members, notably Jerry Portnoy on harmonica, update the Chicago blues formula with fresh numbers like "Streamlined Baby." They do some jump blues on "Loverboy" and stay close to the roots on Leroy Carr's "Come Back Baby." With Duke Robillard.

After Hours **Blind Pig 73088**

In 1988, at age 75, Perkins cut an album under his own name for the first time. Little Mike and the Tornadoes do a good job in supporting a snappy tour through the Chicago blues book, including "Anna Lee" and "Got My Mojo Working." Perkins makes certain that the emphasis is solidly on boogie-blues piano. Every song has its Perkins solo, and they are impeccable. One of the best, Jimmy Yancey's "Yancey Special," is an easy-rolling keyboard blues with just a taste of harmonica accompaniment. "The Hucklebuck" is also fun; it's done up in an electric rock style. Also here is a very dramatic performance of "Pinetop's Boogie Woogie." Very nice work.

LINK➤ *Willie Love — Clownin' with the World* ***Alligator 2700***

Look for this album under either Willie Love or Sonny Boy Williamson. Love's early 1950s sides for Trumpet Records form part of this CD, and he has a great time performing "Feed My Body to the Fishes" and other boogie numbers. The Williamson material is also terrific.

Lucky Peterson

When he was just 5 years old, Little Lucky Peterson performed "1-2-3-4" on *The Tonight Show* and *The Ed Sullivan Show*. The 1968 single and a subsequent album was written and produced by Willie Dixon, a friend of the family. Peterson's father owned the best blues club in Buffalo, NY, and son Judge Kenneth Peterson learned keyboards quickly and easily from Bill Doggett and Jimmy Smith, among others. His adult career started at age 17, when he joined Little Milton's band as organist. During that first year, Peterson became the band's leader and also opened each performance with his own solo set. After three years, he signed on with Bobby "Blue" Bland. Simultaneously, Peterson prepared for his own career as a headliner. He recorded for Florida's King Snake records.With label mate Kenny Neal, he caught the attention of Alligator Records. Peterson later moved to Verve.

Ridin' — Evidence 26033

Melvin Taylor's electric guitar and Lucky Peterson's fast-fingered keyboarding turn out to be ideal partners on this 1984 Paris session. On the title track, the two musicians showboat their way through blues at a breakneck speed. Willie Dixon's "Little Red Rooster" is treated to a slow and sexy organ arrangement and an understated Peterson vocal. Jimmy Reed's "You Don't Have to Go" starts with a flourish, then settles into a traveling rhythm, a funky little boogie. Reed's "Baby, What You Want Me to Do?" is soulful with some scat singing and concert-style piano work. And then there's the old Booker T. Jones and Steve Cropper instrumental "Green Onions." A delightful, entertaining CD.

LINK➤ *Melvin Taylor — and the Slack Band* **Evidence 26073**

Evidence's best-selling CD opens with Larry Davis's "Texas Flood," and Taylor shares an economical, high-impact approach to guitar with the song's most famous interpreter, Stevie Ray Vaughan. There's some Hendrix in Taylor's virtuosity. "T-Bone Shuffle" is also great.

Triple Play — Alligator 4789

Peterson's second Alligator album is marginally preferable to the first. Some of his freshness in Paris has been exchanged for a tidy fit into the Alligator profile. This is fine rocking blues, mixed with stylishly coarse vocals and a guitar that's just a little heavier than before—by 1990, Peterson was playing his own lead guitar as well as the keyboards. There are plenty of nice touches, too: the small-scale keyboard solo on "Your Lies," the funky organ opening on "Let the Chips Fall Where They May," and the extra horns on "Funky Ray." Ideas like the overblowing supplied by Ray Anderson's trombone and Bruce Staelens's trumpet set Peterson's music apart.

LINK➤ *Lucky Peterson — Lucky Strikes!* ***Alligator 4770***

This album happened because King Snake owner Bob Greenlee was looking for a creative spark for Kenny Neal's Big News from Baton Rouge!! *(Alligator 4764). The gig set Peterson up for a solo career. Musically similar to* Triple Play.

Henry Roeland Byrd (or Roy Byrd) was born in Bogalusa, LA, in 1918, and spent most of his life in New Orleans. He tap-danced for tips in the French Quarter and later performed in a minstrel show. Byrd also worked as a boxer and a card sharp before turning to music in the 1930s. After serving in WW II, he became a local leader on the New Orleans club scene, working under various names, including Professor Longhair and His Shuffling Hungarians. ("Professor" was sometimes shortened to "Fess.") Byrd began recording in 1949 and had an R&B hit, "Bald Head," for Mercury. He recorded for many other labels and was locally famous. By the 1960s, Byrd was working as a janitor to make ends meet. During the 1970s, renewed interest in R&B once again made him a local star; Fess became a fixture at the annual New Orleans Jazz and Heritage Festival. He died in 1980.

Fess: The Professor Longhair Anthology — Rhino 71502

This 2-CD set starts with 1950's hit single, "Bald Head," by Roy Byrd and His Blues Jumpers. It's a bouncy, jump number. Professor Longhair ("Fess") complains about how a man's wife "ain't got no hair," and the band shouts back "bald head." Harmless fun, it was his biggest hit. "Tipitina," from 1953's *New Orleans Piano* album (Atlantic 7225) is more like the Fess that New Orleans loved: the song features a rhythmic piano and a vocal style that simultaneously resemble blues, R&B, zydeco, and 15 other influences. "Ball the Wall," which is similar, includes an Alvin "Red" Tyler baritone sax break that will shake the pictures off your wall. "No Buts, No Maybes" was recorded for Ebb in 1957; it's unusual because the song is performed by the entire band in the foreground (most of the time, the band plays behind Fess, except for the occasional solo). It's an energetic, solid R&B horn workout. "Big Chief, Part 2" is a large-scale venture—a Mardi Gras march celebrating Indian culture that later became a regular part of the Neville Brothers' repertoire. Most of CD2 is devoted to Fess's comeback work in the post-1970 era. The first seven tracks are from 1974 and feature an interesting combination of New Orleans and blues tunes. A 1978 club date provided "Everyday (I Have the Blues)" and "Got My Mojo Working," but the essence of this music—a mix of blues, R&B, and New Orleans spirit—permeates every moment of this fine box.

LINK➤ *Allen Toussiant — Allen Toussaint Collection* — ***Reprise 26549***

An hour of music from one of New Orleans' leading pianists, producers, and songwriters. Toussiant's influence is most often heard in music by the Meters and the Neville Brothers, among others; here his darker, more profound take on New Orleans R&B is even very appealing.

A pioneer in the development of blues harmonica, James Edward Pryor was born in Lambert, MS, in 1921. John Lee "Sonny Boy" Williamson was an important early influence, though Pryor adapted much of the music he heard while picking up work around the Delta. He joined the Army in the early 1940s; after serving time in the Pacific, Pryor ended up at Fort Sheridan, which was close enough to Chicago to permit weekend gigs. Pryor performed in the Army, too, and it was here that he experimented with the effects of amplification on his harmonica. Pryor recorded often in the postwar years and scored several minor hits, some with guitar player Moody Jones. Commercial success, however, was elusive. As work faded away in the 1960s, Pryor left the scene. He returned in the mid-1980s with a Blind Pig album and has since recorded several more in addition to performing.

Snooky Pryor **Paula 11**

Although these recordings were made mostly from 1947 until the mid-1950s, they sound much older. (Sadly, this is typical of Paula releases.) On 1947's "Stockyard Blues," Pryor performs on harmonica and dominates a song sung by guitarist Floyd Jones and bassist Moody Jones. A completely capable lead instrumentalist, Pryor shines. Jumping ahead to 1952, Pryor is now leading a five-man band with Sunnyland Slim on piano. He starts right in on harmonica, then offers a relatively high-pitched old-style vocal on "Going Back on the Road." Sunnyland Slim and Pryor do a fine light boogie, "Harp Instrumental," from 1952. It's the best available from younger Pryor.

LINK➤ *Various Artists — Low Blows: An Anthology of Chicago Harmonica Blues* *Rooster Blues 2610*

Good album, but most of the artists are unknown outside the Windy City. Try, for example, Big Guitar Red & Good Rockin' Charles, or Golden Wheeler. Mostly mid-1970s. A find.

Snooky **Blind Pig 72387**

Although 1991's *Too Cool to Move* and 1994's *In This Mess Up to My Chest* may be preferable, their distribution status is questionable (the two were on Antone's). This CD is a good alternative. Pryor does a nice job with his harmonica solo on "Nine Below Zero," but his vocal is not as tight as it could be. The instrumental work on Bill Broonzy's "Key to the Highway" is unassailable; Pryor's vocal work here is every bit as effective as the fine guitar accompaniment that Chicago's Steve Freund provides. Most songs are originals, and Pryor's songwriting ability nicely suits his vocal style. "Broke and Hungry" is good, too. From 1987.

LINK➤ *Bobby Parker — Shine Me Up* *Black Top 1119*

A 1995 follow-up to the fine 1993 Bent Out of Shape *(Black Top 1086), these albums showcase a guitar player who started in L.A. in the late 1950s. He had a small hit in 1961 with "Watch Your Step." Parker is a musician's musician, a hero to Carlos Santana and others. Good soulful voice, too.*

Gertrude Pridgett was born into a show business family in 1886. She grew up in Columbus, GA, and at age 18, married minstrel performer Robert "Pa" Rainey. The couple performed together as Pa and Ma Rainey, or as Rainey and Rainey: Assassinators of the Blues. They traveled as part of the South's popular Rabbit Foot Minstrels as well as in traveling tent shows. In 1923, when she signed with Paramount (a subsidiary of a Wisconsin furniture maker with a line of phonographs), Ma Rainey had been singing professionally for 25 years. Through the 1920s, Rainey was one of black America's most popular recording artists; she was also one of the most popular performers on the TOBA vaudeville circuit. Tastes changed in the 1930s, and eventually Rainey packed it in and went home to Columbus. She supposedly spent her final years working as a domestic. Rainey died of a heart attack in 1939.

Ma Rainey **Milestone 47021**

In the 1920s, the distance between the blues and the music we now call jazz was almost nonexistent. Ma Rainey was an expert vocalist who straddles show business and honest downhearted blues; the warmth of Louis Armstrong's cornet and the scattered phrasing of Buster Bailey's cornet help Rainey's character seem deranged and hopeless on "See See Rider Blues." She's a very effective storyteller on "Prove It on Me," with Georgia Tom Dorsey on banjo and (probably) Tampa Red on kazoo, a principal instrument on several songs with washboard (uncredited). Through these remarkable recordings, Rainey taught hundreds of blues singers how to sing. While the sonics on these recordings are not perfect, the repertoire and entertainment value are supreme.

LINK➤ *Var. Artists — Blues Masters, Vol. 11: Classic Blues Women* ***Rhino 71134***

Rainey rates two of the 18 tracks, taking her place beside Trixie Smith, Mamie Smith, Bessie Smith (none of whom were related), Victoria Spivey, Billie Holiday, and others.

Ma Rainey's Black Bottom **Yazoo 1071**

With slightly better sound, most of these tracks were cut in 1924, 1926, and 1927. There's an excellent version of "Oh Papa Blues," a vaudevillian crowd pleaser with a terrific melody. In particular, the bass provided by the tuba is stunning. The familiar "Black Eye Blues," classic in its 12-bar structure, features the familiar chorus "you low-down alligator, just watch sooner or later, gonna catch you with your britches down." Most of these songs are accompanied by a small jazz band. Rainey's world-weary voice is smart in its phrasing and expressions of misery. She is fabulous, in fact, on every song. The many highlights include "Booze and Blues," "Blues, Oh Blues," and "Screech Owl Blues." Also essential.

LINK➤ *Original Cast — Ma Rainey's Black Bottom* ***Capitol 53001***

You'll find the music from this off-Broadway show only on cassette (or, if you haunt used record stores, on LP perhaps). It's spirited and fun, and captures Rainey's era.

Jimmy Reed is possibly the most confounding artist in the history of blues. He's also one of the all-time best-selling blues artists. Reed was a legendary backstage drunk who was at times incapable of remembering lyrics or parts. Somehow he managed to captivate audiences with his mild blues, which were completely the opposite of the aggressive electric Chicago style. Reed was born in a small Mississippi town in 1925 and became part of the Chicago blues scene following World War II. Married to his hometown sweetheart, Mary (better known as his songwriter, Mama Reed), he partnered with guitar player Eddie Taylor, a boyhood friend. Reed recorded for Vee-Jay from 1953 until 1966, then worked into the 1970s with ABC-Bluesway. By then, the combination of alcoholism and epilepsy (treated years too late because its symptoms were attributed to drinking) had ruined his chances. After years playing festivals, Reed died in Oakland, CA, in 1976.

The Classic Recordings — Tomato 71660

After the "Carnegie Hall" set, it's tough to know where to turn. This 3-CD behemoth—the second best choice in Reed's discography—includes 55 songs whose sound quality is often just adequate, and whose liner notes don't provide details about musicians, recording dates, and so on. Some songs are extremely memorable. "Ain't That Lovin' You, Baby" is tasty. "You Don't Have to Go" is simple but catchy. "When You Left Me" follows the tried-and-true road song tradition. "I Don't Go for That" is a tightly constructed piano blues, and "I Wanna Be Loved" is stirring; when Reed is on his game, he's irresistible. For every good song here, there are three marginal ones.

LINK➤ *Jimmy Reed — Jimmy Reed* — ***Paula 8***

A so-so collection filled with 1966, 1967, and 1971 recordings for ABC-Bluesway and Exodus. Reed was past his prime, and the recording quality is not what it should be.

At Carnegie Hall — Mobile Fidelity 566

This isn't a live album; instead, it's Reed singing songs he sang in a 1961 Carnegie Hall concert. It opens with one of his biggest hits, "Bright Lights, Big City" and soothing blues like "Found Joy" and "Kind of Lonesome." That's half the album, anyway. The other half recreates Vee-Jay hits under ideal studio conditions. "Baby What You Want Me to Do" (with its famous lyric, "You got me running, you got me hiding, you got me run, hide, hide, run, anyway you want to let it roll") is spectacular, with Mama Reed's harmonies and Jimmy Reed's terrific harmonica solo. "Honest I Do" and "Big Boss Man" are among other hits. Start here.

LINK➤ *Slim Harpo — Scratch My Back: The Best of Slim Harpo* — ***Rhino 70169***

Slim Harpo (James Moore) performs with an easier style than Reed, but also injects the occasional rock song into his repertoire. As usual, Rhino has done a terrific job in assembling the best material into a convenient package. Many of these songs have been covered by pop artists.

Rhodes was born Clarence Brown in Smithville, TX, in 1940. He started playing guitar just after his eighth birthday and received a guitar for a Christmas present just a month or so later. Rhodes's parents were sharecroppers; music was his ticket out. By the time he was a teenager, Rhodes was working in Austin. In the late 1950s, he did some recording and backup work. He joined the Navy after high school and worked part-time entertaining shipmates as a disc jockey. Rhodes spent the 1960s in Fresno, CA, and then in Oakland. He recorded, but didn't make much money with his music; frustrated, he formed his own record company, Rhodesway. It wasn't until the late 1980s that Rhodes found his audience. He tours as a way of life, reaching out to a growing audience of blues fans who support big-city clubs.

Just Blues — Evidence 26060

Extremely skillful electric blues makes Rhodes's self-produced, self-distributed 1985 album a worthy excursion. He starts with the optimistic "I Can't Lose," a bright, quick-stepping rocker. It's followed by the over-modulated guitar and stabbing vocals that lead into "The Things I Used to Do," a song whose trump card is not Rhodes's well-chosen guitar riffs, but his gutsy vocal. "Cigarette Blues" begins with "I loved a women, but she got cancer from smoking cigarettes," a line repeated within a standard blues song structure. Rhodes describes her habit as "four packs before noon, four more in the afternoon and evening." Ultimately, "nothing I did could make her stop." Here, as elsewhere, Rhodes is very effective.

LINK➤ *Roy Buchanan — Sweet Dreams: The Anthology* — *PolyGram 517-086*

Buchanan was one of the most promising guitar players of the 1970s—pumping out pure energy, but with a certain poetry amidst the madness. He worked through alcohol and drug problems until 1988, when he committed suicide. This is very steady work, worth owning.

Disciple of the Blues — Ichiban 9002

Rhodes recaps "Cigarette Blues" on this 1990 album, recorded for Florida's King Snake productions and licensed to Ichiban. Rhodes's songwriting is rock solid. "You Can Look for Me" is a simple tune that he sings persuasively while balancing Dwight Champagne's piano with the rhythmic strokes of his superbly contoured electric guitar sound. Rhodes allows space for the horns to shape the song on "Blue Funky Down"; it's a sort of talking blues with a funk attitude. "Ain't Nothing But the Blues," with a theme of poverty and illness, takes its cues from Chicago blues; Lester Chambers's harmonica carries the sympathetic feeling. Honest, straightforward, passionate blues.

LINK➤ *Bob Margolin — Up & In* — *Alligator 4851*

Another hard-working contemporary blues musician, Margolin, like Rhodes and a handful of others, probably won't become a major label star. In "Alien's Blues," he sings about an extraterrestrial death ray: "I may be green, but I love those blues." "Go Girl" is another highlight.

Robinson was born near Greenwood, MS, in 1935; his career took off as a result of a move to Memphis 16 years later. By then Robinson was a fine guitar player, and he started working immediately as a session man. In 1952, Robinson debuted on Modern Records. Not much happened as a result. Robinson kept working sessions and clubs. He played in the 1950s with Larry Davis, and the two cut several successful records including "Texas Flood" (credited to Davis) and "As the Years Go Passing By" (credited to Robinson). By 1962, Robinson was a Chicago musician, a South Side sideman behind Otis Rush, Sonny Boy Williamson, and others. Finally in 1967, he scored a hit record, "Somebody Loan Me a Dime." Unfortunately, two years later, Boz Scaggs recorded it and claimed to be its composer. Legal fights ensued. By the 1970s, Robinson was a viable recording act for Alligator. Cancer took his life in 1997.

Somebody Loan Me a Dime — Alligator 4705

From the first few bars of "Somebody Loan Me a Dime," it's clear Robinson owns this song. His integration of voice, rippling guitar, and lyric line is completely unified; even after hearing the song dozens of times, the tonal quality of Robinson's guitar still shivers the spine. Throughout this 1974 album, Robinson sings with the utmost sincerity. He's a very talented guitarist with a wonderful sense of detailing (check out "Going to Chicago"). Robinson is also one of the most skillful blues arrangers in the business; every sound, every emphasis is skillfully placed. Check out the sculpted interplay between piano and guitar on "Country Girl," for example. This is one gorgeous—and underappreciated—blues album.

LINK➤ *Jimmy Dawkins — Me, My Gitar and the Blues* — ***Ichiban 24909***

Although this album was recorded in the mid-1990s, Dawkins's sound hasn't changed much since the 1970s. He's got more energy here than on other recent works, but his signature buzz tone and his style of fingerpicking his "gitar" with his thumb make him unique.

I Hear Some Blues Downstairs — Alligator 4710

Despite high expectations, Robinson's second Alligator effort shows only flashes of 1974's brilliance. The title track is original—he's caught between a desire to spend quality time with his woman and a simultaneous urge to play blues with his friends—but Robinson's own lyrics and arrangement let him down, not by much, but by just enough. He's pretty effective in the T-Bone Walker homage "Tell Me What's the Reason," one of several songs where pianist Bill Heid plays an important role. There's zest in the fast-paced "I Wish for You," a track that is also finely produced. As slow melancholy memory songs go, "As the Years Go Passing By" is a warm-hearted delight.

LINK➤ *Willie Kent — Ain't It Nice* — ***Delmark 653***

Mississippi-born Kent was a top Chicago bassist in the 1950s. He returned to music full time in 1988 and cut two fine ensemble albums with his Gents band. This one, from 1991, is marginally better than 1994's Too Hurt to Cry *(Delmark 667).*

Rogers grew up in Atlanta, GA, and taught himself guitar and harmonica by listening to radio programs and records. He moved to Memphis when he was a teenager to make his way with the blues. Rogers occasionally performed with Robert Nighthawk and Robert Jr. Lockwood. He performed with Sunnyland Slim in the St. Louis area in 1940, then moved to Chicago the following year. By now the 17-year-old Rogers was an experienced hand. After a decade of playing with various musicians, he joined Muddy Waters as bassist in 1950; a healthy series of hit records followed. Rogers's solo career became a full-time endeavor in 1955 and lasted five years. Rogers quit the business in 1960 to manage a clothing store and raise a family. He came back in 1971, and gradually built a new career by touring, appearing at festivals in the U.S. and Europe, and recording for small labels.

The Complete Chess Recordings **MCA 93722**

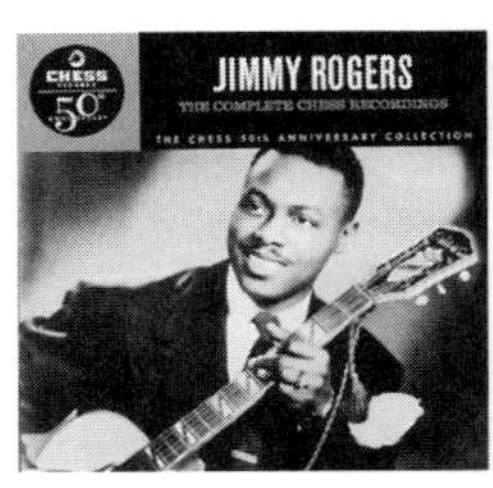

Chicago blues doesn't get better than this. Rogers supplies vocals and guitar, and plays with a variety of sidemen. Little Walter is most often the harmonica player; his interaction with Muddy Waters's guitar and Rogers's vocals, along with bassist Big Crawford on 1953's "Act Like You Love Me" is a prime taste of Chicago. Pianist Otis Spann and bassist Willie Dixon provide the rhythm for 1955's "You're the One," also a showcase for Little Walter and Rogers. "Money, Marbles, and Chalk," from 1951, is an appealing slow blues that begins with the familiar lyric "In the evening, after the sun goes down, the womens all tell me I'm the sweetest man in town." Everything here is perfect—particularly Rogers's voice and his superb songwriting. "Sloppy Drunk" shows the fine Chicago ensemble at its peak: "I would rather be sloppy drunk than any thing I know." Mighty Joe Young's powerful guitar provides the accents on 1958's cutesy "Don't Turn Me Down," and Reggie Boyd's picking provides an original texture for 1959's "Rock This House." The best material includes "That's Alright," the deep rhythm on "Walking by Myself," and Henry Gray's piano on "Chicago Bound." The heart of this 2-CD set is material also available on *Chicago Bound* (Chess 93000), but this package includes three times as many tracks (admittedly, more than a dozen are alternates). The liner notes are extensive, providing a clear explanation of why Rogers was so important to the Chicago blues.

LINK➤ *Chuck Berry — The Chess Box* ***Chess (MCA) 80001***

Everything changed during the mid-1950s. While Jimmy Rogers and others played electrified juke-joint music for a primarily black audience, Chuck Berry made music for car-crazed rock 'n' rolling teenagers. Rogers was old news. Berry was the future—then he, too, faded. Most of this 3-CD set presents Berry at his best.

Chicago Blues Masters, Vol. 2 **Capitol 33916**

Rogers revisits some classic material ("Act Like You Love Me," "Sloppy Drunk," "That's Alright") on these 1972–73 sessions, but also explores other material. In fact, this CD compiles three sessions. In Chicago, J.J. Cale produced 1972's "Broken Hearted Blues" (with David Myers providing a rock-solid bass line) and the simmering "Bad Luck Blues," as well as "Gold-Tailed Bird," Rogers's best slow blues. Freddie King co-produced eight more tracks in L.A., including "Brown-Skinned Woman" and the very fast "Live at Ma Bee's," both distinguished by Bill Lupkin's harmonica. Four tracks cut in Tulsa, OK, in 1973 include "Slick Chick," and the grieving "I Lost a Good Woman." Three solid outings.

LINK➤ *Jimmy Rogers — Ludella* ***Antone's 12***

Kim Wilson's harmonica and Pinetop Perkins's piano are behind this labor of love—a recreation of Rogers's best Chicago blues (plus additional treats). The recording is half studio, half live, and all very well done. From 1990.

Feelin' Good **Blind Pig 5018**

With the exception of three tracks, this album was recorded for the small Murray Brothers records in 1984. Rogers gets excellent support from Honey Piazza's piano, which ripples through a robust version of "Rock This House," and from Junior Watson, who plays a mean guitar. Rogers revisits a lot of the Windy City's blues scence from "Chicago Blues" to "Angel Child," and "You're So Sweet," in which he shares the lead spot with Rod Piazza's harmonica. Piazza, who co-produced the album with Rob Murray, provides the necessary emotional depth along with the craftsmanship. The band is tight, the songs are superb, and the production is flawless. There is plenty to recommend here.

LINK➤ *Johnny Young — Johnny Young and His Friends* ***Testament 5003***

Chicago-based Young, who played guitar and mandolin, appears here with Robert Nighthawk, Otis Spann, Little Walter, and others. Made in the early 1960s, these recordings blend earlier music with Chicago blues.

Blue Bird **Analogue 2001**

Rogers got plenty of attention in the audiophile press for this 1994 release. It was engineered with very special care. As a result, the instruments are clearly defined both in their stage positions and their tone, and Rogers's guitar sounds live. His voice appears to be a little tired, but there are no issues with his instrumental work, or his great backup band: Carey Bell (harmonica), Johnnie Johnson (piano), Jimmy D. Lane (lead guitar), Dave Myers (bass), and Ted Harvey (drums). This labor of love covers such standards as "Walkin' By Myself," "Smokestack Lighting," and an especially sweet, slow rendition of the title cut (also Rogers's best vocal performance).

LINK➤ *Billy Boy Arnold — Eldorado Cadillac* ***Alligator 4836***

Along with 1993's Back Where I Belong *(Alligator 4815), this 1995 album presents a veteran Chicago blues harmonica player on his comeback trail. Noted for his work with Bo Diddley in the 1950s, Arnold's career subsequently lost momentum. These two albums brought him back.*

Rogers grew up in the San Francisco Bay area community of Redding. Playing a guitar in a high school band led to work with a variety of bands that played Bay Area bars. At age 26, in 1976, Rogers and local harmonica player Dave Burgin cut an album for the tiny Waterhouse label. Rogers formed his own band, the Delta Rhythm Kings, in 1980. His growing reputation attracted John Lee Hooker's attention, and in 1982, Rogers joined Hooker's Coast to Coast Band. Rogers's first album, recorded in 1986, was nominated for a W.C. Handy Award. Meanwhile, Rogers continued his relationship with Hooker, serving as both session guitarist and producer. He won a Grammy for 1991's *Mr. Lucky* and a nomination for 1989's *The Healer*. In the 1990s, Rogers has recorded and performed with Norton Buffalo, an R&B harmonica player. Rogers also tours regularly.

Slidewinder — Blind Pig 72687

The big news here is Roy Rogers's slide guitar, an instrument he employs to great effect on "Tip-Walk," a pleasant musical stroll of a duet with pianist Allen Toussaint. The two are at it again on "Red Hot." Rogers's guitar also sounds mighty fine when backing John Lee Hooker, as the gravel-voiced vocalist masters Robert Johnson's "Terraplane Blues." Rogers is just terrific, a model of versatility on the one-man band number "Down in Mississippi." And if Rogers's voice can at times be a bit too friendly, too high, or too lightweight, his version of "Walkin' Blues" should silence the doubters. The musical craftsmanship here is impressive, too. Accessible, nonthreatening blues. From 1988.

LINK➤ *Ari Eisinger — You Don't Understand*
Second Mind L-1011

Eisinger is a Philadelphia-based acoustic guitar virtuoso, a big fan of Blind Blake, and a devotee of fine country blues. He plays with a ragtime feeling with a constant flow of interesting, well-articulated ideas. Highly recommended, but hard to find (Second Mind: Box 987, Landsdowne, PA 19050).

R&B Blind Pig 74491

The emphasis here is on vocal harmony as Rogers sings some peppy duets with harmonica player Norton Buffalo (who gets joint credit). This isn't quite blues—it's more like Wild West meets vaudeville. The music is energetic, fun, and for all of the pair's effusiveness, it works. A song like "Is It Love?" provides insight: Rogers's guitar work is pleasant, friendly, and inviting. Add room-filling fancy dancing from Buffalo's harp, and the resulting sound is difficult to resist. Best is "Tender Heart," partly because Rogers does not attempt to fill the open space, allowing a cello and fiddle to create the mood. The lyrics are innocuous, and the songs are mostly originals.

LINK➤ *Various Artists — Jackson Blues, 1928–1938* ***Yazoo 1007***

The highlights of this Mississippi collection include three tracks by Tommy Johnson, one by the Mississippi Sheiks, and one by Carter. Walter Vincent, who performs "Overtimes Blues," grew up with Carter. (In fact, all of these Yazoo compilations are worth owning.)

Duke Robillard formed Roomful of Blues as a Rhode Island bar band in 1967. In the early years, the band played everything—blues, R&B, jazz, rock—and did it well enough to get bookings in many East Coast cities. After a decade of road work, Roomful of Blues was signed to Island/Antilles, a reggae label. In the late 1970s, Robillard left to form Duke Robillard and the Pleasure Kings. In 1980, Ronnie Earl took his place, and stayed for eight years. (Earl also made records on his own, and left in 1988 to devote full-time energy to Ronnie Earl and the Broadcasters.) For two years in the 1980s, LuAnn Barton was also a lead vocalist alongside singer and sax player Greg Piccolo. The band also collaborated on acclaimed albums with Big Joe Turner and Eddie "Cleanhead" Vinson. The band continues today despite numerous personnel changes, with recordings on several labels.

Dressed Up to Get Messed Up — Varrick (Rounder) 18

Several early Roomful of Blues albums are worth a listen. These include 1979's hard-to-find *Let's Have a Party* (on Antilles) and 1987's *Live at Lupo's Heartbreak Hotel* (Varrick/Rounder 24). This 1986 album is representative of the group's middle period, when Ronnie Earl and Greg Piccolo dominated the band. The songwriting is good, but not always great; the execution, however, is always enthusiastic and capable. "Money Talks," for example, is a midtempo tune with a pleasant beat and some clever touches. "Dressed Up to Get Messed Up" is sleazy fun. "The Last Time" is one of several tunes with a 1950s R&B veneer. Sound quality is okay.

LINK➤ *Duke Robillard — Turn It Around* **— *Rounder 3116***

Robillard's fat guitar launches "Down by the Delta," a conspiratorial Memphis duet with Susan Forrest and sings lead with her come-hither, tough-babe style. Mostly, this is an album about guitar, with occassional nods to the 1950s.

Turn It On! Turn It Up! — Bullseye Blues 66001

Much cleaner sound, plus interactive content (for Windows or Macintosh) should encourage an audition for this 1995 album. Sugar Ray Norcia's vocals are out in front, with Chris Vachon's lead guitar also in a starring role. The band gets off to a powerful start with "Blind Love," a rocking R&B tune, then winds down for a 1940s big band sound on "I Left My Baby," with muted trumpets and Matt McCabe's jazzy piano. "If You Know It" is a terrific hybrid swing, jump blues and rock number—an effective update on an old style. These guys are having a great time making music.

LINK➤ *Little Charlie & the Nightcats — Deluxe Edition* **— *Alligator 5603***

A best-of compilation detailing the history of one of Alligator's most popular acts. The heart of the band is the bounce and enthusiasm of Little Charlie Baty on lead guitar and his associate of 20 years, harmonica player Rick Estin. It's jump blues brought up to date.

Despite his enormous talent and his popularity in the Chicago area, Otis Rush never became a star. Rush was born in Philadelphia, MS, in 1934, learned guitar, and moved north to Chicago. He started slowly in the late 1940s, but eventually attracted Willie Dixon's attention. Dixon arranged for a Cobra recording contract in 1954, and this led to a top 10 R&B single on the very first try: "I Can't Quit You, Baby." When Cobra went out of business, Rush signed with Chess and then with Duke, but neither deal was productive. Through a friendship with Mike Bloomfield and Nick Gravenites, Rush was represented by Albert Grossman, whose clients included Janis Joplin and Bob Dylan. Grossman arranged a deal with Cotillion, but Rush's album flopped; he recorded another with Capitol, which never bothered to release his best work. Eventually Rush gave up recording and simply played in Chicago's clubs.

1956–1958: Cobra Recordings — Paula PCD01

These are seminal moments in the development of Chicago blues—even the four alternate takes are essential. Rush's R&B band is hard-edged and barroom tough. It's characterized by honking horns, athletic drumming, and a spicy piano. Make no mistake, however: Rush is the center of attraction. His disappointed city vocals, the hopeless sting of his old guitar, and the complexity of his arrangement make the utterly bleak "Double Trouble" sound more like late 1960s—not 1950s—blues. This is Rush at his best. Half the history of the blues is packed into Rush's vocal nuances, ringing guitar, and echos from the past on "All Your Love." It's a style that has been copied by hundreds of rock-blues bands. This CD clearly belongs in every collection.

LINK➤ *Various Artists — The Cobra Records Story* — ***Capricorn 42012***

The small Cobra label didn't last long (just two years, from 1956 until 1958), but Willie Dixon's talent and artistic judgment encouraged Rush, Buddy Guy, Magic Sam, and other Chicago artists to do some of their best work. An essential slice of blues history.

Right Place, Wrong Time — Hightone 8007

Rush's presentation here is smoother; there's less competition between his band and his guitar. In short, everything works beautifully on this previously unreleased 1971 Capitol session. Rush sings like he really means every word. Rush's electric guitar sends out little spikes of pain and anger on "Right Place, Wrong Time," which also features silky-smooth horns painting layers of sadness. It is, quite simply, perfect blues. Compare Rush's "Rainy Night in Georgia" to Brook Benton's hit version. Rush's sincerity is a revelation, and the cut is tastefully underproduced. On song after song, Rush is tight, on the money, and exciting. He's a brilliant performer who should have been a major star.

LINK➤ *Various Artists — Chicago/The Blues/Today! Vol. 2* — ***Vanguard 79217***

The first five tracks are performed by "Jimmy" (James) Cotton's band with pianist Otis Spann. The second features Rush (he does "It's a Mean Old World," among others). Homesick James, who isn't as often heard, performs "Dust My Broom" and three others. Important and satisfying.

Cold Day in Hell **Delmark 638**

The crosscut edge of Rush's guitar juts into rock territory with this 1975 release. "Cut You Loose" finds Rush so involved that his instrumental work sounds like a jam; it's a collection of riffs that fit together in a larger context, but don't much satisfy commercial considerations. "You're Breaking My Heart" starts with a two-and-a-half minute razor-sharp guitar solo with horn and rhythm accompaniment (definitely for the advanced class) that leads into Rush's vocal. Rush picks up some standards here, including "Mean Old World," "All Your Love," and "Midnight Special." His sophistication, however, transforms these songs into something new. Highly recommended.

LINK➤ *John Scofield — Liquid Fire* ***Gramavision 79501***

Scofield is one of the best contemporary jazz guitar players, but his work is clearly influenced by blues guitarists like Rush. This set collects several albums recorded in the mid-1980s. To continue, try Best of John Scofield: Blue Note Years *(Blue Note 53330).*

So Many Roads: Live in Concert **Delmark 643**

Tokyo's Hibiya Park was the setting for this summer 1975 concert. Rush is in absolute top form, and the recording is generally excellent (with a few engineering mistakes). Earl Hooker's "Will My Woman Be Home Tonight (Blue Guitar)" is the basis for a lengthy opening improvisation that sets Rush apart as a guitar giant. He makes all the right moves, following with Peter Chatman's famous "Everyday I Have the Blues." Rush also aces the popular B.B. King number "Gambler's Blues" with a sparkling guitar solo. R.G. Ford's "Crosscut Saw" and Rush's own "Three Times a Fool" are also well worth a listen. Mostly, Rush leans on standard blues repertoire, works his guitar hard, and delivers a crowd-pleasing knockout punch.

LINK➤ *Dave Specter — Blueplicity* ***Delmark 664***

Specter came up by playing as a sideman at Chicago's popular B.L.U.E.S. club. This 1994 release concentrates mostly on guitar. His music ranges considerably from low-down dirty blues to jazzier pieces. Lately, Specter has been heading in the jazz direction.

Live in Europe **Evidence 26034**

This is a straightforward 1977 concert taped at a festival in Nancy, France. Rush is backed by a trio: Bob Levis (rhythm guitar), Bob Stroger (bass), and Jesse Green (drums). The three are attentive, hard workers, but as always, it's the strains and ideal tones that Rush coaxes from his guitar that's the source of wonder. While many of these numbers appear on other albums, Rush's knack for improvisation makes each one seem new. Titles include "I Can't Quit You Baby," "Society Woman," "Crosscut Saw," "All Your Love," and "Cut You Loose." The sonics are predictably adequate for a live rock recording. Not Rush's best, but his top-quality guitar, just the same.

LINK➤ *Otis Rush — Live & Awesome* ***Genes 4131***

This 1996 release features several Rush favorites, such as "Right Place, Wrong Time," "Cold Day in Hell," and "Let's Have a Natural Ball." There's a good version of T-Bone Walker's "Stormy Monday" here, too. Nice chats between the songs, with a receptive audience.

A big man with a voice large enough to take over a room, Rushing defined the term "blues shouter." He became famous singing for big bands, but he was also an important figure in the Kansas City blues scene. Rushing was born in Oklahoma City, OK, in 1902. His first instrument was the violin, and he received a serious musical education before moving on to Wilberforce College. When the industry beckoned, Rushing quit school to make his name in California. He worked briefly with Jelly Roll Morton in the early 1920s before returning to Oklahoma and then to Kansas City, where he became the lead singer for Walter Page's Blue Devils. Rushing followed Page and pianist Count Basie to Bennie Moten's band, then joined Basie in his own band; he remained there until 1950. These were his greatest years.

The Essential Jimmy Rushing — Vanguard 65/66

There's very little that Rushing can't do, and do well. He's a fine blues shouter from the very start: "Boogie Woogie (I May Be Wrong)" is a flashy tune he wrote with Count Basie. It's plotted somewhere between big band jazz and jump blues. Rushing's better still on the slower material: a gentle piano and a muted trumpet on "How You Want Lovin' Done," a classic blues tune like Leroy Carr's "How Long How Long Blues," or Sam Chatman's "Every Day I Have the Blues." Rushing's got both the pipes and the expressiveness to define the way these songs should be sung. From the mid-1950s.

LINK➤ *Count Basie — The Complete Decca Recordings* **Decca Jazz 3-611**
Handsome 3-CD history of one of the bluesiest jazz bands. The period covered is from 1937 to 1939. In addition to the phenomenal precision of the horn arrangements, it's worth listening to Jimmy Rushing doing the best work of his life alongside Coleman Hawkins, Helen Humes, Lester Young, and other top artists.

Gee, Baby, Ain't I Good To You — New World 80530

Old friends come together for a 1967 session that's considerably heavier on jazz than blues. It's a bit sloppy, but Rushing sounds terrific (he always did). The selections fall into the "old favorites" category: "St. James Infirmary," "One O'Clock Jump," "I Ain't Got Nobody," and "Good Morning Blues." There's even a respectable version of "Who's Sorry Now?" The album is credited to the Jimmy Rushing All Stars, an informal ensemble of former Basie greats including Buck Clayton (trumpet), Jo Jones (drums), and Dickie Wells (trombone). Rushing recorded a plenty of albums between 1955 and 1971; nearly all are out of print (a few have been released on CD).

LINK➤ *Chuck Willis — Stroll On: The Chuck Willis Collection* **Razor & Tie 2055**
Atlanta-born jump rocker Willis is probably most famous for "C.C. Rider" (which he didn't write), but he was the composer of "I Feel So Bad" (which was recorded by many artists, from Elvis to Little Milton) and lots of other fine tunes. An R&B innovator, shown here at his best.

Saffire is a trio inspired by the sassy female blues singers of the 1920s and 1930s and by their own unpredictable muses. Born in 1944 in Virginia, Gaye Adegbalola worked as a biochemical researcher and an eighth-grade science teacher while spending spare evenings in a local theater group. Ann Rabson was born in 1945 in New York, but grew up in Ohio. Her passion was blues guitar. She moved to Virginia in 1971 and worked full time as a musician. A few years later, she took a job as a computer analyst. Rabson met Adegbalola around this time, but they didn't get together as a duo until 1984. By then, Rabson was also a skilled pianist. They quit their day jobs in 1988 and released their first album in 1990. Two years later, bassist Earlene Lewis was replaced by Andrea Faye McIntosh (who also plays fiddle, mandolin, and other instruments). Saffire is still going strong today.

Hot Flash — **Alligator 4796**

There's an appealing purity about this 1991 album. Apart from some occasional help from Billy Branch's harmonica, it's just the three women (Earlene Lewis is still on bass). And when they all gather around to harmonize on "One Good Man," Saffire's music refreshes the soul. The trio does some signature sassy blues and open with "Two in the Bush Is Better Than One in the Hand," with Ann Rabson playing a whole lot of piano. "Tom Cat Blues" has a nostalgic country blues quality, and the peppy little boogie "Sloppy Drunk" is one of many memorable tunes. "Dirty Sheets" is also typical: it's sheer frustration expressed in musical form.

LINK➤ *Saffire — Old, New, Borrowed & Blue* — ***Alligator 4826***

In addition to the usual Saffire originals, some tunes associated with female blues singers are also here: Bessie Smith and Billie Holiday's "T'aint Nobody's Business"; Etta Jones's "The Richest Guy in the Graveyard"; plus good stuff from Jelly Roll Morton and others.

Broad Casting — **Alligator 4811**

The third Saffire album introduces Andra Faye McIntosh. Bessie Smith meets Ma Rainey on "One Hour Mama," a song complete with those impossibly sexy long vocal lines so popular on the vaudeville stage. And although it's a torch song, "Seemed Like Such a Good Idea at the Time" comes from the same school. Saffire has some fun with boogie-woogie by way of jump blues on "Dump That Chump." The most distinctive song is "OBG Why Me Blues," a surprisingly literal report on a visit to a gynecoloist (sample lyrics: "It's tough to let a stranger take a gander at these thighs"). As always, Rabson's piano is a treat. From 1992.

LINK➤ *E.C. Scott — Hard Act to Follow* — ***Blind Pig 5044***

Scott came up through the gospel world, listening to Shirley Caesar and also to pop singers like Gladys Knight and Dinah Washington. She's got the same brazen attitude as Saffire, and a big voice, too. Try also her wonderful debut album, Come and Get Your Love *(Blind Pig 5019).*

"Satan" is Sterling Magee. He was born in 1936 in Mount Olive, MS, where he played piano at church services. Magee left home for the Army and served in Germany as a paratrooper. During the mid-1960s, he worked in NYC as a Brill Building songwriter who wrote songs for Etta James, Marvin Gaye, and King Curtis, among others. He later led his own quartet. Magee left the business by the late 1970s, and worked in Florida as an auto mechanic. Reinventing himself as Mister Satan, he next worked as a Harlem street musician. One day in 1986, 28-year-old Adam Gussow stopped by. Gussow, with a Princeton undergraduate degree, an M.A. from Columbia, an apprenticeship with blues harmonica wizard Nat Riddles, and street performance experience, became Magee's partner. The pair recorded a demo and sold it to Flying Fish. Satan and Adam hit the road, worked hard, and found their audience.

Harlem Blues — **Flying Fish (Rounder) 70567**

The sound is so overwhelming and frenetic that it's nearly out of control. At its center is the wild feral voice of Satan. It's hoarse, gravely, and frightening—until you get to know him. "Groovy People" is a slower, welcoming love song to the audience; it's performed in a kindly, embracing way and features the sounds of Adam's pleasant, inviting harmonica. "I Create the Music" is another accessible song with a direct link to the heart of the audience. Many of the original songs on this 1991 debut album are innovative in their use of rhythm and raw vocals; even such blues classics as "Sweet Home Chicago" get a new spin. Altogether, this is a deeply involving, wonderful piece of work.

LINK➤ *Ted Hawkins — Happy Hour* — ***Rounder 2033***

With a knack for memorable melodies, a voice that goes down easy (with a touch of Jimmy Buffett), and a pop sensibility, Hawkins somehow never made it. This 1987 release is delightful, and so is 1985's Songs from Venice Beach *(Evidence). Hawkins died in 1995.*

Mother Mojo — **Flying Fish (Rounder) 70623**

Although Satan's voice continues to resemble coarse sandpaper, the whole veneer of this 1993 album is silky smooth. "Seventh Avenue" is especially sweet; it's a memory of a faraway lost love. Satan's expressive "Aw, she was pretty" and Adam's lengthy harmonica solo (with a quote from the Beatles' "Get Back") rank among the pair's best work. The song is followed by a lovely ballad, "Ain't Nobody Better Than Nobody." Unafraid of honest sentimentality, this music comes straight from the heart; it's the essence of street smarts, and yet it's sophisticated, too. "Thunky Fing," for example, exposes Satan's Brill Building experience; it's one of several with pop roots. "Silly Little Things" is another fine bit of songwriting.

LINK➤ *Satan & Adam — Living on the River* — ***Flying Fish (Rounder) 666***

This 1998 album shows the duo in a familiar, comfortable groove. Satan drifts from street madness and old blues ("Stagga Lee") to golden oldies ("Proud Mary," "Ode to Billy Joe," "I'm a Girl Watcher"). Adam embroiders with his endlessly fresh harmonica work. The combination works.

Frank Seals was a blues musician who owned the Dipsy Doodle Club in Osceola, AR. Little more than a roadhouse joint, it was frequented by traveling blues heroes like Sonny Boy Williamson and Albert King. Frank's son, who everyone called "Son," listened and learned from the bluesmen. By age 13, in 1955, he was playing the drums behind Robert Nighthawk. Five years later, Seals had his own working band in nearby Little Rock. He opened for many big acts when they were in town, and picked up some work playing guitar behind Earl Hooker. By 1971, Seals was trying to make it in Chicago; on a tip, Bruce Iglauer caught his act at the Expressway Lounge and signed him for Alligator. Iglauer became Seals's manager, and the two worked together for a decade; they separated after a dispute and reunited in 1991. Seals is one of Chicago's current guitar legends.

The Son Seals Blues Band — Alligator 4703

Nowhere near as slick as his later work, this 1973 album was Seals's recording debut. Made in the days before outrageous guitar amplification and blaring horns, it's still one of his best. Seals's training as a Southern bluesman is especially evident in his slower blues. "Sitting at My WIndow" is an original, but it sounds like a Southern blues from decades ago; the moody guitar solo is supported by organ and the low voices of fellow band members acknowledging that Seals is doing just the right thing. Seals's voice is quite expressive and soulful on "All Your Love," and Johnny "Big Moose" Walker's organ creates the perfect rainy-day feeling. Recommended.

LINK➤ *Johnny Winter* — ***Columbia 9947***

Winter's aggressive combination of Texas rock and Texas blues is essential. An exquisite guitarist, Winter tries on various types of blues on this 1969 debut, from the hard and heavy pain of "I'm Yours and I'm Hers" to the raw jangle of Mean Mistreater."

Midnight Son — Alligator 4708

The first ten seconds of this album tell you something special is happening: a jangly electric guitar solo, twangs perfectly spaced, and horn accents jumping in at just the right time. This conversation begins "I Believe." The rhythm section kicks in about 20 seconds later, and then Seals sings slowly with steely confidence. The whole package works. Seals chooses his guitar licks with perfect taste and varies them just enough to conform to his gutsy songwriting. Three horns pump plenty of fuel into a rocking mix, but Seals knows just when to change the formula; for example, "On My Knees," with its emphasis on drums. Solid work from 1976.

LINK➤ *Various Artists — Blues Masters, Vol. 9: Postmodern Blues* — ***Rhino 71132***

There's a lot of good guitar on this survey of post-1968 blues: Albert King, B.B. King, Magic Slim, Son Seals, Albert Collins, Robert Cray, and so on. Also, there's soulful vocal work from Bobby Blue Bland and some earthshaking from Koko Taylor. Great collection.

Live & Burning **Alligator 4712**

Compare "Hot Sauce" on this 1978 live album to its more gentle predecessor on his first album, and you'll see how Son Seals has transformed himself from just another talented guitar player to one of the loudest, fastest, meanest voices around. When he tackles a slow song, he's got the top-notch blues saxman A.C. Reed beside him to set things up. Seals is in command of his singing voice, too. He digs into the lower ranges, messing with phrasing on "Blue Shadows Falling" and gives the crowd at Chicago's Wise Fools Pub a fine laid-back performance. There's plenty of variety here, from Southern blues in "Help Me, Somebody" to smart urbanity on "Call My Job."

LINK➤ *A.C. Reed — I'm in the Wrong Business* ***Alligator 4757***

Stevie Ray Vaughan and Bonnie Raitt guest on Reed's debut album as a leader. He's been on plenty of blues albums (five with Albert Collins, more with Buddy Guy and others). On this 1987 workout, Reed delivers the goods on sax; his songwriting is clever and funny, too.

Bad Axe **Alligator 4738**

It's 1984, and Seals is working with a studio band. The emphasis is now on his voice, with his guitar in second place and a pleasant rhythm section filling in with a sound suggsting R&B and country blues. "Don't Pick Me for Your Fool" is centered by an anthemlike guitar riff that bores into the soul. Diversity within a formula has always set Seals apart. With Billy Branch on harmonica, he straddles country music and blues on "I Can Count on My Blues." It's delivered in a singing style that's sometimes close to rhythmic speech. Still, there's nothing like the full-fisted ripping anger of "Going Home."

LINK➤ *Carl Weathersby — Don't Lay Your Blues on Me* ***Evidence 26075***

Pungent electric guitar from the next generation of Chicago blues; Weathersby is half of the popular Sons of Blues. This is his 1995 album, notable for a devastating "Killing Floor" and many good originals, including "Rock Your Town" and the title song.

Living in the Danger Zone **Alligator 4798**

Seals is considerably more relaxed, less showy, and allows more room for instrumentalists throughout this 1991 effort. On "Ain't That Some Shame," the open space permits an appealing groove. Seals is facile, as his super-fast guitar fingering proves on "Four Last Nickels." He's at his best on "My Life," with Sid Wingfield's organ, Johnny B. Gayden's bass, and Sugar Blue's harmonica accompaniment. After a really slow harmonica and guitar duet, Seals's fine voice nearly prays as it faces mortality. He evaluates his beliefs, his worries, and the promise of getting his reward some day. Seals is sincere and credible, but a bit long-winded during the 8-minute piece.

LINK➤ *Carl Weathersby — Looking Out My Window* ***Evidence 26089***

With extremely clear sound (HDCD, for those with properly equipped CD players), Weathersby's 1997 effort is his best yet. After a strong start with the street-smart "If That Ain't the Blues," he runs down compositions by Chuck Willis, Paul deLay, John Hiatt, and Elmore James.

A determined realist who refused to earn his living on street corners, Shines was born near Memphis, TN, in 1915 in the small town of Frayser. He learned guitar, performed at local gatherings (mostly in Arkansas, where he grew up), and rambled with buddy Robert Johnson in the 1930s (not only in the Mississippi Delta region, but as far north as Canada). By the 1940s, Shines was working in Chicago, but his country-blues style was old-fashioned, so he didn't get much work and his records didn't sell. He gave up music in the late 1950s and found a steady job as a construction worker. Shines was rediscovered in the mid-1960s, but kept his day job for a few more years. He spent most of the 1970s on the road, playing colleges, clubs, and festivals. A 1980 stroke hurt Shines's dexterity, but he kept singing. He died in 1992 in Alabama.

Johnny Shines and Robert Lockwood — Paula 14

Although they were friends, Shines and Lockwood do not play together on this album. Instead, Shines plays ten songs, which are terrific, and Lockwood trades lead chores with Sunnyland Slim on ten more, which are not as good. The key cut here, from 1952, is the hootin' and hollerin' tune "Rambin'," but the B-side, "Fish Tail," is equally satisfying for its falsettos and guitar imitations of his vocals. Six sides with harmonica master Walter Horton are better still. The boogie feeling of 1953's "Evening Sun" is terrific early Chicago blues. Shines and Horton are even better on "No Name Blues." Sadly, this great music was not a money-maker, and Shines left the business.

LINK➤ *Elmore James & John Brim — Whose Muddy Shoes* — *Chess 9114*

Vintage Chicago blues from 1953 (and four cuts from 1960). Guitarist/vocalist Brim is good, but James's intensity and emotion is on another level. His country style on the title song, those extended vowels, and J. T. Brown's searching tenor sax are among many classics. Very fine.

With Big Walter Horton — Testament 5015

Walter Horton's harmonica is a big part of this show; his soulful musings wrap in and around this music so completely that it's easy to listen only to his work. The two guitars belong to a young (and very talented) Luther Allison and to Shines. It all comes together on "Hello Central," but some of the other cuts (like "Sneakin' and Hidin'" and "Fat Mama") fall a little short on either songwriting or energy. "I Cry, I Cry" and "If It Ain't Me" are better. These songs come from a 1969 session. Five others, including the upbeat rocker "You Don't Have to Go" (with Fred Below's pseudo-military drumming), are from 1966.

LINK➤ *Johnny Shines — Masters of Modern Blues* — *Testament 5002*

Here's the principal release from June 1966, whose additional cuts filled out the 1969 album above. Great version of "Rollin' and Tumblin'" and "Mr. Tom Green's Farm."

Last Night's Dream **Warner Brothers 45285**

In the mid-1960s, Shines gave the music business another try, this time with some success. He was coaxed back by British blues enthusiast Mike Rowe, who produced this album. Shines is in good company with an excellent, attentive, imaginative band: Walter "Shakey" Horton (harmonica), Willie Dixon (bass), and Clifton James (drums). Shines is superb—his vocals are emotional, articulate, and captivating, proving him to be a world-class blues singer. "Pipeline Blues," with Otis Spann on piano, is among the best Chicago blues on record. There's plenty of fine guitar work, too, on mellow classics like "I Had a Good Home" and "From Dark 'Til Dawn."

LINK➤ *Various Artists — Bottleneck Blues* ***Testament 5021***

One of the best Testament collections, this one concentrates on slide guitar in its various forms. There's a healthy dose of Big Joe Williams, a track by Shines, Nighthawk, McDowell, and others. Discoveries include Napoleon Strickland, Mott Willis, and John Lee Ganderson.

Traditional Delta Blues **Biograph 121**

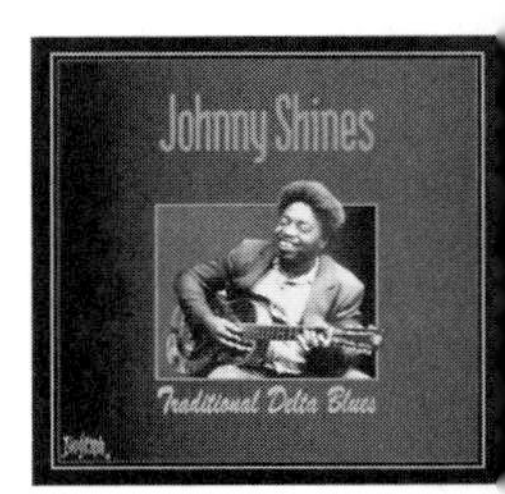

An extraordinary 1974 collection of vintage songs associated with Robert Johnson and other Delta artists, this album should be a part of every blues library. Shines is brilliant as both a vocalist and guitar player, and the material is among the best available. The Johnson set includes "Dynaflow Blues" (based on Johnson's "Terraplane Blues"), "Milkcow Blues," and "Tell Me, Mama," a fine song that Johnson never recorded. "Pony Blues" is a Charlie Patton tune, and "Sittin' on Top of the World" is a popular song by the Mississippi Sheiks. Shines also sings his own classic, "Ramblin' Blues." He also fits a few contemporary originals into the mix, notably "Glad Rags," about getting high.

LINK➤ *Johnny Shines — Hey Ba-Ba-Re-Bop!* ***Rounder 2010***

Don't miss this 1971 live acoustic solo album for a good sampling of Shines's repertoire. It includes some Robert Johnson music, some Shines originals, and, just for fun, Lionel Hampton's title tune.

Too Wet to Plow **Blues Alliance (Concord) 13001**

Shines left behind an impressive catalog of work, but no single album presents his talent as effectively as this 1975 release. Louisiana Red, an ideal partner on guitar, embellishes Shines's flashier work with a solid, consistent line. Sugar Blue's harmonica is offered more as support than as a lead instrument. The title song is among the best work here, but the extended notes on "Moanin' the Blues" set up a very effective soul searcher. Similarly, the heated guitar and harmonica blend on "Red Sun" stands with Shines's best on record. Throughout this album, there's a sense of depth and control, the feeling that an artist is developing his legacy work. Highly recommended.

LINK➤ *Louisiana Red — The Best of Louisiana Red* ***Evidence 26055***

With a gruff vocal tone and a muscular approach to guitar, Louisiana Red recalls an earlier, rough-and-tumble era. These recordings were made mostly in 1965, when he was around 30 years old. He's a good storyteller, and very much an original performer.

Bessie Smith

One of the century's finest voices, Bessie Smith was born in 1894 in Chattanooga, TN. Her parents died while she was a child, and young Bessie learned to sing and dance from her brother, Clarence, who later became a vaudeville performer. By 1912, she was dancing in the Moses Stokes Company (her brother was also in the troupe). Blues singer Ma Rainey was also part of the show, and the two women became friends. Smith became well known among black audiences, and by the early 1920s, she was based in Philadelphia. She first recorded in 1923, and gained fame when one of her early records, "Down-Hearted Blues," sold 750,000 copies in a year. Smith recorded for Columbia through the 1920s, but blues went out of fashion late in that decade; by 1931, Smith was without a recording contract. She continued to perform, mostly in he South but also in NYC at the Apollo Theater. Smith died from injuries related to a Missouri car crash; medical attention was likely delayed because of her skin color.

The Complete Recordings, Vol. 1 — Columbia 47091

Bessie Smith probably made some records prior to 1923. She may even have recorded hem for Columbia, but they're gone, lost to history. This box picks up with the earliest known side, "Down Hearted Blues," recorded simply with Smith and pianist Clarence Williams. It was coupled with "Gulf Coast Blues," and became a huge hit. Those early sessions also yielded "'Tain't Nobody's Bizness If I Do," a Smith anthem presented here with only Williams's piano. Her vocal stylizing, the way she holds notes for emphasis, intonates for bite and depth, and phrases her lyrics are distinctive; Smith was enormously influential for generations of singers. Most of Smith's songs were decidedly unlike the country blues that were popular at the time. Her voice, her rrangements, and her choice of material more strongly suggest stage music, night-lub or tent show performances and are closely related to early jazz. Smith has some attitude on "Aggravatin' Papa," a jazzy tune with clarinet, banjo, and piano accompa-iment. By late 1923's "Mistreatin' Daddy," she was attracting top-notch accompani-ment: Fletcher Henderson on piano and Don Redman on clarinet (the three are also esponsible for the silly novelty, "Haunted House Blues"). Harry Reser's guitar quiets he mood on "Easy Come, Easy Go Blues," and Robert Robbins plays violin on "Rock-ng Chair Blues" as this new music finds its way. Start with the later material, which is more consistent, then return to this box for her early work.

INK➤ *Louis Armstrong—Portrait of the Artist as a Young Man* Columbia 57176

his 4-CD box begins in 1923 with Armstrong's first recorded solo (for King Oliver's Jazz reole Band), and ends in 1934 with Louis Armstrong and His Orchestra. Excellent ommentary and track selection by historian Dan Morgenstern.

The Complete Recordings, Vol. 2 Columbia 47471

The decidedly old-fashioned sound on the first box and on the first CD in this box are partly due to the use of a horn, not a microphone (admittedly, much of this musical style is also vintage 1924–25). "Weeping Willow Blues" features Joe Smith's sweet cornet and particularly expressive singing from Smith. "Reckless Blues" boasts a far superior cornet player: Louis Armstrong. On January 1925's "St. Louis Blues," Smith sings a slow duet with Armstrong's horn. By May 1925, a microphone added some fidelity, bringing (Fletcher) Henderson's Hot Six (with Coleman Hawkins) alive on "Cake Walkin' Babies (From Home)"; Smith delivers the lyrics with robust conviction. Armstrong returns for "Careless Love Blues," a standard; he's joined by Fred Longshaw, a favorite piano accompanist. Smith gets to the heart of the matter with a pair of recordings made in the summer of 1925: "He's Gone Blues" and "I Ain't Got Nobody." Vaudeville legend made "Nobody" famous, and the song has been performed by many black performers, but Smith's desperate grasping at dignity is without equal. Not everything she recorded was brilliant, though. Her duet with singer Clara Smith (no relation) on "My Man Blues" is awkward, although their harmonizing on the finale forgives a sloppy performance. And then there are the simple, straightforward songs, like the sad poetry of "New Gulf Coast Blues"; it's effective because Smith sings so very well. Listen carefully, and don't try to digest all 37 songs in one sitting.

LINK➤ *Mamie Smith — Complete Recorded Works, Vol. 1* **Document 535[illegible]**

Smith (no relation) was the first female singer to record a blues song, and she made histor[illegible] in 1920 by creating a market for "race records" with her OKeh recording of "Crazy Blues." That song is included here; the series continues, but later volumes are clearly not blues.

The Complete Recordings, Vol. 3 Columbia 4747[illegible]

Writer Chris Albertson's liner notes deserve a special mention. With each volume, th[illegible] notes become longer, describing Bessie Smith's life and detailing her slice of the enter[illegible]tainment industry. After returning to the road with a new tent show she called "Bessi[illegible] Smith's Harlem Frolics," Smith continued recording. Although she's primarily remem[illegible]bered as a blues singer, blues represented only part of a larger repertoire. Smith growl[illegible] the novelty (hokum) song "Jazzbo Brown from Memphis Town" and at the sam[illegible] session (March 1926), she cut one of her best blues, "The Gin House Blues." Th[illegible] slow drag "Hard Driving Papa" brings back Joe Smith's cornet; it's one of many Smit[illegible] songs that is, essentially, country blues dressed up for city audiences. (Many of Smith[illegible] fans were Southerners who had recently moved up north.) To stay fresh and becaus[illegible] blues was beginning to lose favor, Smith recorded some Tin Pan Alley songs in Marc[illegible] 1927, including an effective "After You've Gone" and a reasonable "Alexander's Rag[illegible]time Band." The obvious attempt at crowd pleasing also resulted in "There'll Be a Ho[illegible] Time in the Old Town Tonight," but Smith soon settled back into her own musi[illegible] "Lock and Key," accompanied by the remarkably talented James P. Johnson, is stun[illegible]ning. The same 1927 session yielded the proud "A Good Man Is Hard to Find"; a da[illegible] later, Smith cut "Homeless Blues." Her voice is fine, her expressiveness is fantasti[illegible] and this music has lost none of its magnetic power after 70 years.

LINK➤ *Ruth Brown — Blues on Broadway* **Fantasy 9662**

A heartfelt, under-the-skin presentation of classic female blues songs, like "Good Morning Heartache," "Tain't Nobody's Business If I Do," and "I'm Just a Lucky So-and-So." Nice jazzy accompaniment from Bobby Forrester's organ and a top band. Brown is an extraordinary singer.

The Complete Recordings, Vol. 4 — Columbia 52838

Bessie Smith recorded her very best material in 1928 and 1929. "Spider Man Blues" and "Empty Bed Blues" are rich with sexual innuendo, lending themselves to a grittier, somewhat humorous treatment. But Smith is deadly serious on 1928's "You Ought to Be Ashamed," in which she berates herself for loving the wrong man. (There was much truth in this, incidentally.) The spooky darkness provided by clarinet and saxophone on "Devil's Gonna Git You" is simultaneously tongue-in-cheek and biting. Through every one of these songs, Smith's command, her complete control over the music, her natural swing and grace, and her style make her music work so very well. Still, the best is yet to come. The groveling low notes of Joe Williams's trombone capture the dreadful happiness of drink; in fact, the trombone becomes the liquor on "Me and My Gin." May 1929 was a miraculous month for Smith. In two sessions, just a week apart, she recorded five of her finest songs. "I'm Wild About That Thing" is handled as a novelty number with Eddie Lang slightly overdoing it on the guitar as Smith snakes around the lyrics. It's her most overtly sexual song, and she sings it beautifully; "You've Got to Give Me Some" follows a similar format. Andy Razaf's "Kitchen Man" is set up as a ballad, using food items for innuendo ("Oh how that boy can open clams," "His baloney's really worth a try, never fails to satisfy," etc.). The melody is distinctive, bringing Smith's vocal to a higher level than usual. Singer Ida Cox is credited as songwriter for Smith's most remarkable song, recorded just months before the Great Depression: "Nobody Knows You When You're Down and Out." No other song ever suited Smith's voice so well. The slight growl in her voice, her extended phrasing, even the long hums that replace the lyrics in the second verse—it's all perfect. More so, because of the expert backup instrumentation (especially Cyrus St. Clair's tuba). After a few good songs with James P. Johnson, notably "Dirty No-Gooder's Blues," Smith seemed to lose track of the best material. She tried some pseudo-spirituals ("On Revival Day") and pop ("Baby, Have Pity on Me"), and although she sings wonderfully, the quality of the songwriting on the second CD falls short of the first.

LINK➤ *Billie Holiday — Quintessential Billie Holiday, Vol. 3 (1936–1937)* **Columbia 44048**

Along with Vol. 4 in this series (Columbia 44252) and perhaps Vol. 5 (44423), this 2-CD set presents Holiday during her peak period. The connection from Smith is direct, but Holiday's music is more jazz than pure blues. Best songs include "(This is) My Last Love Affair."

The Complete Recordings, Vol. 5: The Final Chapter

Columbia 57546

The first song on this final set was recorded in 1931. Smith sounds more mature, reflective, almost as if she's looking back over her life and savoring its finest moments. The slow blues called "I Need a Little Sugar in My Bowl" begins with the line "Tired of being lonely, tired of being blue, I wished I had some good man to tell my troubles to." It's a beautiful song. Times were bad for Smith. She was drinking heavily, and there wasn't much work available, even for a former star of Smith's status. Two full years passed before she was invited to return to the studio. In 1933, her style had become more modern. She's still a blues singer, but there's a lot more Broadway and jazz in her delivery. The same session produced "Gimme a Pigfoot," which became one of Smith's best-known songs ("Gimme a pigfoot and a bottle of beer"), a rouser about a Harlem rent party. The mood for these recordings was generally upbeat, and even on the sad "I'm Down in the Dumps," Smith never really plays the part of a dejected lover. She keeps the feeling light, but it's here that the story ends. It was her last session. The first CD continues with some unissued takes, mostly from 1925, and the soundtrack from a (disposable) film appearance. A second CD contains two interviews, one with singer Ruby Smith (Smith's niece, who traveled and performed with her) and another with knowledgeable writer Chris Albertson.

LINK➤ *Victoria Spivey — Complete Recorded Works, Vols. 1–4*

Document 5316-5319

Four volumes, all very special. Like Bessie Smith, Spivey was an extraordinarily gifted musician and interpreter. Spivey made her deepest impact in the 1920s and 1930s (these sets cover 1926-37), but kept working until 1976. Why isn't her work available on a major U.S. label?

The Collection

Columbia 44441

What the world probably needs is a 2-CD set covering the best of Bessie Smith. This bargain-priced CD is a reasonable substitute. It contains 16 fine songs, and inevitably, it misses some personal favorites. Still, the most important material is here: "Downhearted Blues," "T'ain't Nobody's Bizness If I Do," "Weepin' Willow Blues," "Empty Bed Blues," "Nobody Knows When You're Down and Out," "Do Your Duty," and "Gimme a Pigfoot." This collection was not put together in a haphazard way; it's a nicely produced package that clearly benefited from the investment made in the five boxed sets. Also, Smith's growth as a musician is more clearly stated in this telescopic career view.

LINK➤ *Dinah Washington — First Issue: The Dinah Washington Story*

Mercury 514-841

This 2-CD set emphasizes Washington's work as a jazz singer and only touches on her R&B experience (she blurred the line between the two related genres). Washington is just a notch below Billie Holiday and Bessie Smith in any list of the century's top female jazz-blues vocalists.

Spann became famous as the piano player in Muddy Waters's band and later secured his reputation as a successful solo artist. The son of a minister, Spann grew up in Jackson, MS; he taught himself to play piano. Spann was also a serious athlete who earned money boxing and playing football. After a few years in the Army, the 21-year-old Spann ended up in Chicago in 1951. He spent two years on his own before joining Muddy Waters, where he remained through the early 1960s. This was an extraordinary period; Waters and his band defined the rocking sound of Chicago blues. While playing on occasion with Waters, Spann recorded a critically acclaimed series of albums for a variety of labels. He also appeared at many blues festivals, sometimes with Waters and sometimes with his own band. At age 40, Otis Spann's time was over. He died of cancer in 1970.

Otis Spann Is the Blues — Candid 9001

Otis Spann may be the blues, but Robert Jr. Lockwood deserves a little credit here, too. This 1960 album is a collaboration between two of Chicago's best; it's a series of duets on good material that hasn't been heard too often. Spann is an extraordinary pianist. His effortless integration of rhythm, energy, and intelligence are without equal in the blues catalog. He's at his best on "Beat-Up Team," in which he sings, very effectively, about farming. The delicacy of Lockwood's guitar and his more aggressive vocal style is magnficiently counterbalanced by Spann's keyboarding on "My Daily Wish." Spann shows off on the boogie-woogie "Great Northern Stomp," a solo piece.

LINK➤ *Johnny Jones — With Billy Boy Arnold* — ***Alligator 4117***

Pianist Johnny Jones had two claims to fame: he played behind Elmore James, and he was regularly employed by Sylvio's, a top Chicago blues club. He was also a busy session man. This exciting set of piano-harmonica duets was recorded live in 1963 at Chicago's Fickle Pickle.

Good Morning, Mr. Blues — Analogue 3016

When Spann was on tour with Muddy Waters in the early 1960s, he cut an album for the Storyville label in Copenhagen, Denmark. Fortunately, the engineer was attentive and skillful, for the original master tapes provided the Analogue Productions team with loads of piano and vocal information. Remastered, this sounds like a new recording. It's simple enough: just Spann and a piano. Spann is in fine voice, a soulful interpreter of his own slightly R&B, slightly boogie, slightly blues tunes. When he sings out and pumps that piano, it's goosebump time. His original "Must Have Been the Devil" and the clever keyboarding behind Lonnie Johnson's "Jelly Roll Baker" are among many exquisite moments.

LINK➤ *Various Artists — Barrelhouse Blues 1927–1936* — ***Yazoo 1028***

Another great Yazoo collection, this one starts with Cow Cow Davenport doing his "State Street Jive" and includes tracks by such well-known artists as Little Brother Montgomery. Also included are numbers by more obscure artists such as Raymond Barrow and Jabo Williams. Enjoyable music.

The Blues Never Die! **OBC 530**

The first thing you notice is the rip of James Cotton's harmonica, and the next is how effective Spann's vocals had become by 1964. There's some extraordinary guitar playing from "Dirty Rivers" (in fact, the whole backup group is Muddy Waters's band). The combination of Waters's guitar and Cotton's ecstatic vocal chants of "gonna boogie!" make "Feelin' Good" a classic. The whole deal comes together with Spann's piano and deeper vocals, Cotton's punctuating harp, and Waters's strokes on "Come On." The instrumental "Lightnin'" gives each player solo space and allows the band as a unit to shine. This is very solid Chicago blues, and should not be missed.

LINK➤ *Johnny Young — Chicago Blues* ***Arhoolie 325***

Performing on a hard Chicago street-savvy electric guitar and singing with the grace of an experienced Mississippi juker, Young also plays the mandolin (more common in the old South than in 1965 Chicago). With Spann, James Cotton, other top Chicago players.

Otis Spann's Chicago Blues **Testament 5005**

The piano recording is a bit soft, Spann's voice is a little distant, and the overall ambience recalls a so-so session from the early 1950s. Spann's performances are fine. The rolling misery of "Nobody Knows My Troubles" tells his tale with the usual keyboard hijinks, borrowing some from Fats Waller and some from Little Brother Montgomery. It's one of a half-dozen solo tunes with just voice and piano. James Cotton's harmonica shares the spotlight on another five tunes with an adequate electric band. Notable is a St. Louis blues called "Sarah Street." The band's much better on the last track: "G.B Blues," the only one with Johnny Shines and top drummer Fred Below.

LINK➤ *Feelin' Down on the South Side: Bluesville Years, Vol. 2* ***Prestige 9906***

Truly excellent collection with a great performance of "Come On" from Otis Spann, followed by work from Billy Boy Arnold, James Cotton, and Homesick James. Probably the best in this series.

Down to Earth: The Bluesway Recordings **MCA 11202**

Two sessions are captured here: a live-in-studio date from 1966 and a studio session from 1967. Guitar players Muddy Waters, Luther Johnson, and Sam Lawhorn are featured on both. There is plenty of intense energy, rock-solid city blues, vocals from the heart, and, thankfully, superlative engineering. There's a definitive "Down On Sarah Street" here with a very aggressive harmonica, guitar, and vocal mix. Smith sets up "T'ain't Nobody's Bizness If I Do," Waters comes in to set the mood, and Spann then delivers a vital, haughtily independent vocal on this Bessie Smith chestnut. "Heart Loaded with Trouble" is one of many good examples of live work successfully captured in a recording studio. Very, very good music.

LINK➤ *Various Artists — Chess Blues Piano Greats* ***Chess (MCA) 9385***

Unlike most of these 50th Anniversary sets, this 2-CD collection focuses mainly on the work of two men: Eddie Boyd and Willie Mabon (famous for "The Seventh Son"). Otis Spann contributes just four tracks and Lafayette Leake, three. Very fine work throughout.

Like many blues players of his generation, Sumlin was a native of the area near West Memphis, AR. He was born in 1931, and his hometown was Greenwood, MS. The first guitar Sumlin learned to play was one he built himself. He teamed up with James Cotton in the South, then moved to Chicago in 1954 to begin a sometimes stormy relationship with Howlin' Wolf. During his years with Wolf, Sumlin worked his way up from rhythm to lead guitar and became known as one of the best. Beginning in the mid-1960s, Sumlin did some solo work at European festivals. After Howlin' Wolf's death in 1976, Sumlin's solo career took shape, both as a guitarist and a vocalist. He started recording in Europe in the late 1970s, but his late 1980s U.S. recordings for Black Top and Blind Pig have provided him with a second career.

Blues Anytime! — Evidence 26052

Here's the set of 1964 sides that Sumlin laid down in Berlin when he was just starting a solo career. His sidemen are Willie Dixon (bass, acoustic guitar) and Sunnyland Slim (piano). Both men also sing. The drummer is Clifton James. After a Chicago blues rouser called "It's You Baby," sung by Sunnyland Slim, Sumlin does a solo on "Love You, Woman" and coaxes magic from his acoustic guitar. Sumlin also does "When I Feel Better" on his own in a similar style, as well as "Hubert's Blues." Willie Dixon also performs an unaccompanied acoustic number, "Big Legged Woman." The group material, like "My Babe" and "Blues Anytime," is spirited and well played.

LINK➤ *Hubert Sumlin — I Know You* — ***AcousTech 2004***

A remarkable 1997 release finds Sumlin in peak form with endless energy. He blazes through "Smokestack" (similar to "Smokestack Lightning") and nods to his old boss on "How Many More Years?" This audiophile recording features Sam Lay (drums), Carey Bell (harmonica), and others.

Hubert Sumlin's Blues Party — Black Top 1036

Sumlin's guitar is on the left, and Ronnie Earl's is on the right. Besides being an extraordinary lesson in comparative blues guitar, this album features singer Mighty Sam McClain and keyboard man Bruce Katz at their best. The album's concept comes together beautifully on Earl's "A Soul That's Been Abused." Tenor saxophone player Greg Piccolo does a slighty comic vocal on "Letter to My Girlfriend," a party song with a nice sax solo. It's balanced by Earl Hooker's inspiring blues instrumental, "Blue Guitar" and the jagged street nastiness of Howlin' Wolf's "Down in the Bottom," done up by McClain. A winning combination of 1960s Chicago and Earl's more modern take on the blues.

LINK➤ *Vance Kelly — Call Me* — ***Wolf 120.877***

Solid workingman's blues by an earnest voice, backed by Eddie Shaw's saxophone, and aided by John Primer's production. Kelly is Chicago through and through, one of many Wolf releases emphasizing that city's best modern-day players. Recommended.

A beloved Chicago legend, Sunnyland Slim was born Albert Luandrew in 1907 in Vance, MS. He learned organ and piano while a teenager, and worked his way through Arkansas to Memphis, TN, where he settled around 1927. Slim played regularly on Beale Street beside Little Brother Montgomery and Ma Rainey; he picked up his nickname from an often-performed tune called "Sunnyland Train." In 1938, he followed the action to Chicago. He worked as a piano player, accompanying Sonny Boy Williamson and others. He introduced Muddy Waters to the Chess brothers in 1947. For the next four decades, Slim persevered. He helped young artists, played extended gigs at clubs (12 years at B.L.U.E.S., for example), recorded mostly for small labels with little national exposure, and performed at festivals. He died in 1995 after a nasty fall on an icy sidewalk.

House Rent Party — Delmark 655

Around 26th Street and South Prairie, Sunnyland Slim maintained a basement hangout frequented by Chicago's blues musicians. From 1947 until 1954, Jimmy Rogers, Big Bill Broonzy, Little Walter, Johnny Jones, Louis and Dave Myers, and others spent time there rehearsing and shooting craps. Usually, someone was banging on the piano. That's the atmosphere this 1949 album recalls: Willie Mabon spelling Slim on "Boogie Man," and adding some rich harmonica; St. Louis Jimmy picking up the vocals on "Chicago Woman"; and Slim singing and playing piano on "Bad Times (Cost of Living)." It's a relaxed session or two among friends—nobody works too hard. For these guys, the blues came easy.

LINK➤ *David Maxwell — Maximum Blues Piano* — ***Tone-Cool (Rounder) 1160***

Maxwell developed an outstanding reputation as a blues sideman; he worked with Freddie King, Bonnie Raitt, James Cotton, Buddy Guy, John Lee Hooker, and others. Boston-based, Maxwell rocks on this 1997 solo debut.

Slim's Shout — OBC 558

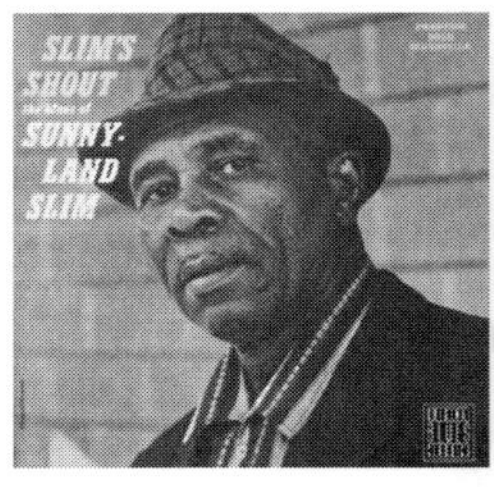

It's 1960, and Slim's slick and sharp; he finds the heart of each groove and takes the music as far as it will go. On "Slim's Shout," for example, he's pumping hard next to Robert Banks's great blues organ (a terrific complement to Slim's keyboarding). Then King Curtis jumps in with a full-blooded tenor saxophone solo. This is blues, but it's also close to jazz or R&B. "Brownskin Woman," so often covered by other artists, debuts here. Slim sails through this material. Curtis's elegiac saxophone opens "Decoration Day," and if there's an authenticity in Slim's vocal, it's because he's singing about his wife, Freddie Lee, who died a year earlier.

LINK➤ *Sunnyland Slim Blues Band — Chicago Jump* — ***Evidence 26067***

An honest representation of Sunnyland's Sunday club nights. The 77-year-old pianist works out with his regulars: Steve Freund (guitar), Sam Burckhardt (tenor sax), Bob Stroger (bass), and Robert Covington (drums). Steady rolling . . . and riveting.

Roosevelt Sykes

Sykes was born near Helena, AR, but grew up around St. Louis. Brimming with humor and a knack for show business, he learned his craft on the church organ, but perfected his style during his teen years by working in brothels and barrelhouses. Sykes had an easy and charming way with the ladies; he was nicknamed "The Honeydripper." By 1929, at age 23, Sykes was under contract to Okeh; he also signed several other contracts under assumed names. A Decca deal followed in 1935. Sykes spent the 1930s in St. Louis and the 1940s in Chicago, recording for RCA's Bluebird subsidiary. He often backed up other musicians and sometimes arranged gigs and record deals for them. When Chicago fans demanded electric blues in the 1950s, Sykes moved to New Orleans, which became his home base. After many club and festival appearances in the U.S. and Europe, Sykes died in New Orleans in 1984.

Roosevelt Sykes: 1929–1941 **da Music 3542**

Here's the authentic Sykes singing about women, sex, and the realities of black life in the 1930s. Typical is the bouncy "She Showed It All" ("Me and my gal was walking fast, she fell down, and I saw her leg, and she showed it all . . . " and "her legs fell open like a country well"; the lyrics go on to describe the woman's body odor and so on). While there are more like that, notably "The Honeydripper" ("don't you let nobody wet your honeycomb but me"), the style of these piano blues and Sykes's dramatic technique sets them apart. "44 Blues," a song about a dark chase for his woman and her lover, is one Sykes's best.

LINK➤ *Fats Waller — The Middle Years, Part 1 (1936–1938)* ***Bluebird 66083***

The sextet recordings here include well-known rousers like "The Joint Is Jumpin'," "Havin' a Ball," and so on. Waller was an enthusiastic showman, a superb pianist, and this is his fun-loving, toe-tapping best. He's as full of life as Sykes, but much jazzier.

The Return of Roosevelt Sykes **OBC 546**

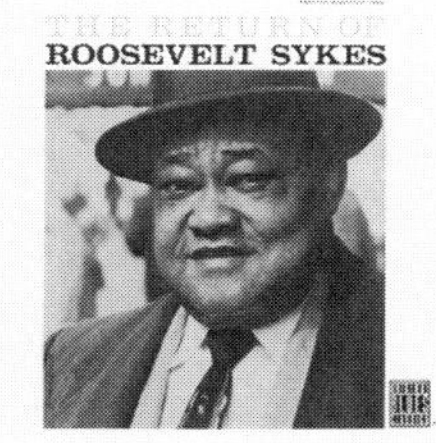

It's 1960, and Sykes has transformed himself in accordance with contemporary tastes. His voice is hoarse, the setting has evolved into jazzy R&B, and the songs are politically correct. The dominant sound on many tracks, like "Number Nine," is not Sykes's vocal, but Clarence Perry, Jr.'s soulful tenor saxophone. "Night Time Is the Right Time" is typical; Sykes's rascal days are through, so now it's sincerely about "the one you love." He has some fun with the guitars on "Hey Big Momma," but sounds a little old and tired. The best number is the opening tune, "Drivin' Wheel," a very solid mid-tempo country blues with a good piano break.

LINK➤ *Bumble Bee Slim — 1934-1937* ***Best of Blues 6***

Twenty-three tracks demonstrate Amos Easton's interpretative skill as a singer; backup musicians include some of Chicago's best, notably Big Bill Broonzy on guitar. The sound on this series is generally reliable, and so, the "B.O.B." series should be seriously considered.

The Honeydripper **OBC 557**

Lots better. "Mislead Mother" keeps Sykes at the center of an adultery song ("Daddy put things on my mother she just couldn't stand . . . that started my mother on cheatin' on my dear old dad"). Sykes sings the verses and chorus, then hands off to a rocking band. Sykes plays a tough piano against Robert Banks's equally aggressive organ, and both trade licks with King Curtis's tenor sax. It's hot stuff, followed by a mellow piano-organ duet, "Yes, Lawd!" Sykes is back to some of his old tricks on "Jailbait" (complete with lascivious mouth sounds) and returns to familiar blues grooves on the slow-paced "Lonely Day" and "I Hate to Be Alone."

LINK➤ *James Booker — Classified* ***Rounder 2036***

A prime New Orleans pianist with an expansive style, Booker easily flits from Fats Domino ("One for the Highway") to Lloyd Price ("Lawdy Miss Clawdy") to Leiber and Stoller ("Hound Dog") to Roger Miller ("King of the Road"). He's popular, it all works, and it's worth a listen.

Blues by Roosevelt "The Honey-Dripper" Sykes

Smithsonian Folkways 40051

Memphis Slim produced this 1961 album featuring Sykes, accompanied only by his piano, filling the room with sound. Sykes's barrelhouse piano could hardly be finer than on the instrumental "R. S. Stomp," but everything here is thrilling. He's best on "Ran the Blues Out of My Window," whose tricked-out piano rhythm on the line "the train they call the Cannonball" is distinctively Sykes. "I Got a Woman in Elaine, Arkansas" is a slow, sexy tribute to a woman whom he respects—and enjoys in bed. "The Mistaken Life" doesn't turn out as well (she "cut my pleasure in two" with a pocket knife). With printed lyrics and unusually high fidelity.

LINK➤ *Henry Townsend — & Henry Spaulding* ***Wolf 117***

Country blues, recorded from 1929 to 1937, by one of the leading performers in St. Louis. Most tracks feature just Townsend and his acoustic guitar (these are the best); others include Sykes on piano. Two more are by Spaulding; Townsend doesn't play on these two.

Gold Mine **Delmark 616**

Recorded in Europe in 1966, this is another voice-and-piano delight. "Springfield Blues" contains some glistening keyboard work and a healthy dose of bragging about having a gal in each of several cities. Even at age 60, Sykes still performs "I'm a Dangerous Man" with humor, credibility, and gusto. That feisty demeanor even translates effectively when Sykes sounds grandfatherly as on "Whole Lot of Children." He's so full of himself and his showbiz bravado that he easily sells every song—and ultimately, it's personality that makes this album work. An older man's wisdom and contemporary sensibility make "Big Ben" the best song here. ("She's much too wise to be abused.")

LINK➤ *Var. Artists — Raunchy Business: Hot Nuts & Lollypops* ***Legacy 46783***

There's a long history of blues artists singing suggestive songs—some with very explicit lyrics. Vocalist Lil Johnson used this gimmick to win fame on "Sam—The Hot Dog Man." Others who did so included Lucille Bogan ("Shave 'Em Dry") and Bo Carter ("My Pencil Won't Write No More").

Hudson Whittaker was born in Georgia in 1904. A red-haired boy raised in Tampa, FL, he migrated to Chicago in the 1920s, and established himself as a significant slide guitar player. At first Red made music on street corners for spare change, but a 1928 partnership with Georgia Tom Dorsey made him famous. The pair recorded bawdy songs and humorous novelties, and were sometimes billed as "The Hokum Boys." When Dorsey left the act (to become gospel singer Thomas A. Dorsey), Tampa Red continued with a new partner, Big Maceo (Merriweather). His apartment—and his wife's fried chicken—became popular with local blues musicians, and became central to Chicago's scene; his home also became a safe harbor for rural Southern musicians settling into the new urban environment. Red partied heartily and performed everywhere, from burlesque houses to rent parties. Health problems due to alcohol abuse slowed him down, but he lived until 1981.

The Guitar Wizard — Columbia 53235

Tampa Red and pianist Georgia Tom Dorsey recorded several versions of their popular "hokum" song "It's Tight Like That" in the fall of 1928. The one that begins this collection features the two musicians as accompanists. The pair takes off as a duo act on 1932's "No Matter How She Does It" and "You Can't Get That Stuff No More," two good-time songs with suggestive lyrics. About half of these tracks were made by the two friends in 1932. The other half feature Tampa Red recording in 1934 as a solo with more traditional blues material. The best in this group is "Turpentine Blues," about earning a decent wage. Solid work throughout.

LINK➤ *Thomas A. Dorsey — Precious Lord* **Columbia/Legacy 57164**

This CD begins with Dorsey speaking, making sense of his transition from blues to gospel. And then, he sings. And he prays and testifies with a fervor. With many of the century's finest gospel performers, including Alex Bradford, the Dixie Hummingbirds, and Marion Williams.

Bottleneck Guitar: 1928–1937 — Yazoo 1039

Tampa Red performs a masterful guitar solo on "You Got to Reap What You Sow," one of a half-dozen of his own songs on this collection. The toe-tapping "What Is It That Tastes Like Gravy?" is a crowd-pleaser (but it's not played in the bottleneck style). Tampa Red's voice is pleasant and warm on "The Duck Yas Yas Yas," as is his sense of humor and melody. A lot of the best work here is accompaniment, the best and fastest is on singer Madlyn Davis's "It's Red Hot." On the violent story "Black Eyes Blues," sung by Ma Rainey ("you low down alligator, gonna catch you sooner or later"), Tampa Red's guitar nearly sings a vocal duet.

LINK➤ *Country Blues Bottleneck Guitar Classics 1926–1927* ***Yazoo 1026***

The best thing about this CD is the number of songs not often heard on other guitar collections. There's Weaver and Beasley drifting through "Bottleneck Blues," Bo Weavil Jackson doing "You Can't Keep No Brown," and Ramblin' Thomas performing "So Lonesome." Fine stuff.

Bluebird Recordings 1934–1936 **Bluebird 6672**

With the Great Depression's grip loosening, RCA signe Tampa Red and got him back into the recording studio. Th repeal of Prohibition in December 1933 opened an impor- tant new market for Red's music: jukeboxes. The recordin quality here is far better than before, and Red's performance are entertaining and just plain fun. A rip-roaring kazoo sol begins the set on "I'll Kill Your Soul." Red adds character t the lyrics with lots of engaging chatter and with periodic shouts and calls on "Yo Don't Want Me Blues" and other songs. There's some pop material, including a ver good kazoo solo on "Nobody's Sweetheart Now" and some solid scat singing here too—Tampa Red could put on a spectacular show. On "Happy Jack," a bit of po nonsense, he merrily yodels and plays the kazoo. It doesn't take long to understan Tampa Red's game—he's working blues structure, piano boogie, and other establishe forms to create modern pop music. On song after song, Tampa Red really performs he sounds as though he's in an MGM musical. As a result, even traditional blues lik "Don't Dog Your Woman" become sophisticated and urban through his articulatio and phrasing; in time, Red's work would provide a foundation not only for Mudd Waters, but Bobby "Blue" Bland, Johnny Adams, and many soul singers. "Singin and Crying Blues," recorded in 1935, is sweet soul music. Most of the 46 songs o this 2-CD set were recorded with Black Bob on piano and an uncredited string bass- ist. Some were recorded with the Chicago Five, a small combo. Tampa Red recorde with Bluebird and Victor until 1950; look for more multi-CD collections in the fu- ture.

LINK➤ *Big Maceo Merriweather — The King of Chicago Blues Piano*
Arhoolie 700

Top Chicago pianist Merriweather recorded these tracks with his friend and frequent part- ner Tampa Red in the first half of the 1940s. Mostly it's just the two of them laying dow mellow blues (Big Maceo is the vocalist). The recording quality is just fine. Very nice work

Bluebird Recordings 1936–1938 **Bluebird (RCA) 6672**

Forty-five tracks by one of the best. "Stormy Sea Blues," from 1936, is a duet wit Willie Bee James on guitar; they were frequent partners. And Tampa Red raises th kazoo to the level of a legitimate melodic instrument on the self-deprecating "I Hat Myself." He was not limited to one particular type of song. On "Blue and Evil Blues," Tampa Red addresses misery in a far more direct way. As Arnett Nelson's clarine quietly performs the siren song of another lost love, Tampa Red sings "I'm not drink- ing because I want it, I'm drinking to ease my evil mind" and "I'd rather see a dea body than see her with somebody else." A 2-CD set.

LINK➤ *Charles "Cow Cow" Davenport — 1926-1938* ***Best of Blues***

Davenport sings and plays piano with great conviction. It's a thrill to hear his origina "Cow Cow Blues," an instrumental recorded in Chicago in 1928. Most tracks here wer recorded prior to 1930, but sound just fine. Lots of spirit and magic here.

:ddie Taylor taught himself to play guitar by standing outside Mississippi juke joints s a child and copying what he heard from Charlie Patton, Robert Johnson, and other nasters. As a teenager, he worked local parties and picnics, then moved on to greater pportunity in Memphis in the early 1940s. By the end of the decade, Taylor had noved to Chicago. He started playing in the Maxwell Street area there and then earned living in the clubs and studios. Taylor first became well known working behind immy Reed. He teamed up with Reed for some Vee-Jay sessions in 1953 and contin-ed working with him. During this time, he also served as a very capable sideman for irtually every significant Chicago blues headliner. Taylor also did some recording on is own. He was inducted into the Blues Foundation's Hall of Fame in 1987, two ears after his death at age 62.

Iasters of Modern Blues — Testament 5001

'his 1966 CD is credited to Taylor and his friend Floyd Jones, who perform together n each other's tracks. Both bluesmen grew up in the South and moved to Chicago in ne 1940s. Completing the ensemble are Otis Spann on piano, Big Walter Horton on armonica, and Fred Below on drums. "Stockyard Blues" is a song of frustration by a nan (Jones) who can't keep up with the rising cost of living. Taylor's railroad song, Train Fare Home," is about money and leaving a lover. "Playhouse" is typical of the tyle: street smart with a clear memory of juke joints. Sound is good, not great.

INK➤ *Eddie Taylor — My Heart Is Bleeding* — ***Evidence 26054***

'he first nine tracks were recorded in Chicago; they're notable mainly for good guitar work. 'ive more were recorded in Europe with Carey Bell, Sunnyland Slim, Hubert Sumlin, and thers. This isn't Taylor's very best work, but there are many special moments. From 1980.

Feel So Bad — Hightone 8027

traight-ahead Chicago blues, with especially fine guitar playing, makes Taylor's al-ums a pleasure. Guitar duties are shared with Phillip Walker; the sound is filled out 'ith piano, bass, drums, two percussionists, and George Smith's harmonica. "I Feel o Bad" is a representative track: it's uptempo, thick with rhythm, dominated by 'aylor's sincere vocal, and made special by a plaintive electric guitar. Taylor wrote nost of the songs himself, and although he tends toward full-blooded rocking blues, e also presents an occasional acoustic blues, like "Stroll Out West" and "Bull Cow lues." Both are sung in a comfortable rural style with glowing guitar accompani-nent. "Wreck on the 83 Highway" combines both styles. From 1972.

INK➤ *Brewer Phillips — Good Houserockin'* — ***Wolf 608***

'hillips and Taylor were longtime friends with some similar musical tastes. Most of this lbum was recorded in 1982 for a solo album called Ingleside Blues*; the rest is a variety of ve performances with J.B. Hutto and Cub Koda. Fellow Houserockers drummer Ted Iarvey shares credit. So-so sound.*

Hound Dog Taylor

Theodore Roosevelt Taylor came from Natchez, MS. He wa born there in 1917, but didn't take music seriously until the lat 1930s, when he pieced together a living by performing on hi guitar at picnics and other local events. In time, Taylor rамble to Helena, AR, did some spots on the King Biscuit Time radi series, and landed in Chicago in 1942. He became very popula in West Side and South Side clubs, but recording opportunitie were few. By the late 1950s, Taylor finally quit his day job an became a full-time musician. In 1971, after failing to convinc his boss, Delmark Records chief Bob Koester, to sign Taylo Bruce Iglauer formed his own label to record Taylor and th noisy pair of sidemen called the Houserockers. The record succeeded, as did Alligato Records, the new label. After cutting two more albums, Taylor died of cancer in 1975

And the Houserockers **Alligator 470**

Raw and authentic, wiry and dangerous, Hound Dog Taylor's trio recreates the splin tery simplicity of a juke joint. He teases that guitar—that poor, muffled, old-sound ing, overmodulated guitar—until it's the voice of the ages on "Walking the Ceiling. This was Taylor's first album, and Alligator's debut, too, in 1971. It's low budget an sounds as though Taylor's guitar is zapping every amp of the house's electrical powe on "Wild About You Baby"; everything's kept compact and nasty, like a bantam weight in heat. The boogie beat and Taylor's feisty, miniature vocal range transmi "She's Gone" to the heart. Taylor wrote almost everything, except "44 Blues," one o the album's tightest tunes.

LINK➤ *Various Artists — Genuine Houserocking Music* ***Alligator 10***

Alligator's first sampler is still the best. The artist list is terrific (Johnny Winter, Kok Taylor, Lonnie Mack, Roy Buchanan, James Cotton, among others), and the choice c music is very strong indeed. From 1986.

Natural Boogie **Alligator 470**

Taylor's second album is every bit as riveting as the first. "You Can't Sit Down" ge the room shaking with its stop-start beat, fuzzed-out rhythm guitar, and Chuck Berr licks. Great dance music! Taylor built his reputation on hard-hitting up-tempo slash and-burn numbers like "Roll Your Moneymaker" and "One More Time." Both ar reminiscent of 1950s rock 'n' roll guitar heroes. Taylor's slower material, however, i not to be missed. He's back in that seedy, dirt-floored juke joint for "Sitting at Hom Alone," crying with his electric guitar while two backup musicians track the beat. Th painful "Sadie" digs way down with a devastating slow rhythm that spirals into th darkest part of the soul. From 1973.

LINK➤ *Maurice John Vaughn — In the Shadow of the City* ***Alligator 481***

1993 outing by a versatile bluesman, born and bred in Chicago. Optimistic and fresh. H got a good funky sense, and understands R&B, but he goes down easy. Entertaining.

Beware of the Dog! **Alligator 4707**

Since the Houserockers' fame was based on its live shows, it made sense for Alligator o release some live sessions. These were made in 1974 at Chicago's Northwestern University for WXRT-FM, and in Cleveland's Smiling Dog Saloon for WMMS-FM. It's the same down-and-dirty band. Memories of Elmore James are evident not only in a version of "Dust My Broom," but also in the rawboned "The Sun Is Shining." Not many bluesmen could follow "Comin' Around the Mountain" with "Let's Get Funky," but nothing stops Taylor. His roughshod guitar just takes over, making every song his own. This barbed-wire approach to music making is surprisingly compelling.

LINK➤ *Various Artists — Living Chicago Blues* ***Alligator 7701-4***

Alligator has been unusually successful with its collections. The company's four volume Living Chicago Blues series is spectacular. Jimmy Johnson and Eddie Shaw highlight Vol. 1; Lonnie Brooks and Johnny "Big Moose" Walker spice Vol. 2, and A.C. Reed's the best man on Vol. 3. Queen Sylvia Embry and harpist Big Leon Brooks shine on Vol. 4.

Genuine Houserocking Music **Alligator 4727**

Fortunately, producer Bruce Iglauer recorded more of Taylor's music than he released; Taylor's outtakes are far better than most artists' buy takes. He wraps his brain around Ray Charles's "What'd I Say," digs those coarse guitar riffs way down into the heart of the song, and furiously repeats notes to make his point. When a real blues singer, such as Taylor, fights his way through Leiber and Stoller's "Kansas City," it becomes difficult to take the lounge act version seriously. Taylor is similarly credible on a tattered highway version of "Crossroads," mainly because he's a guitar player who doesn't take nonsense from anyone. "Blue Guitar" is even more solid.

LINK➤ *The Alligator Records 20th Anniversary Collection* ***Alligator 105/6***

Taylor starts off this low-priced 2-CD set with "Give Me Back My Wig," setting a course or metallic electric blues; he's followed by James Cotton ("No Cuttin' Loose"), Tinsley Ellis "Double-Eyed Whammy"), Katie Webster ("Pussycat Moan"), and other top Alligator acts.

Have Some Fun **Wolf 120.300**

Joe's Place, in Cambridge, MA, was the home of some raucous blues concerts in the 1970s. There's a hard-to-find album called *Live at Joe's Place* (on New Rose), and two more on Wolf. (One is called *Freddie's Blues* [Wolf 120.600].) While some points might be deducted for recording under the influence, and for some shaky tuning, these albums are mostly great fun. This particular CD, which is actually the second volume in the trio of albums, includes "The Things I Used to Do" and "Phillips Stomp" (named for lead guitar player Utah Phillips). The third volume features "Freddie's Blues" and a searing version of "Dust My Broom."

LINK➤ *Eddie Shaw — Home Alone* ***Wolf 120.879***

Another great Chicago session from Wolf (in fact, this is Vol. 33 in the series of Chicago Blues Sessions). Recorded in 1994, it features a rocking Shaw singing a gravel-riden, optimistic lead, hitting hard on his saxophone. His son Vaan Shaw is part of the band.

Cora Walton's father was a farmer who sharecropped in the Memphis area. Her family attended church regularly, and Cora sang in the choir. She became a skillful gospel singer, but a 1953 move to Chicago with Robert "Pops" Taylor (who later became her husband and manager) changed all that. By day, Taylor cleaned other people's homes; at night, she and her husband went out to blues clubs. These bars were small, and the performers weren't far removed from the audience. It wasn't long before Koko Taylor was sitting in with Chicago's best. Under Willie Dixon's wing, she started recording for Chess in 1962 and remained a favorite throughout that decade. After a few slow years, Taylor picked up again with Alligator in the mid-1970s; she hasn't stopped. Taylor's won dozens of awards, performed at the presidential inauguration of George Bush, and has appeared in several films. She still tours and records.

What It Takes: The Chess Years — MCA 9328

Seventeen of the 18 tracks on this essential retrospective were written and produced by Willie Dixon in the late 1960s. Taylor's thick, gutsy voice is immediately familiar as she growls through the definitive version of "Wang Dang Doodle." Lots of songs follow a straightforward Chess formula: street-smart rhythm, a vocal delivery that borrows from rock 'n' roll, and a bluesy soul. "Twenty Nine Ways" is one of those songs, and "All You Need" is another. Divergent songs are even more interesting, like Taylor's macabre duet with Dixon on "Insane Asylum" or the blazing chorus on "Fire." Her duet with Muddy Waters on a live "I Got What It Takes" is also special.

LINK➤ *Big Time Sarah — Lay It on 'Em Girls!* **Delmark 65**

With impeccable credentials (she's worked for Buddy Guy, Junior Wells, and Sunnyland Slim), Sarah Streeter serves up full-bodied versions of tunes by Gershwin and Willie Dixon. She even performs a credible version of Bill Withers's "Ain't No Sunshine."

I Got What It Takes — Alligator 4706

Taylor's an original, but she also knows how to absorb influences. She's got some Ruth Brown in her performance of "Mama, He Treats Your Daughter Mean," and there's a trace of Bessie Smith in "Trying to Make a Living." Mostly, Taylor improves on her own fine work on this 1975 Alligator debut; evidence includes a down-tempo rendition of "I Got What It Takes" that seethes with sex. Taylor also makes good use of Mighty Joe Young's distinctive guitar and Bill Heid's keyboards on Otis Spann's "Blues Never Die." The arrangements are also stronger than before; the funky Denise Lasalle tune "Find a Fool" features saxman Abbe Locke. Considerably better sound, too.

LINK➤ *Denise LaSalle — Hittin' Where It Hurts* **Malaco 744**

Malaco specializes in 1960s-style Southern R&B, and there is no better practitioner of the form than singer-songerwriter LaSalle. This is a good representative effort—a strong voice a feeling that recalls Stax at its best. Worth exploring.

From the Heart of a Woman **Alligator 4724**

It's always gratifying to hear a top artist progress to a more sophisticated level of performance. On this Grammy-nominated 1981 album, Taylor takes on a range of material suitable to her maturing voice. She sings a fine torch song, nicely colored by Sammy Lawhorn's guitar, on "I'd Rather Go Blind." She also tries some Louis Jordan vith the bouncy "Sure Had A Wonderful Time Last Night," smiling through the ronic lyrics. The band gets on a roll for "Keep Your Hands Off Him," an update of he old Chess formula (A.C. Reed contributes the tenor sax workout); "Never Trust a Man" is in the same vein.

.INK➤ *Masters of Jazz, Vol. 5: Female Vocal Classics* ***Rhino 72472***

Part of an essential collection of the very best jazz on record, this 1996 CD is a good ntroduction to Mildred Bailey, Etta Jones, Chris Connor, Nina Simone, Anita O'Day, Betty Carter, and others.

The Earthshaker **Alligator 4711**

Koko Taylor singing blues and R&B standards is a mighty good idea. It's 1978, and he does a very credible job with Willie Dixon's "Spoonful," Floyd Dixon's "Hey, Bartender," and "Wang Dang Doodle." Taylor also handles "I'm a Woman" in strict Chicago blues style with a rigid rhythm pattern and a harmonica break from Mervyn Harmonica" Hinds. (She avoids the "w-o-m-a-n" convention and stays with the hard tuff.) "Walking the Back Streets" is desolate and spooky, with excellent Johnny B. Moore and Sammy Lawhorn guitar. Listen carefully and you'll hear what Janis Joplin probably borrowed from Taylor's style. Nice Pinetop Perkins organ in this mix as well.

INK➤ *Koko Taylor — Queen of the Blues* ***Alligator 4740***

Although Taylor's 1980s albums were as distinctive as those that came earlier (and later), he combination of her slick band, her spirited delivery, and some guest appearances comnend this 1985 release. Notables include Lonnie Brooks, Albert Collins, James Cotton, nd Son Seals.

Queen of the Blues **Alligator 4740**

's 1993, and Koko Taylor's again bringing it all up to date. On "Mother Nature," as the rhythm section works a groove, he pumps equally hard. Taylor's 58-year-old voice exudes nore of a weathered hum than a streetwise growl, and she eaves more open space for soloists like Criss Johnson (lead uitar) on "Mother Nature." Taylor takes on Leiber and toller's "Hound Dog," not as an Elvis remake, but as an onest R&B song. Buddy Guy joins in for "Born Under a Bad Sign," proof that aylor's still got more chops than most singers ever see. Score lots of points for perfornance, and a bonus for repertoire selections.

INK➤ *Trudy Lynn — 24 Hour Woman* ***Ichiban 1172***

bluesy R&B singer with guts and a gift for singing ballads, Lynn does an equally good job ith Isaac Hayes's quietly angry "Your Good Thing" and Merle Haggard's "Just Because." Most songs on this 1994 CD get the full treatment: guitars, horns, and backing vocalists.

Saunders Terrell was born in Greensboro, NC, in 1911. His father was a musician and taught him to play harmonica. Blinded by two boyhood accidents, Terry's ability to perform allowed him to earn a living on the street corners of nearby North Carolina cities, where he often worked with Blind Boy Fuller. Terry traveled with Fuller to NYC for some recording sessions and returned there to be a part of John Hammond's From Spirituals to Swing concert at Carnegie Hall. He met Brownie McGhee in the late 1930s, and when Fuller died in 1941, they became a duo. Terry followed McGhee to NYC, and both musicians developed friendships and alliances in the burgeoning folk movement. He also appeared in several Broadway plays, notably *Finian's Rainbow*, where he played a significant role. As folk music gained popularity during the 1960s and 1970s, Terry and McGhee became popular performers. Terry died in 1986.

The Folkways Years 1944–1963

Smithsonian Folkways 40033

From the folk heart of the 1950s, rock-solid Americana. "Harmonica with Slaps," from 1958, is simply a spirited harmonica solo, with J.C. Burns slapping his body to provide percussion. "The Woman Is Killing Me" is a vocal with an assortment of percussion that includes washboard, washtub, even a frying pan. Terry sings with Pete Seeger on "Right on that Shore," but the finest material is with Brownie McGhee. The duo's at their harmonizing best on "Dark Road." Add Coyal's call-and-response on the irrestible "Pick a Bale of Cotton" and Seeger's guitar on a surprisingly fresh "Skip to My Lou." "Shortnin' Bread" features the engaging twang of a jaw harp.

LINK➤ *Various Artists — Harmonica Masters* **Yazoo 201**

Hammie Nixon was Sleepy John Estes's partner, and he's often heard on his Delmark releases. Jaybird Coleman was hugely successful in the South in the 1920s. And nobody knows much about Kyle Wooten. An interesting mix, mostly fine work.

Whoopin'

Alligator 473

After breaking up with McGhee, Terry worked with some unexpected co-horts. This 1984 album finds Terry, age 73, chops intact, hanging with bassist Willie Dixon (age 69), guitarist Johnny Winter, and drummer Styve Homnick. Terry's harmonica is remarkably smooth and tasty, and his signature vocal whoops add spice on the Chicago-style instrumental "Sonny's Whoopin' the Doop." "Roll Me Baby," which features Winter's gritty guitar and Terry's rough vocal, is more like a Texas electric blues, not much like the slick-and-smooth folk blues that made Terry famous. Some very hot harmonica here. Kudos to Terry for taking some risks!

LINK➤ *Buster Brown — Raise a Ruckus Tonight* **Relic 70**

"Sugar Babe" is one of those rough tunes that gets you moving, but somehow wasn't commercial enough for radio play. This album's full of such songs, performed by an ace harmonica player and singer (who also whooped).

Sonny Terry & Brownie McGhee

Sonny Terry was a harmonica player from Greensboro, NC, and Brownie McGhee was a guitar player from Tennessee. In the 1930s, they met up in Durham, NC. At the time, Terry was backing up the popular Piedmont blues singer Blind Boy Fuller. Both traveled to NYC from time to time, and in the early 1940s, when Fuller died of blood poisoning, they became a NYC duo. Their style was immediately accessible to the likes of Pete Seeger, Leadbelly, Josh White, Woody Guthrie, and others who were inventing contemporary folk music. The two began to attract notice by the 1940s and remained a fixture at coffeehouses, folk clubs, blues clubs, colleges, festivals, and special events for decades, particularly in NYC and in the Berkshires. These activities led to time in such 1950s Broadway plays as *Cat on a Hot Tin Roof.* The partnership showed signs of friction in the 1970s and eventually dissolved.

At the 2nd Fret — **Original Blues Classics (OBC) 561**

To further confound record collectors, this 1962 album is credited to Brownie McGhee and Sonny Terry. Recorded live at a Philadelphia coffeehouse that catered to folk audiences, it's a good performance. On "Evil Hearted Me," for example, Terry's harmonica solos run just a little longer and get a little wilder than they might in the studio. McGhee is a bit more adventuresome on his guitar breaks, attentive to Terry's misery on "Sick Man," but willing to try some new ideas. The combination of harp and guitar glimmers as it sets the dark rural mood on "Backwater Blues," a flood story associated with Bessie Smith. Start your collection here.

LINK➤ *Josh White — Blues Singer: 1932-1936* — ***Columbia/Legacy 67001***

Although White became known on the college circuit in the 1960s (singing mainly folk music), this is strong stuff. His style is light and easy, but the material addresses the loneliness of migrant workers ("Friendless City"), welfare, evil, and sex. There's also some gospel blues. Superb.

Just a Closer Walk With Thee — **OBC 541**

Two experienced hands laying their burden down on a dozen fine gospel blues tunes. It's 1957, but the sound is excellent. It's just the two of them, trading vocals on one song after another, singing and playing their hearts out. Best tunes include "Children Go Where I Send Thee," and an up-tempo "Glory, Glory" with an outstanding, toe-tapping harmonica solo from Terry. The higher and raspier voice of Terry combined with McGhee's smooth vocal tones make for a distinctive sound. Their voices alternate on a very persuasive "I Shall Not Be Moved," which became a folk anthem. And even the slow numbers have some pep, as on "If I Could Hear My Mother Pray." Fine work throughout.

LINK➤ *Holmes Brothers — In the Spirit* — ***Rounder 2056***

With their no-nonsense gospel harmonies and their ease in shifting from sacred music to contemporary blues, the Holmes Brothers have been popular throughout the decade. Unadulterated by the needs of contemporary radio, they pour it on. Great album! From 1990.

Brownie's Blues **OBC 505**

Although this 1960 album is credited only to McGhee, it's a fine duo album. McGhee is the singer and composer on most selections, hence the title. The pumping and puffing of Terry's harmonica and the seamless connection it makes to the tricky pacing of McGhee's vocal on "Jump Little Children Jump" show how closely aligned these two musicians can be. McGhee's talent for singing a sad song provides heart for "Lonesome Day" and "The Killing Floor." A more careful listen reveals McGhee's exquisite guitar work. The utter simplicity of two talented musicans performing fine blues makes this album one of their best. Bennie Foster adds some guitar fill.

LINK➤ *Frank Frost & Sam Carr — Keep Yourself Together* *Evidence 26077*

Frost is the harmonica player, Sam Carr's the drummer, and Fred James plays lead guitar and Hammond organ. Their sound lays somewhere between early Chicago blues and the likes of Terry & McGhee. With a good beat. Recorded in 1993.

Back to New Orleans **Fantasy 24708**

On "Betty and Dupree's Blues," Brownie McGhee lays down one of his best story-song vocals. He's a riveting storyteller with a slightly roughhouse voice. Here, McGhee sings a duet—not with Terry's voice, but with his harmonica. The eloquence of their combined sound makes this song outstanding. It's hardly the exception. Terry's harmonica reaches for the heart time and again, transforming even a simple topical tune like "Pawn Shop" into a work of art. This is pure magic and deserves to be heard by a much wider audience. In fact, this CD combines two albums: 1959's *Down Home Blues* and 1960's *Blues in My Soul*. Wonderful sound quality, too.

LINK➤ *Various Artists — Blues Sweet Carolina Blues: Bluesville Years, Vol. 6* *Prestige 991*

These aren't old recordings, but rather early 1960s sessions with Terry and McGhee ("Ida Mae," "Callin' My Mama") and also with Pink Anderson (a guitar player from the 1920s) and Baby Tate (same credential).

Midnight Special **Fantasy 24721**

Another CD that combines two excellent 1960 albums: *Blues and Folk* and *Blues All Around My Head*. It starts with a very hot harmonica number, "Sonny's Squall," with lots of honest whooping; McGhee knows well enough to stand aside and just play the rhythm. Leadbelly's "Midnight Special" is performed as a vocal duet—a relatively uncommon format for these two musicians. It's a bit show-biz, a toe-tapper suggesting vaudeville, but their combined vocal sound is invigorating; they also give the instrumental breaks their all. "Tryin' to Win" is pure coffeehouse music (the song was covered by Peter, Paul and Mary); it's also a vocal duet. Lots more good material, all well recorded.

LINK➤ *Peter, Paul and Mary —See What Tomorrow Brings* *Warner Bros. 2665*

Connecting the dots between '60s folk and Terry-McGhee's blues, the trio sings "Betty & Dupree" and the blues duo's "Tryin' to Win." In fact, most PP&M albums included one or two blues and often a gospel song, too. Miraculous sound quality for 1965. Nice harmonies, as well.

Jimmy Thackery & the Drivers

Thackery was born in Pittsburgh, PA, in 1953, but he grew up in Washington, D.C. A pianist before he learned guitar, Thackery started taking music seriously in the late 1960s, when he was part of a high school band that included Bonnie Raitt's brother, David. Thackery supposedly decided to pursue a music career after seeing first Buddy Guy and then Jimi Hendrix in concert. Thackery became well known as the lead guitar player for the Nighthawks, a powerhouse blues band he cofounded in the early 1970s. After years of touring (300 nights on the road in the busiest years), he left in 1986 to start a six-piece R&B group called the Assassins. The band recorded three acclaimed albums and stayed together until 1991. That year saw the beginning of the three-piece Jimmy Thackery and the Drivers, a blues band that occasionally adds rockabilly and some jazz to its mix.

Empty Arms Motel — Blind Pig 5001

On "Paying the Cost to Be the Boss," Thackery demonstrates his extraordinary talent for blues guitar. His personal electricity charges a midtempo tune with passion, and his hoarse, phlegmy vocal adds just the right touch of anger. On "Rude Mood," a Stevie Ray Vaughan song, the band operates as a unified trio. Thackery dominates with his guitar, but drummer Mark Stutso and bassist Wayne Burdette actively participate in this rocking boogie. The choice of material is interesting, and well suited to Thackery's talent. There's a Jimi Hendrix song ("Red House"), one by Hoyt Axton ("Last Night"), and a slower song with a hypnotizing rhythm, Lowell Fulson's "Honey Hush." From 1992.

LINK➤ *George Thorogood & the Destroyers* — ***Rounder 3013***

The 1977 debut album for a minor-league baseball player turned musician and his Boston-based blues-rock band. "Move It on Over," the group's only big hit, is on the inferior second album; and the MTV favorite "Bad to the Bone" is on the fourth album. This album is the best, though.

Drive to Survive — Blind Pig 5035

With Michael Patrick in the bass position, this 1996 album starts with the 1970s-style rock anthem "Drive to Survive." The energy says "road song," with a nod to Chuck Berry's influence in parts of Thackery's early solos. Thackery wrote the majority of songs on this album, and it's fun to hear him connect with earlier blues-rockers; "You've Got Work to Do" contains more than a few touches familiar to Boz Scaggs fans. Thackery takes it slow and makes good use of open space on "That's How I Feel"; it's perhaps his most pleasant vocal. The grain and texture of his voice is admirable, as he achieves a kind of quintessential rock-blues weariness.

LINK➤ *Eddy Clearwater — The Chief* — ***Rooster Blues 2615***

Clearwater's not a Native American, but he does wear a chief's headdress onstage (hence the absurdist cover art). This 1980 debut album is about his sharp, heated guitar, and not his voice, which is earnest, but uncompelling. Skillful Chicago accompaniment from top names.

Willie Mae Thornton was born in 1926, the daughter of a minister in Montgomery, AL. As a young girl, Thornton frequently sang in her father's church, one of seven children singing prayers to the Lord. By 1940, Thornton was already on the road with the Hot Harlem Revue; she stayed until 1948. When the tour played Houston, Thornton left to pursue opportunities in the city's popular club scene. Don Robey, a local music entrepreneur, signed her to a record and management deal in 1951. Two years later, Thornton scored a number-one R&B hit with Leiber-Stoller's "Hound Dog." She also toured with label mate Johnny Otis and with many other musicians through the 1950s. Thornton stayed with Peacock until 1957. After her career slumped in the early 1960s, she moved to San Francisco. Thornton eventually established herself as a tour and festival attraction, working until shortly before her death in 1984.

Hound Dog: The Peacock Recordings **MCA 10668**

Thornton slashes the lyrics of "Hound Dog" with genuine anger; she even barks and howls like a mongrel. She not only has more fun than Elvis Presley, but the junkyard guitar in the background adds a low-down charm to the song, too. Thornton's sassy attitude comes through on the fast R&B sizzler, "They Call Me Big Mama," one of many songs Thornton recorded with the Johnny Otis Orchestra. She's at her best on "My Man Called Me." The song features several fawning male chorus members in the background, an occasional vibes break from Otis, punctuation from several horns, and a good beat. "Yes, Baby," Thornton's duet with the popular singer Johnny Ace, is also a highlight.

LINK➤ *Johnny Otis — Spirit of the Black Territory Bands* **Arhoolie 38**

Otis was an entertainment businessman who covered all the bases. Here, he's leading a big band. The music is swing, or more accurately, a memory of swing recorded in 1990. It's sweet and notable for the inclusion of his son, guitarist Shuggie Otis in the band.

Ball 'n Chain **Arhoolie 30**

Thornton is in excellent voice for these 1965–66 sessions. In fact, she's very much her own woman, not just the vocalist standing in front of Don Robey or Johnny Otis's conceptions. Thornton wails on "Hound Dog" and hits hard on "Ball 'n Chain," a song later popularized by Janis Joplin, who mimicked Thornton. That's Buddy Guy on guitar for the extremely fine "Sweet Little Angel" and a handful of other cuts. When Guy's not playing, Thornton's accompanied not only by Muddy Waters's guitar, but by his whole band. As you listen to this CD, one thing becomes clear: it's one of the finest blues albums ever recorded.

LINK➤ *Sister Wynona Carr — Dragnet for Jesus* ***Specialty 70***

Carr was a gospel singer from Cleveland, OH, who pushed jazz, blues, jump blues, and R&B into the sacred repertoire. A remarkable singer, some of her best work is presented here. Highly recommended.

azz, R&B, and blues vocalist extraordinaire Turner was born in 1911; he grew up inging in Kansas City churches and on the streets. Turner started his career early, ending bar and performing blues. He partnered with boogie woogie pianist Pete ohnson around 1930; the two men worked together for the better part of two de-ades. Turner also sang with big bands passing through Kansas City, notably Count Basie's band. Turner and Johnson's 1938 Carnegie Hall appearance during John Hammond's Spirituals to Swing Concert ignited a boogie woogie craze that lasted everal years. They settled in NYC and became regulars at the upscale jazz club Cafe Society. As times changed, Turner shifted to a rocking version of R&B, signed with Atlantic in 1951, and recorded hit after hit for the next five years. He later reteamed vith Johnson, played some jazz, and appeared at many festivals. Turner died in nglewood, CA, in 1985.

Jumpin' with Joe: The Complete Aladdin and Imperial Recordings

EMI 99293

Four "battles" between Turner and Wynonie Harris, another blues shouter, begin this CD. The first two, called "Battle of the Blues," come from 1947. As a big band grinds away in the background, the Turner and Harris go on about "how long can a chick be rusted?" and jive their way through a stagey performance. The entertaining jump blues of "Roll 'Em Pete," "Blues Jump the Rabbit," and "Ice Man Blues" are nicely balanced by slow blues. "Nobody in Mind" is a masterpiece of saxophone sadness and he magical expressiveness of an electric guitar. Turner rivals Bessie Smith in his ability o put over a truly sad song. Sound quality is just okay.

LINK➤ *Big Joe Turner — Tell Me Pretty Baby* **_Arhoolie 333_**

Recorded with Pete Johnson's orchestra mostly in 1948 and 1949, this collection sounds better than the Aladdin/Imperial collection and provides more opportunities to hear Johnson's piano at its best. Turner is also in excellent voice, and the material is consistently fine.

Big, Bad & Blue: The Big Joe Turner Anthology

Rhino 71550

As a rule, Rhino's anthologies are comprehensive and both skillfully produced and packaged. This 3-CD Turner collection is one of Rhino's very best. Turner's 45-year journey begins in 1938, when along with pianist Pete Johnson, he was a regular headliner at NYC's Cafe Society. "Cherry Red" was Turner and Johnson's kind of song: "Hot Lips" Page blasts a lowdown fanfare, Johnson makes time, and Turner wails, "Your loving proposition would get somebody killed." He then backs off for "Buster" Smith's brief alto sax solo. It's followed by a longer Johnson piano solo. The year 1941 brought a hit Turner performance of "Careless Love" accompanied by pianist Willie "The Lion" Smith. It's followed by some "typical Kansas City blues," such as the top-selling "Piney Brown Blues" with shouter Turner, boogie-woogie pianist Johnson, and muted trumpeter Page. "Sally Zu-zazz Blues," from 1946, has a bigger sound and some additional patience and confidence, too. By now the label was National. Turner's in full jump blues style in "New Oo-wee Baby Blues" with its "pat-chee, pat-chee, pat-chee all da long" chorus and jazzier accompaniment. His first single for the new Atlantic Record in 1951 changed everything. Suddenly, Turner was a sophisticated balladeer—a proto soul singer whose material made much better use of his enormous vocal capacity. H followed with "The Chill Is On," "Bump Miss Susie," "Sweet Sixteen," and "Don You Cry," one of songwriter Doc Pomus's first hits. Turner's first number-one record "Honey Hush," came in 1953. Somewhere between R&B and jump blues, Turne was riding on the edge of the emerging rock 'n' roll. Next came "Shake, Rattle an Roll," a number-one R&B tune covered by a white group, Bill Haley and the Comets Along the way, the original sexy lyrics were sanitized and made wholesome. (Still Haley and Turner become personal friends.) As the 1950s progressed, Turner remaine steady on his R&B course, scoring some pop hits like the spirited "Corinne Corrina in 1956. Even on an often-heard song like this one, Turner's phrasing and intona tions, his easy style in front of a few background singers, the smile on his face, and th manly control of his voice combine to make him great. The story ends in 1959. By th early 1960s, Atlantic had dropped Turner's contract. Two tracks from 1973 and on from 1983 recap Turner's glorious past.

LINK➤ *Big Joe Turner — Greatest Hits* **Atlantic 8175**

The essential collection of Turner's hits for Atlantic Records. If you're unwilling to spend th extra dollars on the 3-CD box, this is a reasonable alternative. Hits include "The Chill I On," "Chains of Love," "Crawdad Hole," "Corrine Corrina," "Flip, Flop and Fly," an 16 more seminal tunes.

Nobody in Mind **OJC 72**

This CD finds Turner aging: he's still fine in his intonation and phrasing, but lack the hurricane force that made his younger vocals so phenomenal. It's not that Turne doesn't sing well here (and it's not like he's an old guy who didn't know when to quit either), it's just that he's a little muted, a bit distant, not as in-your-face as before. Thi is Turner in a mature, jazzier setting with some formidable partners: jazz trumpete Roy Eldridge, jazz vibraphone wizard Milt Jackson, and blues guitarist Pee Wee Crayton There's some pleasant funk in "Juke Joint Blues," mostly from Crayton, but also fron Turner's easy interaction with Eldridge's horn. From 1975.

LINK➤ *Little Johnny Taylor — Greatest Hits* **Fantasy 451**

On Taylor's big hit, "Part Time Love," he combines touches of Little Richard, lots of othe soulful singers, and always makes decisions based on commercial instinct. When Taylo sings "I Smell Trouble" and "Zig-Zag Lightning," his style shows remnants of a gospe upbringing, too.

Stevie Ray Vaughan

Vaughan, a well-respected guitarist, was born in 1954 and grew up in Dallas. His older brother, Jimmy, was the founder of the Fabulous Thunderbirds. After a stint with the Cobras, Vaughan formed Triple Threat with LuAnn Barton on vocals; a year later, with some personnel changes, the band became Double Trouble. By 1978, the Austin, TX, blues scene counted Vaughan and his brother's T- Birds among its brightest lights. By 1982, Vaughan had been noticed by Mick Jagger and Jerry Wexler, who arranged a Montreux Jazz Festival appearance. This led to a place on David Bowie's *Let's Dance* album, a professional friendship with Jackson Browne, and the involvement of John Hammond, who set up an Epic Records deal. Fighting drug and alcohol problems, Vaughan became very popular, and then tragedy struck. Vaughan and his band were killed in a helicopter crash in 1990 en route to a Chicago concert date.

The Sky Is Crying — Epic 47390

Don't dismiss these ten songs as outtakes; instead, think of them as tracks that never quite fit on any of the band's albums. The best is "Little Wing," a Hendrix song with touches of jazz, blues, and pure magic. Vaughan's guitar has never sounded better than on his update of Elmore James on "The Sky Is Crying." "Boot Hill" is a rocker that seriously considers killing a lover who provided a "first thrill." Vaughan performed "Life By the Drop" with an acoustic 12-string guitar on MTV's *Unplugged*. And "Chitlins Con Carne" is a Kenny Burrell jazz guitar tune with a vaguely rocking edge. Truly masterful guitar playing throughout.

LINK➤ *Lonnie Mack — Strike Like Lightning* — ***Alligator 4739***

Stevie Ray Vaughan produced this 1985 album and also plays second guitar on this comeback effort. Mack was an early Vaughan influence; mostly, he had been working the roadhouses in the midwest, not making enough money in records to bother much.

Greatest Hits — Epic 66217

Just a few seconds of Vaughan's guitar on the introduction to "Texas Flood" set him apart from all but the finest electric blues guitarists. He creates a relentless storm, a flood of angry, sad, desperate electricity, the likes of which point toward only one similar voice: Jimi Hendrix. "Pride and Joy" comes from the same 1982 debut album, *Texas Flood* (Epic 38734). Neither "Cold Shot" nor "Couldn't Stand the Weather" are as catchy, but the snap of Chris "Whipper" Layton's drumming on the latter song is chilling alongside Vaughan's awesome guitar. "Tightrope," from 1989's *In Step* (Epic 45024), addresses Vaughan's abuse problems. This is an essential collection of rocked-out blues.

LINK➤ *Smokin' Joe Kubek — Steppin' Out Texas Style* — ***Bullseye Blues 9510***

Kubek keeps the flame of Texas guitar blues alive with his partner in crime, vocalist and rhythm guitar player B'Nois King. They do Jimmy McCracklin's "Steppin' Out," Big Bill Broonzy's "Hands on It," and Willie Dixon's "That's All I Want," plus originals—and have a great time.

Born on Christmas Day in 1949, Walker's on-again, off-again path to success finally led to renown and some degree of stardom. Starting his career in the 1960s, Walker naturally gravitated toward San Francisco's rock scene. He became friendly with Mike Bloomfield, and the two musicians shared an apartment. Through Bloomfield, Walker met Jimi Hendrix and other performers who frequented the Fillmore auditorium. He worked as a backup musician, then left in 1969 for Vancouver, where he spent a few depressing years playing with bar bands. Walker returned to San Francisco, finished high school, and sang gospel music with the Spiritual Corinthians. In 1985, after completing college, Walker returned to the blues, forming a band called the Boss Talkers. A year later, his first album was released on Hightone. During the early 1990s, Walker was swept up by Verve's sudden fascination with blues. Today he is a top blues performer.

Cold Is the Night **Hightone 8006**

Walker plays his heart out on this appealing 1985 debut album. His methodology is straightforward: soulful blues vocals and electric guitar with an edge. Walker's very much out front, with keyboard, bass, and drums relegated to background status. On nearly every song, he shines with a bright, well-considered guitar solo. "Ten More Shows to Play," for example, contains an extended break with a slighty anxious edge. Walker finds a good hook for the title song, and this knack extends to the boogie-funk "Moanin' Blues" and other tunes. "One Woman" gets its spice from a tenor sax, and "Fuss and Fight" from an organ. Handsome urban blues that go down easy.

LINK➤ *Mike Bloomfield — The Best of Mike Bloomfield* ***Takoma 8905***

Bloomfield was a smart, talented guitar player who died young. Here, he's in two duets with pianist Little Brother Montgomery, and also with former Paul Butterfield co-worker Mark Naftalin. Most surprising cut: a seven-minute session with Woody Herman's band.

The Gift **Hightone 8012**

This sophomore effort from 1988 is even better than the first album. The Memphis Horns provide lift, and consistently excellent material helps Walker soar. "Thin Line," a songwriting collaboration with bassist Henry Oden, gets some funk into the action without sacrificing any blues purity. There's the obligatory guitar solo here, but it's got extra zest, more sparkle. "747" is another of Walker's songs easily identified by the opening riff; nice Jimi Stewart blues piano here, too. The band lightens up for "The Gift," a slow dance praising family ancestry, family unity, and personal integrity. The engineering emphasizes the bass and drums a bit, making this seem more commercial than past efforts.

LINK➤ *Joe Louis Walker — Blue Soul* ***Hightone 8019***

No strenuous objections, but the selection of songs on this 1989 release is somewhat uninspired (and sometimes, as in "Alligator," a little silly). The music is fine; Walker is an extremely consistent performer who never lets his audience down.

ive at Slim's, Vol. 1 **Hightone 8025, 8036**

lim's is a San Francisco club where Walker and the Boss Talkers appeared regularly; ıis recording was clearly a special event for both club and audience. Vol. 1's high-ghts include an austere electric and slide guitar solo in the middle of "Don't Play ;ames" and a funky vocal duet with Angela Strehli on "Don't Mess Up a Good Thing." luey Lewis contributes harmonica on "Bit by Bit (Little by Little)." It's songs like Ridin' High" that make Walker such an appealing performer—a voice that's trying ard to get home, an organ that supports his emotion, and a crackling guitar that ommunicates better than a vocal ever could. Recommended.

INK➤ *Rod Piazza — Tough and Tender* ***Tone-Cool (Rounder) 1165***

ommercial blues by a 30-year veteran, Piazza performs with his Mighty Flyers band ncluding talented wife Honey Piazza on piano). Plenty of great showmanship and catchy ooks; this 1997 CD captures the excitement of a live show.

ive at Slim's, Vol. 2 **Hightone 8036**

'ol. 2 is better still, beginning with a very spirited Ray Charles's "Don't You Know," ıllowed by "Thin Line" and other Walker favorites. Earl Hooker's "Blue Guitar" is a own-tempo, late night solo echoed by Carl Schumacher's organ. Walker's guitar is :d hot, and it works its way deeply under the skin. Blues doesn't get better than this. Shade Tree Mechanic" is a Walker standard with a nice interplay between horns, a ecking beat, and carefully chosen opportunities for guitar punctuation. The finale, Love at First Sight," is a stunner; an amazing guitar solo leads off the song, which ıen slows down before building into a frenzy. Walker's very easy to enjoy.

INK➤ *Clarence Spady — Nature of the Beast* ***Evidence 26080***

ritically acclaimed debut album by Scranton, PA, native Spady. An electric guitarist ith a refreshing repertoire (including covers of Son Seals, Clifford Brown, and Raful leal, Jr.), Spady's reedy voice is well balanced by an R&B section and his own understated uitar.

lues of the Month Club **Verve 527-999**

licker and more commercial, Walker's first major label venture disappointed some ıns. What he's given up in bar band antics, he's picked up in diversity and expansion. ‹e Turner's "You've Got to Lose" keeps all of the old characteristics, but adds a tighter, ıore prominent rhythm section and Walker's old gospel group, the Spiritual ;orinthians, for occasional emphasis in what's definitely an electric blues song. It's ıteresting to note that Walker's solos seem to go on longer—maybe a tad too long— ıan before. The title cut got some airplay, as expected, but the more soulful "Get It ight" is more representative of Walker's 1995 style. Good, but not his best.

INK➤ *Guitar Shorty — Topsy Turvy* ***Black Top 1094***

)avid Kearney's been performing blues for about 40 years. Along the way, he won first rize on The Gong Show *for playing guitar while standing on his head, married Jimi lendrix's stepsister, and perfected a strong brew of updated Chicago blues. From 1993, this his best.*

Born in 1910, Aaron Thibeaux ("T-Bone") Walker became the blues' first great elec tric guitarist and one of its most influential. He grew up in Dallas, TX, where hi stepfather was a bassist. When Walker was 10, he led family friend Blind Lemo Jefferson from clubs to street performances, a job he kept for three years. Walker lef Dallas to play carnivals, then recorded for Columbia in 1929. He worked for a fev jazz dance bands, and eventually established himself in L.A. (first as a dancer, then a a musician). By 1935, Walker was one of the first musicians to perform regularly o electric guitar (complete with stage hijinks). He became famous and recorded hits fo various labels through the 1940s and 1950s. Rock obscured his talents, but Walke continued performing and recording through the early 1970s. His health was weak ened by a 1974 stroke, a bad stomach, and drinking problems. Walker died of pneu monia in 1975.

Complete Capitol/Black & White Recordings **Capitol 2937**

Here's the link between country blues and electric blues, and between blues, soul R&B, and rock 'n' roll. T-Bone Walker was one of the more influential popular artist of the twentieth century. This collection provides ample opportunity to explore thos connections—it contains 3 discs, and over 3 1/2 hours of music. Since no smalle compilation exists, just take it slow to minimize overexposure. CD1 nicely sample Walker's many approaches. He sings 1940's "T-Bone Blues" with a sweet horn an Frank Pasley's Hawaiian guitar. It's an interesting benchmark, for the whole worl changes with 1942's "I Got a Break" and "Mean Old World." Both songs begin wit an extended vamp on electric guitar, then a modern, stylish blend of big band an country blues vocal kicks in. "Don't Leave Me Worry, Baby," from 1946, rocks with stinging guitar, but in a schizophrenic way it jumps back to a big-band horn arrange ment alongside each guitar solo. The same year brought Walker's first hit, "Bobby So Baby" (Chuck Berry would later update this idea as "Sweet Little Sixteen"). The son popularized the electric guitar as a pop instrument. And the late-night lonely son "I'm in an Awful Mood" set the stage for many just like it—and for Walker's greates all-time hit, 1947's "Call It Stormy Monday, but Tuesday Is Just as Bad." The stor continues for about two more years, but by the end of CD1, the ideas are well estab lished. The other two discs offer plenty more along similar lines.

LINK➤ *Matt "Guitar" Murphy — Way Down South* ***Discovery/Sire 7420***

Murphy's been a major blues guitarist since he accompanied Memphis Slim in the 1950 but he's probably best known for his work behind the various Blues Brothers adventure (he's in both films and is married to Aretha Franklin). Murphy emerged as a leader in th 1990s; this CD is his best.

he Complete Imperial Recordings, 1950–1954 EMI 96737

'alker doesn't stay in one place for long. This 2-CD set, which covers the early 1950s, :caps some earlier ideas, then hits hard with a rollicking jump blues, "Strollin' with one." "You Don't Love Me," from 1950, starts with some very fancy electric guitar; Travelin' Blues" is even slicker. It's 1950, and T. Bone Walker is very close to inventg rock 'n' roll. The story advances again in New Orleans with producer Dave artholomew and members of Fats Domino's band. The horns are sharper, and the ocals are grittier. The kinship to jazz becomes clear on some 1954 L.A. tracks. Sadly, 'alker left the scene (due to illness and exhaustion) in 1955.

NK➤ *Various Artists — Blues Masters, Vol. 3: Texas Blues* ***Rhino 71123***

'ne of the best in the series, this story begins with Blind Lemon Jefferson performing Matchbox Blues" through a distant sonic haze; it reaches a kind of adolescence with "Hound og," and matures with Stevie Ray Vaughan's "Texas Flood." Essential blues history.

-Bone Blues Atlantic 8020

his is the closest thing to a T-Bone Walker best-of collection and it's a reasonable ace to start. There is plenty of good news here: these mid-1950s tracks were proiced by Ahmet Ertegun, Jerry Wexler, and Nesuhi Ertegun—the creative forces bend Atlantic Records. Most of Walker's best-known songs are here, but they're prented with wonderfully long, uninhibited guitar solos, a somewhat unusual idea for e era. Jazz guitar player Barney Kessel trades some very effective licks with Walker, it the personnel varies (the album was recorded on three separate dates in 1955,)56, and 1957); the varied settings keep Walker's sound vital and fresh. Overall, the oducers achieve a more modern feel.

NK➤ *Bee Houston — The Hustler* ***Arhoolie 9008***

her later years, Big Mama Thornton was accompanied by Bee Houston, a Texas-born, A.-raised guitar player. Houston's singing voice is on the rough side, but his guitar is eet and direct. A 1970s solo album, plus some tracks with Thornton.

Want a Little Girl Delmark 633

ıe comeback album, cut in 1968. No rehash, this is new work unrelated to past ɔries. Walker's guitar playing is very modern (even by today's standards);in Hal Singer, 's found an entirely sympathetic tenor sax player. Walker is meticulous about every te and vocal intonation, a craftsman whose carefully constructed art achieves preely the right emotional pace and color. On song after song, Walker shows what mmercial music is all about. Listen to the tonal quality of Singer's sax on "Feeling e Blues" and the complementary texture of Walker's guitar and Georges Arvanitis's ano—neither blues nor jazz gets much better than this! Nicely varied repertoire, o.

NK➤ *Wes Montgomery — Full House* ***OJC 106***

guably the best guitar player in jazz, this 1962 live date finds Montgomery sparkling. is rhythm section is world class: Wynton Kelly on piano and Paul Chambers and Jimmy ɔbb on drums. Add saxophone player Johnny Griffin, and the magic takes shape.

One of the L.A. blues scene's longtime favorites, Walker came to California by way c Texas, a common path. He was born near Lake Charles, LA, in 1937, then move with his family to Port Arthur as a child. A local performer named Lover Boy Willi got him started on guitar; within months Walker was hired by Clifton Chenier. Walke stayed three years, until 1956, and frequently accompanied top blues performers o tour. While with Chenier, he befriended Cornelius Green (Lonesome Sundown); thei friendship has endured decades of working and playing together. In 1958, Walke moved to Los Angeles, where he performed with local bands and picked up sessio work. Personal recognition was elusive until he teamed up with producer Bruc Bromberg. Their collaboration began in 1969; after several years of trying, the tw made their way toward success. Bromberg has become a top blues producer, and Walke is now something of a star.

The Bottom of the Top — Hightone 8802

From 1969 and the early 1970s, this collection of singles remains the best of th Walker-Bromberg partnership. "I Can't Lose (With the Stuff I Use)" is an up-temp piece with shades of R&B from a pair of saxes and a trumpet; the bouncy "Hello M Darling" has the same spirit. The slower "Tin Pan Alley," about a rough section c town, is developed mainly by a dangerous guitar (with plenty of fine detailing) an Walker's slightly spooked vocal. "Hello Central," a Lightnin' Hopkins song, gets sparse, lonesome vocal treatment and fine guitar work notable for its economy an clarity of expression. Buck Owens's "Crying Time" features Walker's wife, "Bea Bop.

LINK➤ *Lonesome Sundown — I'm a Mojo Man: The Best of the Excello Single* **AVI-Excello 300**

A decade's work for the Louisiana label yielded "Leave Me Money Alone," "My Home Is Prison," "I'm a Mojo Man," "I'm a Samplin' Man," and other swamp blues classics. Th anthology presents 24 songs recorded between 1956 and 1964.

I Got a Sweet Tooth — Black Top 114

The sharpening of Walker's guitar and the presence of a fuller rhythm on this 199 album show how far Walker has progressed in three decades. The basic formula sti works, but the horns are more prominent and the vocals are blessed with the depth maturity and experience. "On My Way," one of the album's best tunes, is backed by tight Austin, TX, ensemble that includes second guitar Derek O'Brien and Ma "Kaz" Kazanoff's tenor and baritone saxophones. Several other tracks were record in New Orleans. Either way, it's the right blend of tasty guitar, experienced R& horns, and a solid vocal performance that keep the music interesting.

LINK➤ *Sue Foley — Young Girl's Blues* ***Discovery/Sire 724***

The 1992 debut album for a talented guitar player who came to Austin from Ottau Canada. Foley takes on several Earl Hooker tunes and shows some versatility with I. Turner's Latin-sounding "Cuban Getaway." Mostly, this is straightahead rocking blues.

ɜeulah Thomas was born in Houston, TX, around 1900. She became known as "Sippie" ecause of a childhood lisp. Her brother was Hersal Thomas, a popular early blues ianist who died in 1926. Another brother, George, was Clarence Williams's partner n Houston; when George arrived in Chicago, he summoned Sippie, a popular singer t tent shows. She arrived in 1923, and in short order, married gambler Matt Wallace, igned with Okeh Records, and became a recording star. Wallace remained popular hrough the 1920s. In 1935, she lost both her brother and her husband, and found omfort in God. For nearly 40 years, Wallace sang gospel and played organ at a Deroit church. In 1970, after a serious stroke, her health was miraculously repaired hrough a friendship with Bonnie Raitt. By 1972, they were sharing the stage at the nn Arbor Blues Festival. Wallace continued to perform for years; she died in 1986.

Vomen Be Wise — Alligator 4810

onnie Raitt found this 1966 album in a used record store, liked what she heard, and racked Wallace down in Detroit; the two became close friends. It's easy to understand hat Raitt was so excited about. Wallace is classy, sassy, smart and in fabulous voice. Ier version of the title tune is outstanding, and the 13 other tracks are nearly as good. Vith only a piano to accompany her, Wallace fills the room with music. Typically, her ianist is Little Brother Montgomery, Roosevelt Sykes, or herself. "Special Delivery lues" is representative: a hopeful woman looking to the mailman for news of a lover ho has left town. Wallace performs the part like the actress she has always been; her erformance is powerful and affecting.

NK➤ *Bonnie Raitt — Nick of Time* — ***Capitol 91268***

fter years of critical acclaim and just-okay record sales, Raitt broke into mainstream nsciousness with this 1989 album. It's one of her best, with an excellent performance of hn Raitt's "Thing Called Love." Kim Wilson plays harmonica. Don Was produced.

ippie — Atlantic 81592

o be honest, Wallace sounds like an old biddy singing the first verse of her most mous tune, "Woman Be Wise." Bonnie Raitt comes in with her powerful voice, and m Dapogney's Chicago Jazz Band comes on strong. Energized, Wallace returns to omplete the song with a wonderful duet. Remarkably, almost all of the eleven songs n this album are Wallace originals, and she effortlessly updates the 1920s with "Suitse Blues," "You Got to Know How," "Mighty Tight Woman," and others whose rics and style are quaint, sexy reflections of another time. And if her enunciation is ightly 0ff, she's lost none of her enthusiasm or style. Lots of fun!

NK➤ *Various Artists — Roll Over, Ms. Beethoven: Bluesville Years, Vol. 8* — ***Prestige 9916***

his 1961 collection is dominated by Victoria Spivey, who sold more records than any her blues star in the 1920s and continued her confident performances through the 1960s. e's the model of a classic female blues singer. Alberta Hunter and Lucille Hegamin are so included.

Kathryn Thorne came from Houston, TX. Her parents were very religious and ver much against the idea of a career in music. By the late 1950s, despite her parent earnest wishes, the 20-year-old Webster had become one of Louisiana's better R&B piano players. By day, she worked in the Goldband and Excello studios behind Slin Harpo, Lonesome Sundown, Lazy Lester, Guitar Junior (Lonnie Brooks), and man other famous local names. By night, her Uplighters band entertained audiences a small clubs. This led to work as Otis Redding's opening act through the mid-1960 (Webster missed the plane that killed Redding and four Bar-Kays). After a roug decade taking care of ailing parents in Oakland, CA, she restarted her career in 197 and was rightfully known as one of the finest singers and pianists in contemporar blues, until a 1993 stroke forced an end to performing.

Katie Webster — Paula 1

On these 20 sides for the tiny Goldband label of Crowley, LA, Webster seems to b enjoying herself. She sings with that wonderful full-bodied voice, moving from pop t R&B to blues with ease. She's poised with a fifties-style slow dance on "Sunny Side c Love." Webster's a boogie-woogie queen on "Baby Come On" and a rock singer o the old standard "Mama Don't Allow." Accompanied by her own piano, drums, bas and R&B saxophone, she has no trouble rocking the house. Webster also does a goo job with "Glory of Love." Among a great many fine performances, the best is the sass talking blues "No Bread, No Meat."

LINK➤ *Albert Ammons & Meade Lux Lewis — The First Day* *Blue Note 9845*
The title refers to a significant date in jazz history: the premiere recording session of Blu Note Records (January 6, 1939). The music is made by two leading boogie-woogie pia nists, with Lewis's multipart "The Blues" just one of many highlights.

The Swamp Boogie Queen — Alligator 476

One of the best songs on this 1988 album is a robust jaz blues instrumental, led by Webster's piano and very capab framed by her backup band, the Silent Partners. It's an orig nal called "Blue Satin," and it shows off a very talented pi nist. Of course, the real fun here is the familiar R&B tun performed with such skill and genuine enthusiasm. The include "Sea of Love," "Who's Making Love?" and especial Otis Redding's "Fa-fa-fa-fa-fa." Guest harpist Kim Wilso does a marvelous job on her remake of "No Bread, No Meat." Bonnie Raitt joins i for a duet on "Somebody's on Your Case." All this plus Anson Funderburgh, Robe Cray, and a mess of spirited tunes.

LINK➤ *Robert Shaw — The Ma Grinder* *Arhoolie 3*
Texas barrelhouse piano served up in an amazing 1963 album (with more tracks fro 1977) by a man who played at brothels and parties, and then settled down in the 1930s a life as a grocer and barbecue wiz. The richness of his output is awe inspiring.

ımos Blackmore was born in West Memphis, AR; he was earning money as a street nusician by the age of 7 in 1941. By age 12, he was leading a Chicago band called the .ittle Boys. The group eventually became a well-known Chicago lounge act, the Three ıces. In 1952 and 1953, Wells's reputation as a top Chicago blues harmonica player ɾas secured when he replaced Little Walter in Muddy Waters's band. An Army stint ɔok him away from the Chicago scene; when he returned, Wells re-formed the Three ıces and started recording for various Chicago labels. In 1958, Wells teamed up with ›uddy Guy, and the two worked together until 1970, riding the crest of the 1960s lues revival at festivals and rock concerts. Until 1997, Wells maintained a busy conert schedule; he also recorded as an authentic blues sideman for Van Morrison and racy Chapman, among others. Wells died of lymphoma in Chicago in 1998.

unior Wells 1957–1963: Messin' With the Kid **Paula 3**

ecorded for Chief Records and for several other labels owned by Mel London, the ›und here is reasonably good. Amidst a soulful, manly vocal, Wells borrows Tommy ›hnson's falsetto for "Come On in This House," recorded with Earl Hooker on guiır, and Sam Myers on bass. "Little By Little" is an appealing cross between slow &B and Chicago blues, also with Hooker. The title song, "Messin' with the Kid," orks a near cha-cha rhythm, with Hooker slashing his way through the melody with wild, but brief, guitar solo. Not much harmonica here, but the song became a clasc. In fact, Wells downplays his harmonica on most of these tracks.

NK➤ *Delbert McClinton — Classics Vol. 1: The Jealous Kind*
Curb (Warner Bros.) 77664

long with Classics Vol. 2: Plain From the Heart *(77668), here's a reasonably compre-nsive look at one of Texas's best-known musicians, and arguably the state's best har-onica player. McClinton's been around since the 1960s, performing harmonica on many ell-known sessions.*

oodoo Man Blues **Delmark 612**

he ultimate Junior Wells–Buddy Guy album was recorded in 1965. Frankly, it leaves most every other blues album in the dust. Wells's voice takes on the shape of every ng. He growls through "Hound Dog"; he's sleazy and lascivious on "Good Morng, Little School Girl"; and he does a sexy mysterioso routine on the title cut. His ırmonica's tone, emphasis, and phrasing is stunning and perfect, as is everything ›out those short solos. Excellent engineering brings out the details so important to e resonance of "In the Wee Hours." Buddy Guy's accompaniment is tasteful, underıted, and bracing throughout. Billy Warren's drumming and Jack Myers's bass are ı target, offering encouragement and imagination.

NK➤ *Junior Wells — Southside Blues Jam* ***Delmark 628***

ere's the next stop on the Junior Wells express: a 1969 session with Buddy Guy (guitar), tis Spann (piano), Earnest Johnson (bass), and Fred Below (drums). It's a recreation of a ght at Theresa's Bar on Chicago's Southside, and one of the last albums by Spann.

Booker T. Washington White was born in 1909 in Houston, MS, in the hill country west of the Delta. His father, a railroad man and part-time musician, taught him to play guitar. White moved to the Delta as a boy, then rambled by train as far north a Buffalo, NY. He first recorded in 1930, then found a job pitching for the Negro League's Birmingham Black Cats. In 1937 White shot a man in the leg, but jumped bail and recorded a hit ("Shake 'Em On Down") before he was incarcerated at Parchman Farm. Following his 1940 release, White recorded in Chicago, then moved on to Memphis and left music. White was living in Aberdeen, MS, when he received a lette from John Fahey and Ed Dawson (then students at Berkeley), resulting in a second career. White played the folk-blues circuit, recorded, had one of his songs on Bob Dylan's first album, and performed at the 1968 Olympic Games. He died from cance in 1977.

The Complete Sessions: 1930-1940 — Travelin' Man

Fourteen of the twenty songs on this album are duplicated on the Columbia CD, bu the remaining six are significant. The first four were recorded in May 1930 at White first session. "The Panama Limited" is a spirited train song with a memorable refrai and some informal comments along the way. Miss Minnie duets on two spirituals, " Am in the Heavenly Way" and "Promise True and Grand." The other two songs wer recorded by Library of Congress collector Alan Lomax while White was doing tim The recording quality is muffled and harsh, but quite spirited considering that Whit "just gave him the records there for him to get out of my face."

LINK➤ *Various Artists — Georgia Sea Island Songs* — ***New World 802***

At the heart of the blues, there are spirituals. The sea islands of the Carolinas and Georgi have developed their own culture and remained relatively unaffected by mainland progres Because of this, Alan Lomax was able to record an album filled with the music that pr ceded the blues. It's beautiful.

The Complete Bukka White — Columbia 527

White recorded 2 tracks for Columbia in 1937 and 12 more for Vocalion on Marc 7–8, 1940. Most are old-style Mississippi Delta blues; by 1940, that style was bein replaced by newer forms. White's work is somewhat rough, but these recordings pro vide an unusually clear picture of an era. "I Wonder How Long Before I Can Chang My Clothes" is sung in the voice of a Parchman Farm prisoner. "Fixin' to Die Blues" charged with emotion and some desperation, played out with a spooked guitar and hopeless voice. "Shake 'Em on Down" is a classic piece, White's big 1937 hit son and one that's been recapped by some rock bands. (A very memorable rhythm and catchy repeated chorus are the reasons why.) "Strange Place Blues" is sung at his mothe gravesite (Lulu White died in 1933); White recalls the burial, feels very lost, and "ca find a woman to take her place." White spent a lot of time as a train hobo. "Speci Streamline" is a bit like a talking blues; White sings a little, tells a story about a tra trip, and points to a sequence of railroad sound effects he plays on his steel guit (The effects even include air brakes.) Washboard Sam accompanies White (as the on ercussion) on the 1940 sessions, but his sound is mainly fill. The liner notes, by Mark Humphrey, clearly detail the important aspects of every song. All of this is ound on one 1991 re-release CD!

INK➤ *John Jackson — Don't Let Your Deal Go Down* **Arhoolie 378**

rom the Virginia songster tradition comes a series of recordings made by Jackson in the nid-1960s. Twenty years later, he was still recording. Here, Jackson performs blues and lso banjo music, country dance music, and some music from Europe. The emphasis here is n pre-blues.

ky Songs

Arhoolie 323

he best tune on this album is the first one, "Bald Eagle rain." With a persistent railroad rhythm from White's rummed guitar and Big Willie Wayne's washboard, the song onjures images along the way on a train trip from the East California. "Georgia Skin Game" is a slow, wise-talking lues about the time White pretended to gamble away his ife and (almost?) slit a man's throat instead. Both songs are laxed, giving White the space to develop characters. "Alaama Blues" is a quick-tempo traveling song, a duet with White trying out some ncy ideas on guitar while Big Willie Wayne hits those beats hard on his washboard. ecorded in 1963.

INK➤ *Various Artists — Mississippi Masters* **Yazoo 2007**

igitally remastered songs by mostly obscure blues singers like Garfield Akers ("Cottonfield lues"), Mattie Delaney ("Tallahatchie River Blues"), and King Solomon Hill ("Gone ead Train") provide a surprising number of delights. This is among the best of the Yazoo llections.

ig Daddy

Biograph 145

ukka White is one of the few older blues artists whose late work isn't a rehash of rlier recordings. This 1973 album includes a welcome re-recording of "Sic 'Em ogs," which he cut for Alan Lomax in 1937, and a new version of "Aberdeen, Misssippi." Pay particular attention to the fast-paced good-time dancing songs like "1936 rigger Toe" and the sultry slow dance "Jelly Roll Working Man." Illness, pain, and octors show up in several songs, notably "Hot Springs, Arkansas." "Black Crepe lues" is not about death, as its title suggests; rather, it is a song about moving on after failed romance. Interesting overall, but White's beginning to slow down.

NK➤ *Various Artists — Legends of the Blues, Vol. 2* **Legacy (Columbia) 47467**

olumbia's vaults—which contain Vocalion, Columbia, OKeh, and other labels—are seemgly endless. Among the many musicians here who deserve more attention are: Bumble e Slim, Buddy Moss, Casey Bill Weldon, Victoria Spivey, Lil Johnson, and Robert Wilkins. ood selection.

Born in 1903, Joe Lee Williams was one of 16 children raised by a poor farmer i Crawford, MS. By the age of 12, he was working in the nearby logging camps an turpentine mills; Williams earned extra money by performing. In 1918, William went to work for the Birmingham Jug Band, which traveled the South as part of th Rabbit Foot Minstels revue. Williams had made St. Louis his home base by 1934 Along with his cousin, J.D. Short, Williams scraped together a living by performin at parties and an occasional club. His "Baby, Please Don't Go" was a hit record fo Bluebird in 1935. Williams performed with bluesmen coming through town an sometimes left town along with them. He continued this pattern throughout his ca reer. Williams played coffeehouses during the 1960s and performed in festivals durin the 1970s. He died in 1982.

Delta Blues, 1951 — Trumpet 270

Here's an opportunity to hear not only Big Joe Williams (who performs on two track alone and six more with bassist T.J. Green), but also Willie Love (on six more; tw with Elmore James). The sound quality isn't ideal, but it's decent. Williams recorde his tracks while passing through Jackson, MS. Looking like a hobo, he stopped by th local record store, auditioned, and recorded his music in exchange for some cash Williams's dexterous handling of his 9-string guitar presents an otherworldly sound– blues guitar with some Hawaiian steel, perhaps. His vocals are carefree and grounde And check out the four Luther Huff tracks, including two on mandolin.

LINK➤ *Big Joe Williams — Back to the Country* — ***Testament 501***

The sound quality on this 1965 recording isn't all it should be, making the combination Jimmy Brown's fiddle and guitar, and Willie Lee Harris's harmonica an annoying jumb rather than a fine listening experience. For those with the patience, it's a musically rewar ing session.

Stavin' Chain Blues — Delmark 60

Credited to both Big Joe Williams and harmonica player J.D. Short, this 1958 sessio was recorded on the "dingy" second floor of a St. Louis record store. Williams an Short are in the heart of their game. The duo is at its best on "Roll and Tumble notable for Short's extended harmonica performance alongside Williams's pleasant rhythmic guitar and his slightly gritty voice. Rhythm makes the song work. The streetcorner sensibility is evident throughout; it's just one sparkling guitar turn harp solo after another: "You Got to Help Me Some" and "Sweet Old Kokomo" a closely related, gently optimistic blues. Hypnotic with very expressive musicianshi A lovely album.

LINK➤ *David "Honeyboy" Edwards — Delta Bluesman* — ***Earwig 49***

In their Southern days, Williams and Edwards became friends. Edwards was recorded Alan Lomax for the Library of Congress in 1942, and some of that music is here; so a tracks recorded in Chicago for 1979's Old Friends. *They're together here, a meaning montage.*

Mississippi's Big Joe Williams and His Nine-String Guitar **Smithsonian Folkways 40052**

On the liner notes' back cover, there's a photograph of Williams, overweight and in an apron, hunched over a stove in a small apartment with a can of Schlitz beer in the foreground. Here's this magnificent musician, a classic old blues man who captivated audiences for a half-century—and here's a photo of the best his real life ever got. This is Williams's very best album, carefully recorded in 1962 and including "Whistling 'ines," "Bluebird Blues," and a healthy helping of his 9-string guitar. Williams's solo n "Bluebird Blues" is gorgeous, shimmering, and perfect. And his vocals are self-ssured—he sings out and extends those vowel sounds in sheer blues ecstacy.

INK➤ *Big Joe Williams — Blues on Highway 49* **Delmark 604**

n addition to Williams's consistently excellent performance and outstanding guitar work, hree highway songs make this work special. Songs devoted to Highways 49, 13, and 45 rovide a musical geography lesson through Williams's world. With bassist Ransom Knowling.

hake Your Boogie **Arhoolie 315**

'his CD contains two LPs—one recorded in 1960 and the ther in 1969. There's an abundance of excellent work on oth albums. From 1960, "Sloppy Drunk Blues" is based on Sonny Boy Williamson tune. It's completely overtaken here y the bright intricacy of Williams's guitar. "President oosevelt" is a celebration, remembering a man Williams bviously admired. Compare his version of "44 Blues" to oosevelt Sykes's original. Williams's guitar more than ad-quately duplicates Sykes's piano. "Mean Step Father" feels rather personal, too. From 969, there's "So Glad," which Williams would sing whenever he managed to return ome. ("So glad, Lord, I made it back home one more time.") Unlike most bluesmen, Villiams sang about life in the 1960s and its heroes. His pain and sorrow are palpable n "The Death of Dr. Martin Luther King." It's followed by another topical song, Army Man in Vietnam," sung by a father with two sons on the front lines. Guest Charlie Musselwhite's harmonica is particularly stinging on this very emotional song. le's awfully good on straightforward country blues, such as "Killing Floor Blues" and Dirt Road Blues," but never forgets juke-joint dancing, as on "Throw the Boogie Voogie." Willilams's wife, Mary, contributes a vocal on "I Want My Crown," an arnest gospel-blues blend. With so many commendable tracks, this CD is very highly ecommended.

INK➤ *Jesse Mae Hemphill — Feelin' Good* **HMG 6052**

singer-songwriter who's been through the festival circuit, Hemphill moved from acoustic electric guitar while maintaining a Delta blues sound. "Feelin' Good" is probably her est-known song; the album was recorded in 1984 and 1988.

Williams's blues are not as well known as those of his contemporaries with simila stories, but his rough-edged music should not be missed. Williams was born in Zachar LA, in 1914. There weren't many opportunities for a child in a poor, large famil supported by sharecropper's earnings; Williams made barrels, built highways, an often performed for white folks at local parties on weekends. So it went until 195 when Williams killed a man, claiming self-defense. He was jailed with a life sentenc Enter folklorists Dr. Harry Oster and Richard Allen, who recorded Williams as h improvised blues on his guitar. As a result of Oster and Allen's pleading, a pardon wa arranged. In 1964, five years after his release, Allen was allowed to leave the state Louisiana. He performed at the Newport Folk Festival that year, then toured an recorded for the next decade. Williams died in 1980 in Louisiana.

Vol. 1: I'm Blue as a Man Can Be — Arhoolie 39

A rough-voiced singer with an idiosyncratic guitar style, Williams recorded these song while serving time at Angola State Penitentiary in 1959 and 1960. Birds are hear tweeting in the background as Williams sings "Pardon Denied Again." At times, there an otherworldly quality to his presentation; this is particularly true of "Louise," wit its complex, irregular rhythm, and Williams's spare vocal phrasing. Similarities t African music are more pronounced here than on most other blues recordings. Analy sis aside, there's honest pleasure in listening to "This Wild Old Life," pure reverenc in Williams's folk music ("Motherless Children Have a Hard Time"), and plenty straightforward blues (such as "Texas Blues" and "Up and Down Blues").

LINK➤ *Ali Farka Touré — Radio Mali* — ***World Circuit 4***

1970s work by an acoustic musician from Mali, in northern Africa. Touré's instrument work sounds like American blues. Don't obsess about historical connections; just listen to a extremely talented guitar player. And don't miss Ali Farka Touré *(Mango 9826).*

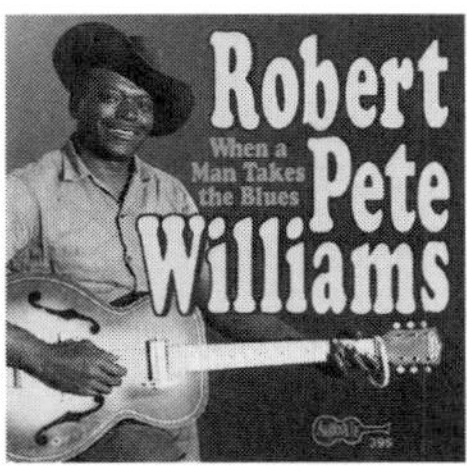

Vol. 2: When a Man Takes the Blues — Arhoolie 39

Start with tracks 3–13 for a continuation of Dr. Oster's Ango recordings from 1959–60. These include "I Got the Blues S Bad," with its understated sparkle of guitar accompanime and prison background noise, and "This Train Is Heave Bound," with its subtle rhythm suggesting a locomotive's fo ward motion. The latter cut is yet another in the lexicon "train I ride" songs, and Williams sings from the heart. Thre tracks were nicely recorded by Arhoolie founder Chris Strachwitz in Berkeley, CA, i 1970. They include a confident-sounding "When a Man Takes the Blues" and th intimate "I Had Trouble." Williams's 11-minute monologue reveals his personality.

LINK➤ *Various Artists — Angola Prisoner's Blues* — ***Arhoolie 41***

Includes "Prisoner's Talking Blues," which encouraged a letter-writing campaign to Gove nor Earl Long and resulted in Williams's parole. Other artists collected by Dr. Oster i clude Guitar Welch and Hogman Maxey.

Sonny Boy Williamson

As the story goes, Rice Miller was the star of King Biscuit Time, a radio series sponsored by the Interstate Grocery Company. To sell more flour, IGC put Miller's face on the bags, and called him Sonny Boy Williamson—the name of a nationally known blues star. In time, Miller adopted Williamson's name as his own. When the real Williamson was killed, Miller became the more famous Sonny Boy Williamson. Miller was born in Glendora, MS, around 1909, worked the plantations with his family until around 1930, then left home after an argument. He earned money with his harmonica, hung out with Robert Johnson and other bluesmen, and by the early 1940s was hosting KFFA's radio series out of Helena, AR. He moved to Chicago and recorded for Chess, but often returned to Helena. By the 1960s, Williamson was a hero to rock bands (especially British ones) like the Yardbirds, with whom he occasionally performed and recorded.

King Biscuit Time — Arhoolie 310

The cover art insinuates an association with the 1940s radio series, but these tracks were recorded in 1951 for the Trumpet label. One of the first songs, "Eyesight to the Blind," became a blues standard. Williamson leads on harmonica and vocals, but the boogeying piano swings an otherwise straight-ahead blues. The fast-footed "Crazy About You, Baby" makes more of the rhythm. "Nine Below Zero" runs deeper; it's empty hearted, and even with so-so fidelity, Williamson's harmonica pains the soul. A steady R&B bass line anchors the barren "Mighty Long Time"; Williamson barely utters the lyrics, and his harmonica communicates the song's sadness. Closes with Williamson backing Elmore James on "Dust My Broom."

LINK➤ *Sonny Boy Williamson (Rice Miller) — Goin' in Your Direction*
Alligator 2803

The title track from this collection of early 1950s sides is a jump blues, rough-hewn from a Saturday night fish fry or a Sunday picnic; it sets the style for the entire set. Three additional cuts feature Williamson with Arthur "Big Boy" Crudup and Bobo "Slim" Thomas.

The Essential Sonny Boy Williamson — Chess 9343

All of Williamson's Chess albums are worth owning, but this 2-CD set contains most of his best material. Williamson recorded for Chess from 1955 until 1964. Adding to Williamson's stylish harmonica and juke joint voice on 1955's "Good Evening Everybody" are members of Muddy Waters's band. The band's four tracks with Williamson are among the best on this collection. Otis Spann (piano), Willie Dixon (bass) and Fred Below (drums) return for a January 1956 session, but Robert Lockwood and Luther Tucker replace Muddy Waters and Jimmy Rogers on guitar—and the style changes just a bit. Still, this is top-flight Chicago blues, centered on harmonica with Williamson's somewhat scattered vocal. One of Williamson's most unique numbers, "Fattening Frogs for Snakes," was recorded in 1957 with the same session men.

Williamson's sound is evolving; he's weaving the harmonic into a thicker, richer arrangement. "I Don't Know" and "Lik Wolf," from the same session, are also progressive. "Unsee Eye," from 1957, is haunted by paranoia. There's some col orful language from a frustrated Williamson before the mu sic gets rolling on "Little Village." The cursing was prob ably an outrage in 1957, but the words are commonplac these days. A striking harmonica solo runs through "Coo Disposition." The song is a good example of the natura ease and fine sense of color and timing that makes Williamson such a standout. Th 1960 "Santa Claus" provides a raw-voiced opportunity to talk a Christmas blues; i includes trouble with the law, sexual innuendo, and the kind of harmonica that Bo Dylan always wished he could play. "Checkin' Up on My Baby" is a formulaic Chi cago blues, but Williamson's coarse singing makes it his own. He's back to the boogi and jump style, but coarser of voice, for "Too Young to Die"; Willilamson's harmonic almost sounds like an R&B saxophone on this number. Toward the end of his Ches tenure, Williamson recorded "Decoration Day," one of his best songs. It's a slow blue enhanced by Donald Hankins and Jarrett Gibson on saxophones, Buddy Guy o guitar, and the very reliable Lafayette Leake on piano. True to the title, every musicia decorates and elaborates with improvisational touches; the heart of the song is a supe rior harmonica solo. It's also a bit slicker than Williamson's past work, and the polis suits his music surprisingly well.

LINK➤ *Sonny Boy Williamson I — Complete Recorded Works, Vols. 1–5*
Document 5055-505

John Lee Williamson (1914-48) was Chicago's best prewar harmonica player, arguably th man who made the harmonica a blues instrument. There's no complete U.S. album, bu you'll find eight tracks on Throw a Boogie Woogie *(RCA 9599); Big Joe Williams com pletes it.*

Keep It to Ourselves **Analogue 303**

An audiophile pressing presents Williamson in an unadorned acoustic environmen with the bit slightest of assistance from an unnamed guitarist. The mood here is caln and relaxed, nothing like Williamson's Trumpet or Chess sessions. Happily, the em phasis is on his harmonica. The positive, friendly beat of "Slowly Walk Close to Me gently wishes for a lover's return. "Once Upon a Time" pays back the investment th remastering producers made in the finest possible equipment: the harmonica's tone i lively and thick, and Williamson sounds as if he's live in the listening room. "Why Ar You Crying?" is reflective; there's no bravado here, just an aging bluesman singin what's on his mind in 1963.

LINK➤ *The Animals — The Best of the Animals* **ABKCO 432**

The Animals were one of many British Invasion groups captivated by American blues; the made Williamson their mentor. This CD was enormously popular in LP form throughou the 1960s; it contains "House of the Rising Sun," "We Gotta Get Out of This Place," an other hits.

Jimmy Witherspoon

ınger Jimmy Witherspoon was born in Gurdon, AR, in 1923. His mother was a ianist who regularly accompanied her Baptist church choir, and it was there that /itherspoon learned to sing. He moved to Los Angeles as a teenager and earned a ving by washing dishes. Witherspoon's break came after serving as a merchant ma- ne during WW II. He was asked to sing with bandleader Teddy Weatherford at a otel club in Calcultta, India. Shortly after Witherspoon returned to L.A. in 1944, he uditioned for Jay McShann, whose band was touring the West Coast. McShann eeded a singer, and Witherspoon got the job. They toured and recorded together, ut Witherspoon broke out with his own 1949 recording of "Ain't Nobody's Busi- ess," which he followed with another hit, "In the Evenin'." As rock 'n' roll emerged, /itherspoon turned jazzier, although he sometimes performed with rock acts. The rategy kept him working for decades. He died in 1997.

lowin' In From Kansas City — Flair 86299

'hese recordings from the 1940s and early 1950s present Witherspoon in perhaps his nest voice, working mostly with early R&B and jump material. If the sound isn't as fined as in later releases, the energy and magnetism more than compensate. Jazzman en Webster lays down a stunning saxophone solo and accompaniment on "Goin' round in Circles" and sets up one of Witherspoon's most heartfelt lost-love blues. Jay 1cShann helps out on "T.B. Blues," and that's most likely Johnny Otis playing the bes during "It's Raining Outside," another excellent sad-eyed blues. With consis- ntly excellent arrangements, interesting material, and one of the best voices in blues r jazz, Witherspoon couldn't miss.

INK➤ *Various Artists — Blues Masters, Vol. 1: Urban Blues* — ***Rhino 71121***

lues moves to the big city, accumulating aspects of jazz, swing, juke joints, and scratchy 'd race records to define itself. That's what Witherspoon was about, and also Bobby "Blue" land, Dinah Washington, Pee Wee Crayton, Joe Turner, Charles Brown, and the rest.

immy Witherspoon and Jay McShann — Black Lion 760173

'he space between jazz and blues is occupied by Jimmy Witherspoon. When his big oice tackles Leroy Carr's "How Long Blues," there's the knowing show business of ightclub jazz in his voice. However, Witherspoon's style is characterized, and 1cShann's sharply defined piano can only support a singular conclusion: it's gotta be lues. When horns start tooting the likes of "Hot Biscuits," it sounds like big band ıusic. Those same horns quickly turn around to the thick dank air of a brothel ante- oom for "Slow Drag Blues," written by McShann and played by him on a honky- onk piano. Read the liner notes carefully, and you'll find that Witherspoon sings on nly half the tracks (all from 1947). Still, this CD is well worth owning.

INK➤ *Jay McShann — Blues from Kansas City* — ***GRP 614***

bout a dozen sides from the early 1940s provide ample evidence of McShann's importance the over-cooked, nonstop, thrilling Kansas City jump jazz-blues sound. Al Hibbler is the ocalist. This is jazz, ultimately, but its impact on blues was enormous.

Spoon So Easy: The Chess Years **Chess 9300**

It's striking to hear a man with a voice as refined a Witherspoon performing with Willie Dixon and other Che session players. Dixon's "Live So Easy" is a fairly typical Che blues, but Witherspoon's enormous talent transforms a simpl song into something that demands riveted attention. He owr "Ain't Nobody's Business," a song much enhanced by a pa of wonderful saxophone solos. It's Harold Ashby on sax wh opens "Goin' Down Slow," with Jay McShann complementing him on piano. Th two provide a sweet setup for the easy swing of Witherspoon's warm delivery. Spice with Chess zest, these late 1950s sessions are among Witherspoon's best.

LINK➤ *Big Blues Honks and Wails: Bluesville Years, Vol. 1* ***Prestige 990***
Six tracks from Witherspoon include "Bad, Bad Whiskey" and "Mean Old Frisco Blues. Sam Charters produced this wonderful series.

The 'Spoon Concerts **Fantasy 2470**

Featured here are two 1959 sessions with such glimmering jazz stars as Gerry Mulligar Coleman Hawkins, Ben Webster, Jimmy Rowles, Mel Lewis, Earl "Fatha" Hines, an Leroy Vinnegar, among others. All dig down deep to find the blues. Witherspoo knows his blues and selects very smart material. For these sidemen, songs like Pete Chatmon's "Every Day," with its rolling choruses, and the traditional "C.C. Rider, with its rocking romps, prove ideal for show-off solos and clever improvisations. Ditt for "Corina, Corina," and "Good Rocking Tonight." Once again, Witherspoon is i great voice, and he treats every song as if it's his biggest hit. A solidly professiona performance, but ultimately it's more about jazz than blues.

LINK➤ *Kevin Mahogany — Another Time, Another Place* ***Warner Bros. 4669***
Mahogony is a huge-voiced natural singer, one of the few successful male jazz/R&B singe in the business (he's just turning 40). He's smooth, powerful, and phenomenally musical. A it happens, he's also from Kansas City. Try also Songs and Moments *(Enja 8072).*

Evenin' Blues **OBC 51**

Call this "Witherspoon meets T-Bone Walker." He also meets the talented organis Bert Kendrix, who plays a big role here. Walker's impact encourages Witherspoon t make better use of open space, allowing a sweet, nearly unaccompanied solo by teno saxophone player Clifford Scott in the middle of "Grab Me a Freight" and from Walke in the grooving "I've Been Treated Wrong." The gem in this 1963 collection is "Evenin', a song often performed by T-Bone Walker and by jazz singer Jimmy Rushing. Wit accents from Walker, Kendrix, and from Scott's understated flute, Witherspoon spin a sleepy, depressing "since my gal is gone" ballad. "Money's Gettin' Cheaper" is als satisfying and fun.

LINK➤ *Sam Cooke — The Man and His Music* ***RCA 712***
Definitive collection by one of the top R&B and soul vocalists of our time. A simply perfe voice. Impeccable taste in material. And it isn't every performer who can carry off "Touc the Hem of His Garment" and "Everybody Loves to Cha Cha Cha" with panache.

he Blues

Smithsonian Collection RD101

'he subtitle of this 4-CD collection is "A Smithsonian Collection of Classic Blues ingers," but there is no particular concentration on vocalists. Instead, this is a wide-inging survey of the development of blues, mostly from the 1920s, 1930s, 1940s, nd 1950s with just a few later recordings. And although it's not perfect, it's the best vailable boxed set on the story of the blues. (For a better selection, invest in all fifteen f the Blues Masters CDs put out by Rhino.) Still, this anthology is extraordinary for l that it does contain—and it contains quite a lot. Blind Lemon Jefferson leads off ith "That Black Snake Moan" and "Match Box Blues," two essential cuts. Bessie mith sings "Back Water Blues" and two others, and Tommy Johnson does "Cool Drink of Water Blues." Others on CD1 include Leroy Carr ("How Long, How Long lues"), Texas Alexander, Barbecue Bob, and Blind Willie Johnson. No big surprises, ut the inclusion of Sara Martin's "Death Sting Me Blues" and Henry Thomas's "Bull Doze Blues" is good news. On CD2, there's more Leroy Carr, plus Charley Patton 'Pony Blues"), Mississippi John Hurt ("Stack O'Lee Blues"), Roosevelt Sykes ("Forty-our Blues"), Skip James ("Devil Got My Woman"), and Big Joe Williams ("Baby lease Don't Go"). Recordings are presented in chronological order; this frames Patton vho seems like an early star) with Sykes (who's more often associated with later de-elopment) in the same year: 1929. CD3 starts out in the mid-1930s, beginning with vo Robert Johnson tracks, "I Believe I'll Dust My Broom" and "Cross Road Blues" om 1936, then looks ahead toward the 1940s with songs by Joe Turner ("Roll 'Em ete") and Jimmy Rushing ("Sent For You Yesterday"). After WW II, the music be-omes considerably more sophisticated, as Charles Brown's "Drifting Blues" and T-one Walker's "Call It Stormy Monday" demonstrate. The music also becomes rougher 'ohn Lee Hooker's "Boogie Chillun") and sometimes swings (as on Wynonie Harris's Mr. Blues Jumped the Rabbit"). Just about all of CD4 is electric. Muddy Waters sets e mood, and he's followed by Howlin' Wolf, Otis Rush, Buddy Guy, and Junior Vells. Singers with distinguished styles also predominate: Junior Parker, Big Mama 'hornton, Jimmy Reed, Ray Charles. Scant attention is paid to the second half of the entury, except for a random track by Cephas and Wiggins, and a few others.

Mean Old World: The Blues from 1940 to 1994

Smithsonian Collection RB0004

'his 4-CD set is a tribute to the diversity of modern blues. Even over the course of ist a few cuts, the differences are profound: Leadbelly sings "Bougeois Blues" accom-anied only by his rudimentary 12-string guitar, and he's followed by T-Bone Walker, oing a slick nearly R&B job on the box's title song, and soon after, Hot Lips Page is nging and trumpeting blues-jazz-swing on "Blood on the Moon." All of that music 'as laid down on record within a single year, from summer 1944 to summer 1945. CD1 here ultimately concentrates on the blues side of R&B, with Dinah Washing-on, Billie Holiday, Amos Milburn, and Charles Brown, but also wanders over Chi-ago way with music from Tampa Red, and Robert Nighthawk. As the modern era nerges, CD2 picks up in 1950 with Muddy Waters performance of "Rollin' and

Tumblin'." He's soon followed by Elmore James doing "Dust My Broom" in 195 and what might be the first rock 'n' roll record, the jump blues "Rocket "88"" b Jackie Brenston and His Delta Cats in 1951. There's a taste of Jimmy Rushing ("Ho Long, How Long Blues") and Joe Turner ("Cherry Red") with his frequent partn Pete Johnson rolling along on piano. The CD ends with a look toward a more moder era with "Three Hours Past Midnight" from Johnny "Guitar" Watson in 1955. CD presents revival music from Fred McDowell ("Shake 'Em On Down"), Mance Lipscom ("Freddie"), and Robert Pete Williams ("Pardon Denied Again"), all from the la 1950s and early 1960s, and all demonstrating an expert's ear in selecting represent tive songs for each artist; the likes of Freddie King ("Hide Away") and Albert Colli ("Tongue Lashing") show where it's going. CD4 includes the most modern high lights, notably Albert King's "Crosscut Saw," B.B. King's "Why I Sing the Blues," an a few artists whose inclusion shows how much the compiler knew about contemp rary blues, notably Junior Kimbrough's "J.R. Blues." Just about every famous name included here, from Little Milton to Jimmy McCracklin, from Lightnin' Hopkins Jimmy Reed. As with all Smithsonian products, the liner notes are both well writte and nicely illustrated. Although some fans may wonder why a particular song or arti is missing, there is no finer (or more wide-ranging) collection of contemporary blu than this boxed set.

Blues in the Mississippi Night — Rykodisc 9015

More than any other single CD, this session explores the heart of the blues. It's conversation and an informal recording by Memphis Slim, Big Bill Broonzy, an Sonny Boy Williamson that's produced and moderated by Alan Lomax. Most whi people knew little about the blues and the culture behind the music when this albu was made in 1946. The musicians speak frankly about "la-la-lu," their nickname fo the ruined scrap food they were forced to eat in order to survive ("'la-la-lu,' if I don like it, he do . . ."). They also talk about enduring the abuse of being pistol-whippe by a white man and tell tales about card sharks and levee camps; most important all, they relate how they used the blues to say in music what could not be said safely i conversation. Roughly half of this CD is spoken, and it is both fascinating and easy hear because the recording quality is decent. The rest contains acoustic country blue performed simply and without adornment. When Broonzy sings "Bama's Stackerlee, with Memphis Slim on piano and Sonny Boy Williamson on guitar, it's one of th great recorded moments in blues (although to be honest, the music's quality is ju adequate). There are many song snippets, but few complete songs. (And yet, this still a marvelous blues album.) Lomax adds some work songs and hymns from h own collection, plays them for the blues singers, and listens quietly as they expla what was heard. Extensive liner notes can be read like a book.

Photo & Graphic Credits

hanks to these record companies for the use of CD cover art. Page numbers follow each credit.

delphi/Genes Records: 134
lligator Records: 29, 55, 143, 151, 154, 171, 173, 188
rhoolie Records: 56, 61, 99, 115, 131, 191, 193, 194, 195
udioQuest Music: 114
iograph Records, Inc.: 37, 121, 156
lind Pig Records: 126, 139
MG Classics: 80, 122, 168
vidence: 105, 107
antasy, Inc. 140, 164, 165
/C Music: 106
[CA Records: 13, 41, 51, 68, 77, 84, 90, 102-03, 127, 128, 129, 144, 162, 178, 196, 198
olyGram Records, Inc.: 34
hino Entertainment: 52, 54, 57, 73, 179
ounder Records: 2, 19, 30, 70, 93, 94, 133
hanachie Entertainment (& Yazoo Records): 7, 11, 22, 23, 45, 47, 74, 78, 98, 135
mithsonian Folkways: 17, 36, 62, 95, 118, 174, 193
ony Music: 64, 79, 82, 119, 158, 160
'elk Music Group: 71, 75, 150

hank you to the photographers and the record companies for photographs used in this book.

:s Gruseck/Alligator Records: 3
enda Ladd/Antone's Record Co.: 5
ul Natkin/Alligator Records: 9
ndro/Alligator Records: 15
kodisc: 16
ichael Terranova/Rounder Records: 18
ck Reinhart/Alligator Records: 24
ul Natkin/Photo Reserve/Alligator Records: 28
ndrew W. Long/Antone's Record Co.: 31
alter Thomson/Blind Pig Records: 35
aren Pulfer Focht/Rounder Records: 38
ul Natkin/Photo Reserve/Alligator Records: 39
ck Olivier/Rounder Records: 42
m Hazeltine/Rounder Records: 44
K. Waller/Rounder Records: 48
Badeaux/Fantasy, Inc.: 60
odern Blues Recordings: 85, 91
ndrew Gallindo: 88
seph Rosen/Alligator Records: 132
ligator Records: 137
n Manville/Rounder Records: 147
ndi Anglin/Alligator Records: 153
ane Allmen/Alligator Records: 170